Catching Moles

THE HISTORY AND PRACTICE

Catching Moles

THE HISTORY AND PRACTICE ...

JEFF NICHOLLS

... and practice makes perfect

Love

Isla x

THE CROWOOD PRESS

First published in 2017 by
The Crowood Press Ltd
Ramsbury, Marlborough
Wiltshire SN8 2HR

www.crowood.com

© Jeff Nicholls 2017

British Library Cataloguing-in-Publication Data
A catalogue record for this book is available from the British
Library.

ISBN 978 1 78500 363 9

Except where stated otherwise, all illustrations are by the
author.

Typeset by Jean Cussons Typesetting, Diss, Norfolk

Printed and bound in India by Parksons Graphics

Contents

Dedicated to the person who investigates further the work contained in this book,
and continues the interest in mole catching for those who come after.

Preface

As a professional mole catcher I have a daily contact with these fascinating mammals, and it is a privilege to have this acquaintance with what is, for too many people, a formidable problem in the garden, field or paddock. My personal association with the mole is further extended as I set cameras in their complex world, and after hours of waiting for these elusive creatures to appear on film, then have the pleasure of being able to watch them on a more intimate basis. This combination of watching them, and then removing them, has provided the information contained within these pages, and I hope will explain the affinity between man and mole that has existed for centuries. It describes the methods, the trials and tribulations, and the history and future of a traditional countryside skill that is still making its mark in this modern world, and which it is to be hoped will continue for many years to come.

Many attacks have been, and still are, aimed at the humble mole, but it has nevertheless overcome all that man has thrown at it. Chemicals and electronics may have superseded old wives' tales and beliefs, but one form of control for moles has survived the test of time, and that is their capture and restraint. These words are chosen carefully, because the nature of the mole catcher's work is not what people have often been claimed it to be in the past. The control of any animal must be carried out with respect and dignity, and must observe a certain level of welfare, and I hope this book will reassure those who query whether mole catching offers a quick and instant demise for the mole.

The reality of what mole catching truly entails is explained, as is what it takes to become a mole catcher today.

This book should be considered as a handbook for anyone working as, or wishing to become, a mole catcher.

From a very young age I was drawn to the occupation of controlling moles, as it was something that I could actually do successfully. Whether this was because I was happy to sit and wait for the bender stick to spring into action, indicating a capture, or because I had an affection for the quarry, I have yet to learn. Over the years I have discovered a personal and private world that it has been a privilege

The mole, Talpa europaea.

to get to know and to understand. My relation-ship with the humble mole has grown over the decades, bringing both sadness and enjoyment. It encouraged a passion in me as a boy, which has grown into the desire to give moles some-thing in return in my latter years. As well as enlightening readers with my written word, educating would-be mole catchers on training courses, and entertaining folk in comedy shows and talks, my message has been that, whether in conflict or study, we should always have the highest respect for this remarkable, rarely seen, never heard, but often spoken about creature: the mole.

My life alongside moles has been pleasur-able, and educational: their ability to avoid being caught brought frustration when I was a young boy, but taught me persistence. When I was a teenager and success in the contempo-rary world seemed remote, their call for me to return to the soil offered an escape route; and they brought me comfort when as a young man I had little hope of a future. Furthermore, their world is so interesting and absorbing, and close contact with them so intriguing, they have given my life significance with each day, and a value that I will cherish until it is my time to lie down amongst them.

Chapter 1

The History of Mole Catching in the United Kingdom

During the eighteenth and nineteenth centuries there lurked a character in the countryside who was as mysterious and elusive as the quarry he sought, someone who worked alone and whose skilful craft was never shared, but was so often required by the owners of land: the mole catcher. The United Kingdom has always had a throng of single soldiers spread across the shires ready to battle the little man in black. These personalities sadly no longer frequent the village's fields and paddocks as they once did. Today, the group term is 'pest control' – the specialist mole catcher, as he once was, is sadly as rare a sight as the mole itself. Nevertheless, mole catchers remain a small but important component in the running of the countryside, a weapon for farmers to call upon and the last resort to gardeners when all else fails.

Man has battled for the supremacy of the soil for centuries, with mole catchers employed to free the land of the unwanted mole, which has in fact dwelled here for many thousands of years. However, the changes made during the Victorian era had a huge impact on the simple, everyday life of both the mole and the mole catcher.

Between the late 1700s and the early 1900s mole catchers went about their daily work of mole control using the only method available to them, as it had been to those who came before them: traps. These were primitive, but achieved the aim of capturing the mole. The word 'capture' is the clue to just how these traps operated, because they did not actually kill the mole, but held or restrained it.

Clearly the mole catchers had to know their chosen quarry to be successful, and the landowners who employed them were keen to see the evidence of the completed task. Many myths were passed around concerning moles, and the mole catchers took advantage of these strange tales to add further mystery to the skill they claimed was required to expose the culprit responsible for the damage caused. The belief that mysterious traits and qualities were required to rule over the moles soon prevailed across the country, adding further to the demand for the mole catcher's apparently enchanted skills. Mole catchers were quick to exploit this demand – but this misplaced belief ultimately contributed to the downfall of the traditional mole catcher typical of those days.

Mole catchers were often employed by the parish to get rid of moles from common land and churchyards, and from the property of those residents whom the parish clerk or sergeant wished to please. In addition, farmers and the gentry, who owned vast acreages of land, augmented this work, which meant that mole catchers could earn a tidy sum during the working year. There is written evidence of this demand and reward in the form of pay tickets – for example we know that a Buckinghamshire mole catcher, a certain Tom Turner, earned enough money in one year to pay for his cottage outright. Even so, the task of working the soil in search of the mole was not that easy, and like so many occupations in Victorian Britain, mole catching often had its problems.

The mole catchers of the United Kingdom, just like the creature they sought, led a solitary life, and although they may never have been seen in the light of day, evidence of their work was clearly displayed in the bodies of the moles that were left tied to fences, gates andposts. These mysterious characters have a story to tell, and I would like to share it with you now.

WHEN DID IT ALL BEGIN?

Mole catchers have been a part of the British countryside for many hundreds of years, dating back to the invasion by the Roman Empire. The desire for neat gardens and flat fields has been foremost in man's land management for thousands of years, and the humble mole has had to put up with sustained attack from man in his efforts to achieve just that; nevertheless the mole has become very proficient at evading these assaults since these early times. Such a formidable foe required specialist attention to eradicate it – and so the services of the mole catcher were increasingly sought. It required someone with patience, a natural instinct, intuition and the ability to be secretive, and such a person found what in today's modern world would be termed a 'niche' in the market.

The capture of the mole was initially by trial and error, with error being the important part, and we can only imagine how the first mole catchers worked out the best way to remove moles. To find out we need to peruse the small parts of this fascinating journey provided by the records, and compare these with the knowledge that has been passed down by word of mouth, and combine these with the clues that may have been deliberately left as time has passed.

There is speculation as to the earliest contact that man had with the mole and its removal – this contact may have come about initially when people realized that the damage they were ex-periencing was being caused by the creature we have come to refer to as a mole, though many names have been used to describe it, both nationally and locally. The name 'mole' comes from the Middle English term 'mouldwarp' or 'mouldiwarpen', which originates from Europe, from the German 'moldewerp' and the similar term 'muldvarp' from the Netherlands. The words refer to the mole as 'earth thrower', but Middle English as a language came shortly after the Norman Conquest, so prior to the terms found in Middle English, the word used to describe the mole would probably have come from Latin. The Latin word that might describe the mole may be 'agger' or 'adger', which means 'earth worker'; other names such as 'neavus' and 'nevus' can also be associated with the mole, as these mean 'a raised mound'. 'Nevus' is still a medical term for a mole found on the human body, but another Latin name, 'talpa', is the name that has survived and is the scientific reference still used today to describe the mole resident in the United Kingdom, *Talpa europea*, the European mole.

Local names can also be found for moles; for example in my home county of Berkshire the mole was always called a 'want' or 'wont', and the 'wanter' was the man who caught them. In other parts the word 'molde' was used for a mole; also in Berkshire 'molde ale' was a drink imbibed at a funeral, where the connection may be the fact that the body is placed in the ground – in the soil below the surface. Whatever word was used to describe the mole then, I am sure that, as today, it was also called all sorts of other names because of the damage it caused, names your mother didn't even know you knew!

Evidence of its subterranean working took the form of strange mounds of soil that appeared as if by some extraordinary magic, or were seen to be mysteriously moving, sometimes with earth being thrown up out of the ground. In this way our descendants discovered they had a problem, and the problem was related to a small creature – they may not have

Not all moles are the same colour.

known anything about it, but because it intruded into their lives in such a way as to cause them some level of annoyance, they decided it would have to be got rid of.

It seems that man feels the needs to control any living species that crosses his path, or that he considers is detrimental to him in any way, so any creature that dares to encroach into his dominion has always been subjected to some form of harm. These measures include violent attack, restraint and despatch, the methodical destruction of habitat, and even capture and removal to another habitat that could be unsustainable to the species. Man with his evolved intelligence has placed himself at the top of the food chain, and uses much the same measures in the control of moles today – in fact our methods may have not changed much since the Romans all those years ago. But as we look closely at these methods, and at those individuals who strove to rid the soil of the little creature in the velvet jacket, we must also consider what changes should be made if this need for control is to continue.

To remove a mole, it is obviously necessary to place some implement into its environment. Historically the Romans had a material available to them that had been used for hundreds of years even before their coming: clay. Man had

been making vessels from clay to hold liquids and other vital commodities, and it was clay that was used to construct mole traps in Roman times. We know this from various pots excavated in archaeological digs and from sites around the world. These experts may have stumbled on such a pot, which we now know was for the capture of moles, and in fact to begin with may not have known the true purpose of such a strange artefact, with the mysterious hole half way up its body. Maybe they thought it was damaged, or an implement designed to retain liquid in some form of cooking or storage where the liquid needed to remain at a certain level.

What must they have thought when they first scraped the dirt away and found a solitary puzzling pot in the middle of a field, with no other fragments of any other pots nearby. But this solitary pot had been placed in soil that previously was maybe part of a field, or a garden, or a patch of land for the growing of food, and had been put there intentionally to control the troublesome mole that had taken up residence there.

We now know that these were in fact mole traps, and not just discarded pots or vessels belonging to another process from our history, because they held the remains of moles. These clay pitfall pots have been found in various places in sites known to have been previously inhabited by our ancestors, as well as the occasional solitary find; in fact the use of a clay pot to control moles continued right up into the early nineteenth century, despite changes in mole control that were available.

The simple clay pot was the first evidence of a direct method to control the mole that we can find. I am fortunate to know Robert Packer, who is a traditional potter in the nearby village to mine of Shottesbroke. His knowledge and enthusiasm for his craft was tested when I approached him with the proposition of making a pot to catch moles. Like a terrier, he trawled through his own library of literature and the corners of his personal knowledge to find references as to how these pots were once made, and the information he collated enabled him to make some simple copies. Following those directions and dimensions, he produced pots that may not have been exactly as the originals, but

were close to those that would have been used, as supplied to the people who sought to get rid of the mole all those years ago.

The pot he made was approximately 8½in (24cm) in height and 8in (20cm) in diameter at its widest point, and the walls were ½in thick (12mm). It is probable that the original pots were constructed from coils of clay, which would have been shaped with the hands and fired in a bread oven. The information available explains that the pots would have been turned on a potter's wheel, and potters have been using wheels as long ago as these mole pot-traps have been around. The pot, whether hand coiled or thrown on a wheel, may have been the brainchild of one individual in his bid to be rid of a mole. Whether this was a personal battle, or an instruction from an employer to whoever was responsible for the land, is something we may never know, but we now understand that this encounter between man and mole had only just begun, and is one that continues today.

The small hole half way up the side of the pot was to prevent it filling with water, and the first pots may not have had these holes. They may have been added possibly after it was witnessed that moles could swim and so were able to escape from pots that had been allowed to fill to the brim with water. This may also have been an important trial and error process as to the final size of the pot, as found amongst Bob's papers and books. Smaller pots may have been cheaper or easier to make, but the mole could get out of them with no trouble. The larger and final size of the pot offers no chance of a mole escaping, and has the added advantage of a possible multiple catch. It was important that the pots allowed the mole to fall in, and therefore it was essential that they were placed so that the mole could not detect their presence, or were located in tunnels that the mole was sure to travel along at speed, so it was captured before it could take evasive action.

Using the pots successfully necessitated calculating the problems involved in confronting

Since early times the clay pitfall trap has been used to capture moles.

the elusive mole, and overcoming them, which would not have been a simple task. This knowledge as to how they would be used, and the changes required, would have meant that whoever began this quest to find a solution to the problem of the mole, had to be dedicated to the task. It would have required much attention to detail and a lot of contact with the mole's environment, and this remains the most important criterion even if you are required to control moles today. To begin with, the catcher may not have had any particular method of fooling the mole into falling into the trap, and the pot was probably just carefully dug into the mole's tunnel with its rim smooth and in line with the run the mole would be using. So whichever direction it came from it would fall into the pot, and then, unable to escape, would die from starvation, stress or exhaustion.

Maybe the pots were originally meant to be dry, but as mentioned above, later it was considered that rainwater needed to be let out, hence the hole. Also, because it was positioned half way up the side of the pot, a quantity of water remained in the pot so any unfortunate mole that fell in eventually drowned from exhaustion – not a pleasant end for any mole. We later learn that a small wooden trap door was placed over the pot, with sides to form a tunnel shape: this would direct the mole over the trap door, and so down into the pot for the same fate.

How this change came about, once more we can only ponder: was it the mole's instinct to survive and its natural ability to solve all that man throws at it? The conflict between mole and man had just begun, and yet their respect for each other seemed to set the rules of combat, the mole providing the lesson, and man needing to understand the mole to solve the problem.

Considering the size, weight and fragility of these clay pots, it is easy to see that they would not have been easy to transport. Also the amount of disturbance involved in placing them in the mole's environment meant that as

a method of control they would have been restricted to a permanent location, unlike those used by the mole catchers we have come to learn about in our history since those times.

Man's conflict with the mole may well have begun even before Roman times as we understand it then, as changes in farming practice were changing the face of the countryside. Domesticated animals such as cattle, goats, pigs and sheep required large areas of grazing, and the much loved woodland habitat of the moles would have been cleared and fenced to provide for this. Man had domesticated animals for his own needs long before the Roman invasion, and the mole would have adapted to these changes. Predators such as wolves, foxes and bears needed to be controlled, and fences and barriers were erected to prevent them preying on man's precious livestock.

But the fences and barriers erected for this protection granted easy access to the moles: rain and dew dripped off these new lines of fences, and the moisture was retained beneath, making tunnelling in the wet soil simple and allowing the moles immediate access to new areas of food. Their main diet of insects, bugs and grubs, and the even more favoured worms, would also be attracted to the newly worked soil, which as a food source they much preferred to the drier woodland floor under the tree canopy. Furthermore the grass with its seasonal changes made for a completely new habitat where the moles could find food, and they now had easy access to such areas from their tunnels dug under the fences of fortification, whilst retaining the dry comfort of the woodlands.

There must have been conflict, and man then may have attempted to understand the reasons for the mounds of soil in his new pastures – and maybe this soil was, like today, utilized by them as the perfect soil in which to grow new crops such as cereals. The farmers then would have been quick to realize that in the new dark-coloured soils produced by the moles, seeds were able to germinate quickly; this is clear to see even today, where the presence of molehills results in an invasive spread of weeds. I would like to think that as long ago as the Neolithic period, man and mole had their moments together, and that the battle of wits began when man first learned of the importance of soil and all it could offer. We know that the clay pots were possibly the beginning of man's quest for supremacy of the soil, but this was only the start: mole catchers had yet to establish themselves, and this was not to happen for hundreds of years.

In between the departure of the Romans and the rise of medieval Britain, it was fashionable to wear fur. Many animals were hunted just for the fur they provided, and we know that nothing ever went to waste: thus the hide from domesticated animals used for food would have been put to use as clothing, bedding and shelter. Moles caught either by chance or targeted would also have been made use of. The skin from a mole is tough and warm, and we are aware that the Romans used the moleskins from any moles they caught as a lining for clothing. The fashion for fur may have had little impact on mole populations, but other animal species were less fortunate; for example the white fur from the belly of the once prolific red squirrel, known as miniver, was the sought-after commodity for royal fashion. And although the mole may have escaped the fashion inclinations of the well-to-do at this point in time, nevertheless to sport a moleskin garment was later to become desired by many.

Both the call for fur and the increasing population during the Middle Ages has been well documented, but for the moles, this would have been a time of respite from the persecution that was to be unleashed upon them. Moleskin was less profitable than the fur of fox, pine marten and even the otter, and the mole was not considered suitable for food, possibly for two reasons: they were difficult to catch, especially in the numbers required to provide a meal; and there weren't enough of them available in any

one location because they tended to live singly.

But the conflict between man and mole would have continued, with man's increasing frustration at the damage caused to grazing and produce. Vast areas of woodland had by this time been cultivated due to the requirement to produce food for the increasing population, and those people responsible for making this a profitable concern would have looked at the mole in a different light.

It is hard to say what persecution moles were subjected to at this time, because during this period of history the country experienced nature's own population control, with outbreaks of disease including the plague slowing down any increase in human numbers. Weather also played its part, with bad harvests reducing the numbers of those dwelling above the soil – but all this had little impact on those that dwelled below. Without the intervention of man, nature can and will overcome all the problems that life confronts it with, and it was the same then as it is now. Moles live in a hostile world in which it competes with life's most difficult adversary, its own species. I have always said that we humans live like moles, and this may be closer to the truth than I first thought.

Following such national devastation, the people of Britain came to appreciate the importance of the food supply. In the mid- to late sixteenth century, human numbers began to increase again, and the demand to provide food likewise increased – and this was a turning point for all animal species, whether they came under the heading of produce or vermin. In human terms the rural population was considerably higher than the population in urban areas, and only the large urban areas such as London, York and Bristol had inhabitants in any substantial numbers. In the country the land had already been divided into manors, and was the property of the very rich or of royalty. The manors and estates employed those who were not so fortunate, who would tend to the land and provide for the needs of the more affluent families; in return, their homes and land could be rented.

During this period villages within the confines of the manor were allocated open spaces called Great Fields; many place names in the United Kingdom still hold the field name, or references to fields, dating from these times. These large fields were worked as a communal effort, but during the 1500s they were divided into strips, which were individually rented and managed. The strips were known as selions, and the owner of each one would have a name to identify it as theirs. A selion of land was an area of approximately one acre, measuring one furlong (660ft/200m) in length, and one chain (66ft/20m) wide. These strips were separated by a mound of earth along their length, which was created just by turning the plough shears in. Different areas would have local names for these mounds, such as 'landshreds' – but whatever their name, the raised mounds were a perfect opportunity for the moles to travel beneath these fields and strips, as their tunnels would never have been disturbed by the agricultural activities.

The owners of these strips had to take what they were offered, and some may have owned more than one strip. To ensure that no one person rented all the fertile land, no one could rent two adjacent strips, so there was an equal share of the fertile and the less fertile land. The moles' activity would also have been dictated by this patchwork of fertile strips. The more fertile land would provide a greater amount of food available to the moles, and those owners who tended their land well would inadvertently encourage the moles to their strips via the mounds or landshreds.

Furthermore, over the years the flow of water running down and off the landshreds created the perfect moisture content in the soil, at a perfect distance down and either out from, or under the mound, for the moles to construct a tunnel that would never be disturbed, especially by the plough. A higher moisture content

would maintain the tunnel, which would be compacted by the moles, prohibiting molehills and so pre-empting any visible evidence of their presence. The sudden appearance of a mole on a land strip would have led to its immediate removal so as to safeguard vital and necessary food production against mole activity.

The main damage would have been caused to new seeds and plants, which were pushed up as a result of the moles tunnelling in the fertile soil beneath in search of food. In addition, the tunnels would displace the soil from around the roots of plants and seedlings, causing them to wilt – but the real culprits were the mice and voles, always quick to share the moles tunnels, and which would chew on the soft succulent roots, with the mole taking the blame.

Farmers and growers may have continued to remove moles with the use of the clay pots, or by opportunistically heaving them out of the ground with a spade or fork if activity was detected in the shallow tunnels – but we now discover that the nuisance value of the mole had begun to raise some alarms.

THE FIRST PROFESSIONAL MOLE CATCHERS

Information identifying the first real mole catchers may be found amongst documents and archives of Tudor times – that is, professional mole catchers who were paid to concentrate on the specific task of getting rid of moles. However, there must have been such designated individuals before this, whose role in the control of moles during their own time must be acknowledged here, and their skill and knowledge recorded for posterity. The methods used by these people during this period may have been similar to those employed from Roman times to the arrival of the Tudors, and they provide the basis of the control methods used today.

It is difficult to be sure that moles were really targeted as a professional concern until the changes made during Tudor times. During the reign of Queen Elizabeth I, the Vermin Act 1566 was passed, which included moles. The Act was an update on the first Vermin Act of 1532, but the revised Act made it a requirement to reward a catcher with a bounty payment if they produced proof that they had killed a vermin species. The churchwardens held the purse for this requirement, and it was their duty to pay one half penny to a catcher for every head of a want (mole) he produced; however, not every parish complied with this Act, or paid the full bounty as required. Further reference to this Act and its impact on the wildlife of Britain may be found in the fascinating book *Silent Fields* by Roger Lovegrove (Oxford University Press).

The traditional mole catchers must have been influenced by the introduction of these Vermin Acts, as the new legislation offered them the prospect of being able to obtain a steady income from the control of moles. The mole catchers must either have worked to control moles prior to the Acts' implementation, or they had already embarked on a journey of research and understanding with the rarely seen quarry. They were without doubt astute and shrewd in their ability to assess their position, and many negotiated lucrative deals. Many details of payments made to people under the Vermin Acts can be found in the churchwardens' records. However, the payments made to mole catchers are few and far between in these accounts compared to the payments made privately for the destroying of moles, which can be found in the accounts and papers of private estates, manor houses and county record offices. This identifies that mole catchers were often in the employment of the more wealthy landowners, and subject to the conditions of those contracts.

The mole catchers quickly identified that they needed to secure their income at a time when under the Vermin Acts every man and his dog was indiscriminatingly taking anything that they could be paid for, ranging from sparrows to red kites and hedgehogs to badgers. The mole catchers specialized in just one species: the mole. This reduced the competition, but they also needed to secure that niche in the market, and they achieved this by refusing to explain how they did control the mole, and with protected agreements. An example is found in the town records of Nottingham Council, which in 1579 paid a mole catcher £3 0s 0d upon engagement, and £1 6s 8d per year; this was a guaranteed income at a time when many were living in poverty following the devastating periods of the early and mid-part of that century. This mole catcher, like so many others, would have still sought the bounty available under the Vermin Act of a half penny a want (mole) for the destruction of moles on common land.

There could well have been resentment amongst the populations of villages, as the mole catchers strove to close the door and prevent others competing for the lucrative trade. Each parish or Lord of the Manor would have employed the services of only one mole catcher, and it was important to ensure that this position was secure; therefore many agreements ran for long periods of time, ranging from one to twenty-one years. These long agreements were often subject to conditions, but to those who took the time to understand the mole and control it, it was security for their family. The mole catchers had to produce the mole bodies as evidence of the completed task, as was required with other species listed under the Vermin Act 1566, and they would boldly display the corpses to the landowners, fixing them on fences and gates as proof of capture.

It was fortunate for the old mole catchers that the Vermin Act remained in force until the mid-nineteenth century, as it deflected interest away from moles, drawing a line between those who controlled moles, and the vermin killers who stopped at nothing for the reward of the bounty payments. Not every parish had a mole catcher, so it was normal for many mole catchers who held the position in their own parish to extend their services to surrounding parishes; when combined with mole catching on some additional private farms and estates, it provided a substantial income.

Examples of these agreements for destroying moles explain clearly the terms and conditions set out by the landowners, and the cost incurred. We can gather much information on just how these wily old mole catchers worked and survived the early part of British history, until their command over the control of moles met its demise in the mid-nineteenth century. Some of these precisely hand-written receipts reveal changes in the names of the mole catchers; by referencing census and other records we can see the reasons for such changes, which may have come about from the death of a mole catcher, or because they moved away, or the services changed from father to son. Many large estates kept meticulous accounts and filed them safely, which helps trace these characters, while others are more difficult to locate as their details can be found on nothing more than a scrap of paper or a line in a village record.

The jigsaw of these important references has provided a window into the lives of these forgotten custodians of rural life, and it has been, and will remain, a privilege to understand their lives. Mole catchers were spread across the whole of the United Kingdom from shore

to shore, and we do know that many a mole catcher travelled from farm to farm plying their trade. They would stay over in the spare room of the farm or the house they were working, and many a record shows that on the night of the national census a mole catcher was staying in the home of a widow in a village.

Some of the payments came from the overseer of the poor, the office of overseer having been created in 1572 to collect alms for the relief of paupers. The Elizabethan Poor Law of 1601 stated that two or three householders were to be overseers each year, and together with the churchwardens would also have had the task of finding work for the unemployed. They were responsible for the relief of poverty within their community, and we can find evidence that some payments for destroying moles in a parish were made by the overseer. This clearly shows the struggle experienced by some, but I include this reference because it must have contributed to the encouragement of interest in mole catching in those less fortunate areas.

The ability to catch moles was without doubt an answer to many people's resources of providing for a family, or as an individual. Whether they were a static mole catcher working the parish in which they lived, and the surrounding

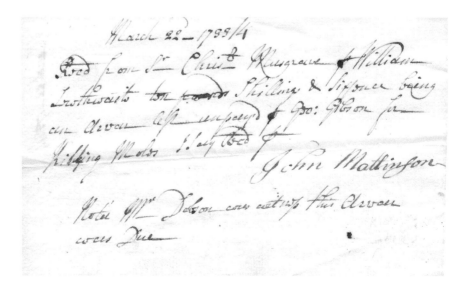

Bill of payment dated 1733. Bills of payment have enabled us to understand the life of the mole catchers.

parishes, or a travelling mole catcher moving across the country as the work demanded, as long as they kept the knowledge a mystery, they had little competition – and to be successful it had to continue that way. There were many hundreds of mole catchers located in every corner of the United Kingdom, and looking at information in different parts of the country we can clearly see into the lives of these people.

Landowners needed the services of mole removal, and the terms and conditions were meticulously written down so that all parties knew the policy of employment. Whether any of the mole catchers could read or write, and whether they fully understood the wording of some of the contents, may be questioned, but they could provide the required service and they completely understood the value of money. According to the content of these agreements, the mole catchers were contracted to destroy the moles from designated land over an agreed period of time and for a fixed sum. With such a term of agreement signed by both parties, the secured income was valid as long as the moles were destroyed. Failure would mean the loss of the income and possible poverty. There are few references to mole catchers in the journals of the workhouses, so until further evidence reveals otherwise, the mole catchers seem to have led a secure and protected way of life.

These locked agreements interested many would-be mole catchers, and also those who thought they might compete in what to most may have seemed a simple way to earn a revenue. The mole catchers' agreements began to include additional terms, and one such term was that failure to destroy the moles would result in the employment of another mole catcher, and a penalty deducted from the contracted payment within the agreement. These penalties were a sum of money subtracted for each mole that the newly appointed mole catcher removed from the designated ground. In a rather lucrative indenture dating from 1834, such a consequence can be found, where two Warwickshire

mole catchers, Francis and Thomas Gibson, would have had three pennies deducted from their annual fee for every mole that another person or persons removed from the said parish. So although mole catchers may well have had profitable agreements, already we can see why they would shrewdly protect their knowledge and thereby lock up their income.

Study of these documents over different years opens a window for us to look into the lives of these individuals of the fields, and to learn of the way they contracted out their skills. Through the medieval period into the 1700s documentation is limited, but during the late eighteenth century details appear frequently in registers and accounts, revealing the existence of mole catchers.

Agreements dated 1708 and 1724 between the parishioners of Belton in Lincolnshire laid out the terms, namely one half penny for each mole destroyed, to be paid by the overseer of the poor. These agreements were not exclusively directed at moles, as they also state that the same payment of one half penny was to be paid for the production of a sparrow.

Therefore, these early documents confirm that many were still working under the Vermin Act of 1566, and for the same payment terms as those over a hundred years previously. Payments in the parishes from the overseer of the poor did not identify the presence of a designated mole catcher, as all could request payment under the Elizabethan Vermin Act. It did, however, inspire those with the inclination to specialize in moles to break away from the norm. With moles being elusive, and their control requiring more dedicated attention, the individual who worked chiefly at mole removal opened up a path for others to follow. Working to destroy moles as a primary target, these mole moguls strove to secure a unique business, and one that with careful nurturing deflected the attention of others and created a personal service for the landowners.

In 1725, in the county of Lincolnshire in

the village of Donington, there is evidence of this change, as John Twell was appointed as parish mole catcher. John could not write, but his mark sealed the agreement between the parishioners and himself, and secured an annual stipend of 15s 8d. These early records quickly disclose the trend for individuals to focus on moles, possibly because of the difficulty in their control and the lack of success by others. Thus to concentrate on one designated target and become proficient in its removal had its rewards. By the late 1700s, the number of mole catchers in Lincolnshire was increasing, and agreements were exchanged for larger sums of money and, more importantly, for longer periods of time. Terms were agreed involving seven and fifteen years of removing moles, with sums of money in pounds rather than the half penny to be had, making the destroying of moles a secure future.

It would be unreasonable for us to assume that every mole catcher was at this time covered under these terms. We find further information from other parts of the United Kingdom where agreements differ slightly, and even payments made to individuals to remove moles during the earlier 1600s, but the number of contractual mole catchers steadily increased in the mid- to late eighteenth century. An example of such early continuing employment of a mole catcher's services can be found in the records of Edenhall, a large country residence in Penrith. Once the home of the Musgrave family, the hall was famous for its artefact the Luck of Edenhall, a glass goblet now preserved for the nation and on display in the Victoria and Albert Museum in London.

Mole catchers were a prominent part of the hall's past history. I have receipts from its records that tell the story of the mole catchers associated with the soil surrounding the hall. The earliest I have is dated 22 March 1733 between Sir Christopher Musgrave and a mole catcher known as Gibson, for the sum of 10s 6d for killing moles. When read in sequence, the records clearly show the names, and the increases in money that changed hands, and despite not having all the records, it was possible to determine that the hall and the Musgrave family certainly employed mole catchers. In 1782 the family member then in residence, Sir Phillip Musgrave, paid mole catcher William Jackson one guinea (£1 1s) for one year's mole catching. My next recorded payment is dated 1796, made by Sir John Musgrave on 17 May, who paid 10s 6d for one year's mole catching, due that Whitsuntide, to the same William Jackson. The same payment to the same mole catcher was again made in April 1797, so although there was a reduction from the payment of one guinea in 1782, the contractual term of one year remained the same.

The one-off payment was not uncommon as an incentive to secure the mole catcher's employment, and possibly to help reduce the population of resident moles to a manageable number. By 1806 the mole catcher's name had changed, and a William Parrington is recorded as receiving the annual sum of 10s 6d. He appears on receipts for 1808 paid to him by the guardians of Sir Phillip Musgrave, while a payment made just two years later on 24 July 1810 was made to a new mole catcher, Thomas

Bill of payment for William Jackson for 1782: William Jackson retained the work but at a reduced payment.

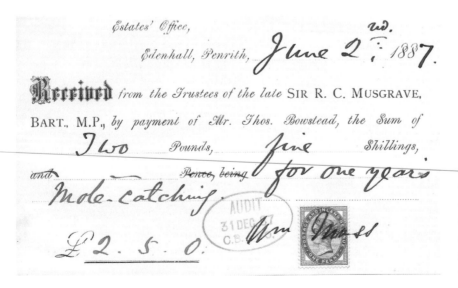

Bill of payment dated 1819 made to William Preston, farmer, but who became the parish mole catcher.

Watson. Thomas Watson was to receive the sum of 2s 6d for killing the moles in one of the estate woods, but only this area.

In the year 1818 Sir Phillip Musgrave was paying his accounts himself, and his mole catcher was William Preston who secured the tidy sum of £3 7s 6d. A year later William Preston, a local farmer from Dacre, was paid an extra £1, but the terms were not, as previously, for catching the moles at just the family residence of Edenhall: it was now clearly stated that the employment was for catching moles in the parish of Edenhall.

Therefore as well as being a farmer, William was now the parish mole catcher, and between 1819 and my next record of 1833 he remains the mole catcher, collecting the annual sum of £2 12s 6d for catching the moles in the lands and woods in the parish of Edenhall. This period amounts to fourteen years, and as we have no evidence to the contrary, it seems he was the mole catcher for Edenhall for that term. Changes at Edenhall saw Sir George Musgrave paying the mole catcher's bill in 1845 of £3 2s 6d, and still that money was being paid to William Preston, as it was until 1851, a confirmed minimum term of service as mole catcher to the parish, lands and woods of Edenhall of thirty-three years.

William's service for removing moles may well have been for longer, as my only other documents show no change until 1869 and

Bill of payment for 1887 to William Moss. The securing of payments and agreements was often made with the mole catcher's signature written over a stamp.

1870; these carry the signature of a new mole catcher, William Moss, whose name is written across a penny lilac stamp, securing the sum of £4 10s for the annual contracts. William Moss continued to hold the post until after 1887. These dates on the agreements confirm their long term, securing a regular annual income to those who could provide the service, and giving good reason for safeguarding the secrets of how to catch moles.

By the turn of the nineteenth century, the mole catchers had a secure hold on the way moles were controlled in the United Kingdom. By targeting the mole, and under the terms and conditions of their agreements, they plied their craft in a different, more methodical way. Working the fields with ingenious home-made traps designed to outfox their soil-dwelling opponent, the mole catchers fought to sustain their lucrative income.

The presence of the designated mole catcher in a parish openly displaying their success on fence and post for all to see, brought further profitable contracts from adjoining parishes and landowners. It was not uncommon for a mole catcher to hold several agreements with different landowners and parish clerks. They dissembled the knowledge gained from any competition, and when new agreements were to be decided, were quick to ruin any other's application that could draw away their agreements of finance for the next term. Most agreements were presented in a meeting of the parish and landowners, with the ongoing annual agreements normally decided on a specific day, maybe a church court day or during an event in the calendar year that was important to that area.

Often the village inn was a preferred meeting point, where the mole catchers would boast of their prowess in their craft, and their skill in catching the moles that had been proudly exhibited around the villages and farms. Any competing mole catcher would have been faced with a barrage of reasons as to why they would not be able to remove the moles, bolstered by constant reference to the success of the current mole catcher. Had they made or prepared their traps properly, and importantly, had they proof that they could keep up with the constant demands of both the mole and the landowners, and successfully fulfil their responsibility of maintaining the land mole free?

Study of the mole catchers, and of their agreements of employment gleaned from parish and church records, enables us to learn how they lived, and we find that not only did they work locally to their place of residence, but some chose to travel further afield to work their skills. Travelling from farm to farm and estate to estate, and as we learn from census records, from county to county, we can trace the mole catchers' journeys, with many crossing the borders of Wales and Scotland. The National Census records began in 1801 to provide the statistics of the population and have been taken every ten years since. The first few surveys recorded only the head of the household, but would have noted his occupation as mole catcher if that were the case.

These records show us the locations of mole catchers in their home villages and parishes, but in 1841 the census details changed and more details were required for submission. Now they included every individual staying in an address over that night. Listing every individual not only identifies mole catchers as head of the family and sons employed as mole catchers, but also anyone staying in the property whose occupation was a mole catcher. Many mole catchers, like other tradesmen providing particular skills, travelled around the United Kingdom removing the moles from one area before moving on to the next. They were granted free lodgings on farms and in households with available rooms; many widows would board them, possibly under the orders of the property owner who required the services of the mole man, or even at the demand of a village desperate to get rid of its moles.

The names of these mole catchers are recorded together with the place they came from, and if they had travelled over the border they would be identified as coming from England. Each census shows that many English mole catchers would have been staying in Scotland at the time, and the reason becomes clear when we consider how seasonal temperature impacts on the mole's life cycle. The climate and the seasonal temperature in the United Kingdom clearly changes as you travel from the south to the north, with the south warming up before the north; thus the life cycle of the mole starts earlier in the south because the weather gets warmer earlier in the year, so the mole catchers are called upon to provide their removal services earlier in the year, moving up the country as the months warm up progressively further north.

Because of this it was once thought that moles had two litters, as the mole catchers would have been called upon to remove moles in the south in the early spring months and were catching pregnant females, only to catch more pregnant females in the early summer months the further north they trekked. Travelling back south again, the tales of two litters would have been passed around, and it was only when it was understood that it was the warmth of the soil that dictated the moles' breeding cycle that this belief was confounded, an observable fact that continues today.

These agreements, census results, and church and parish records contribute to a wealth of knowledge concerning these people. It is impossible to learn everything about them, but we can share further in the lives of some of them, which will help us appreciate the role that such a remarkable person plays in our rural history.

The areas these mole catchers were required to work varied, and today many would shudder at the thought of the task that these old mole catchers took on. In 1884 mole catcher Edward Dixon from Ashby de la Zouch in the county of Leicestershire agreed to destroy the moles from land at the Ingestre estate 30 miles to the west in the county of Stafford. Edward was employed by the landowner, the Earl of Shrewsbury and Talbot, on behalf of the occupiers of property within the boundaries of the estate. Each of the parties was listed on the agreement, along with the acreage of land he was bound to work on their behalf. These land parcels varied from just over 100 acres to over 400 acres, totalling 2,856 acres, for which the sum of one penny an acre was agreed upon for a term of seven years. At the agreed penny per acre, the mole catcher's payment amounted to £11 9s per year.

The agreement had certain terms, including the clause that should he fail to destroy or kill the moles, or should there be reasonable grounds for complaint, then the payments would be suspended. Edward Dixon is recorded as a mole catcher through the census records from 1871 to 1901. An agreement with the agents for the Earl in 1894 shows a reduced acreage of 1,218 acres, with a correspondingly reduced payment of £5 1s 6d. The agreement is worded as follows: '[the agreement] shall continue in force for a term of seven years, should the said Edward Dixon so long live, but in the event of the death of the said Edward Dixon before the expiration of the said term of seven years, then and in that case this agreement shall terminate on the 25th March next after his death.'

This may have been the last agreement Edward held as a mole catcher, as records show that after the term of his last seven years he no longer appears in any accounts in relation to the Ingestre estate, and he sadly passed away at the age of seventy-seven years in 1907. Whether his death was in relation to his age or from a known illness, we may never know. In 1903, Edward's mole duties were taken on by William Oversby, a mole catcher born in Dent in Yorkshire. William appears in the 1881 census, when he was residing at the home of farmer Harriet Wynn in Uttoxeter, Staffordshire.

William then appears in the 1891 and again in the 1901 national census as the resident mole catcher in Cheadle, also in Staffordshire, with his wife and two children. William did not stay in service to the Earl for long, because according to the 1911 census he had returned to Uttoxeter; he died there in 1927.

Mole catchers such as Edward Dixon and William Preston held extensive contracts for their services, and they secured their income by crucially keeping their skills and methods secret, as a way of preventing others from challenging for this employment. By suppressing the knowledge they acquired over their broad periods in service – in the same way that the use of the humble mumble pin is misinterpreted today – they deflected any interest in the control of moles by others. Concealing what they did, and hiding any awareness of it, was their way of protecting their own interests, which I personally can understand. In this century, after the discovery of the internet, combined with the banning of the use of poison against moles in 2006, there was a sudden upsurge of people declaring themselves to be proficient specialists.

There was then, as now, dishonesty in all life-styles, and mole catchers may have been guilty of a certain number of untruths to deter those who claimed they were proficient at removing moles. The reason then was to protect a livelihood; the intention of today's mole catcher is to pilfer one. Wherever we discover evidence of these enigmatic custodians of the mole-catching trade, we also learn that the conditions and terms of the agreements are the same. Cumbria mole catchers John Jackson and Alan Shepherd in 1884 held agreements that paid similar rewards as afforded to those in other parts of the United Kingdom. The landowners of the remote areas of Cumbria paid Alan a penny per acre for the first seven years, and then a half-penny per acre for the succeeding seven years, while John was paid 1½d per acre for the first two years of a five-year contract, reducing to a penny per acre for the remaining three.

In the opposite corner of the country in Sussex, things were no different, as here the agreements also stipulated terms of seven years for a fixed rate of pay. William Dixon, mole catcher, was employed under these terms to kill or destroy every mole he could, and to spread every molehill in the village of Aldbourne, commencing on 25 March 1818. Still in Sussex, Petworth House, once home to the Earls of Egremont and now owned by the National Trust, employed mole catchers to keep the extensive grounds mole free, grounds that during the 1750s were landscaped by the renowned landscape gardener Lancelot 'Capability' Brown. Accounts from the estate show that the sum of 10s 6d was paid each year.

Across the United Kingdom, terms and payments for mole catchers differed very little, and we can trace records from almost every county confirming the presence of a mole catcher who was a noteworthy and essential cog in the running of the British countryside. Rural England was not a place for the faint-hearted, as work was hard to find and a hard existence for its people, with many agricultural labourers who were out of work ending up in the workhouse as the only relief from poverty.

The working year for a country family was repetitive, with many working first in the fields, then in the woods as the seasons progressed, because after the farm harvest many turned to woodland crafts. In one Berkshire village close to my home village, history tells us that many became broom 'dashers', or besom broom makers. Such additional crafts were necessary to sustain any level of income throughout the winter months, until there was employment on the land again. The whole life of a country family was a struggle against poverty, and existence depended on each and every member of that family working. At birth, the country child was probably born into poverty, and not until they were at an age when they could work, at ten or twelve years old, did they start to experience life above the poverty line, as they could then help contribute to the needs of their parents and siblings.

A working person could earn money, but when they chose to marry, they would once again be plunged into possible poverty, as they would have a wife and then a family to provide for. Middle age may have lifted a man over the poverty line, as his own children would then have been old enough to work and could contribute to the family income, as he had to his own parents. But this would have been a short-lived respite, because soon his own children would leave the family home to lead their own lives, and so the pressure on how to survive would return. Finally at around sixty years old, agricultural work would become too hard, and so the country labourer would once again fall into the grip of poverty, until the often welcome release of death.

We have learnt that the mole catchers escaped the levels of poverty of their rural equals because of their skill and reliability in controlling moles, and their success in keeping their methods secret. They rarely appear in workhouse records, and we know that most remained in permanent addresses for long periods of their lives. They maintained a standard of living from a relationship with an animal that many others gave little concern as a source of income, an income that many held until they died, taking the secrets of their success with them.

SO HOW DID THEY DO IT IN THE OLD DAYS?

As already pointed out at the beginning, the use of pitfall traps or clay pots dug into the ground would not have been a practical method, especially for a parish mole catcher or one who was on the move from one location to another. These catchers needed to have methods of control that were practical, low cost to produce, and transportable. The first method was the snare, which was already available, and was be-

ing used for the capture of other species, as it had been for many years. The term 'capture' is significant, as this method, like the clay pots, did not immediately kill the mole but held or restrained it.

The Snare

The snare was simple but effective, a small loop that closed round the mole's body as it passed through it. It was simple to transport, easy to make, and practically invisible in its use as it was set in the moles' tunnels. Those who knew little of the work of the mole catcher would have spoken of how moles were mysteriously brought up from underground by someone who presumably had some magical influence over these strange creatures that were never heard and rarely seen. In fact, the mole catcher simply made practical use of the snare, putting it to work in the moles' tunnels. They studied the moles and how they worked, and because of their daily contact with the little creature's world, soon acquired a personal knowledge of its habits, which they were careful to keep secret. The snares needed to be placed in the tunnels that the moles used to get from place to place; these were the main runs, not the complex network of tunnels that were located under, in and around the obvious visible evidence of the mole's presence, the molehills.

These simple snares were made from horsehair, readily obtainable from the stables, or an unattended horse in a field. The long strands from a horse's tail are strong, and perfect for the task of constructing snares. Horsehair had a wide number of uses in those days, from strengthening plaster, making bows for violins, to creating furniture. The strands of horsehair to make snares were plaited into thin lengths of cord, formed into a loop, and secured to a small peg.

The snare needed to be set directly in the tunnel that the mole was known to use to travel to its feeding grounds. Like those under the landshreds in the Tudor selions, this important tunnel and the general area to search for it soon became known to the mole catcher. A stiff, thin stick pushed slowly into the ground was used to locate it – when a sudden 'give' was felt the catcher knew he had found it. A small hand-held spade or blade was used to open a small shaft just big enough to slide in the snare held in a thin stick – known as a tealer or tiller, and used in snaring other species. Probing around slowly and carefully would confirm the presence of the tunnel and its direction. The aim was to set the loop in the tunnel so that the mole's body passed through it, and set it so it would tighten as the mole continued on its way. The stiffly plaited horsehair held in a split in the end of the tealer made it easier to position correctly.

Once the depth of the tunnel was established with the probe, the snare loop on the end of the tealer could be slid down the shaft: once in the required position the top of the shaft would be squeezed round the tealer, and this would hold the snare loop in the correct position to apprehend the mole. The snare still required some restraint above the ground so that the loop drew tight, so snares were pegged down, in the same way as those used for fox or rabbit.

The shaft of the snare needed to be covered to prevent any external elements from getting into the tunnel, because obviously the mole lived in an almost permanently dark world – so the mole catcher learned that the vertical shaft needed to be covered over at the top with light soil taken from a nearby molehill. In the shallow tunnels that were visible on the surface of the soil or grass these snares were easier to set, as the mole catcher could slice into the roof across the direction of the tunnel and slide the loop into the slot to capture the mole.

The strength of the horsehair was not in doubt, but a mole would soon chew through the snare loop if given enough time, and with the snares set down out of sight often the mole had escaped before the snare could be inspected.

Loops were found empty, or snares were lost as the moles pulled them and the pegs down and along the tunnels. The mole catchers would have been working large fields possibly at various locations in their parishes, which meant it was difficult for them to check the snares frequently enough to collect all the captured moles before they were able to escape.

They overcame this problem by devising a way of holding the snares in the tunnel so that when the loop closed the pressure applied was constant. This also provided a way to see which snares had been sprung. Their solution was to set the loop of the snare within another solid loop made from a thin, whippy stick that was fixed to a small block of wood; this block measured 6 × 3 × ⅜in (150 × 75 × 9mm). Hazel or willow was favoured for the stiff loop; hazel is a forgiving tree when cut, and was readily available from the hazel copses scattered and worked around the countryside. Willow is also excellent and I preferred this, as it is more flexible and therefore slightly easier to work in the hands.

The stick to make the loop was no thicker than a pencil. In fact any stick with a soft central core can be used; it would be whittled down to expose this central core or pith, which would be scraped out to make a natural groove for the

The sticks are whittled to reveal the groove that will hold the snare.

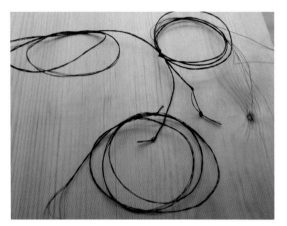

Snares are made from plaited horsehair.

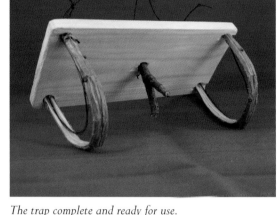

The trap complete and ready for use.

snare loop to fit closely into. In timber with no core, a groove would have been cut with a knife or saw blade, the groove just deep enough to act as a guide for the snare loop. Natural sticks provided exactly what the mole catcher required, and at no cost. Once whittled down, the stick was moulded into a horse-shoe shape, using either steam or the warmth of the hands, to form this snare-retaining loop.

Careful thought had clearly been given as to the best design for these first 'powered' snares for moles. The catcher attached two of these loops to the piece of wood, one at each end, having prepared the wood by drilling five holes, one at each corner and the fifth in the centre. For the snares, as before, they plaited hair from a horse's tail to form a thicker cord: six strands of plaited horsehair would be sufficient to construct a cord.

The cord was threaded through one of the corner holes in the piece of wood, then around the shape of the loop and back up out through the other hole on the adjacent corner to form the cord snare. This procedure was carried out at both ends, and then these cord loops were tied to another central cord, one end of which was passed through the hole in the centre of the piece of wood. The other end of this central cord was tied to the stick that provided the trigger to this first 'powered' mole snare.

They now had a block of wood with a loop made from a small stick at each end, which positioned the snare loops: when released they enclosed the mole's body and pulled tight. To capture the mole the snare had to release at exactly the right moment, when the mole ran into the loop. This was achieved in the following way: when a mole entered through one of the loops and under the block of wood, it pushed on a small twig set in the central hole. To set the twig the mole catcher pushed it up from the underside of the block, pinning the end of the central cord that had been inserted down through the centre hole from the top.

This meant that the snare loops could be formed in the hazel loops, but they would not pull tight until the twig had been dislodged from the centre hole, releasing the central cord. The small twig was hazel or thorn and cut from the hedgerow, and would have been a Y shape so when inverted and inserted it retained the central cord, but the two arms made it more likely for the mole to free it as it pushed through.

This small peg needed to be the correct size for the hole, and had to be cut and carved so it fitted into the central hole in the block of wood. It also had a collar that prevented it from becoming too tight a fit, and which allowed it to release freely; this collar would be made by carefully whittling or rubbing the pin along a rough stone. With the horsehair cord also passing through the hole, the force pulling the cord up resisted by the collar on the pin permitted the snare loops to remain open. When a mole entered and dislodged the pin, the cord would pull through freely and capture the mole as the snare pulled tight.

When setting these snares the mole catcher needed to keep these important pins safe and to hand, so he held them in his mouth. Hence they became known as 'mumble pins', because the mole catcher would have had to mumble, if he'd had to talk to anyone. This mumbled response to any questions summed up the mole catcher's reluctance to share this knowledge, which was the way to a profitable income. Many of those who catch moles today wrongly believe that the mumble pins had to be set like the hairpin trigger of a gunslinger's Colt 45 in the old Wild West, so the slightest interference from a target mole released the trap and captured it. In fact they are quite wrong, and how to set the mumble pin has been misconstrued over the years, as snippets of information on mole catching have been heard, as in a game of children's Chinese whispers – but with experience and understanding, the true setting of the mumble pin can be revealed to those of us who don't know about it.

To set off the snares and capture the mole in the loops, a simple stick was used, called a bender stick. Willow was preferred for this purpose as it was flexible and available, and the bender sticks were slightly thicker than the willow withies used for weaving baskets. These bender sticks were different lengths, but no shorter than a yard – that is, 3ft (1m) – in length, and more often over 4ft (1.2m). The stick was pointed at one end, and this end was forced into the ground so that when the stick was pulled and bent over, the opposite end was directly over where the snares were to be set; this made it easier to position the horsehair snares in the hazel loops held in the piece of wood.

The mole catcher located the tunnel where he wanted to place the snares using a stiff, stout thin stick or thin metal rod. These were thin for a reason, which was so as not to cause too much damage to the tunnel, as any such disturbance to its environment would immediately alarm the mole. I used a stick carefully sourced from the copse with a thick T-shaped top that was comfortable to the hand when in use. All the new growth was trimmed to leave the preferred single probe, except for just one small sprig that was perfect to hold the bender stick in the bent position whilst the snare cord was attached to the end. The tunnel was opened up to the size of the piece of wood, which when lined up in the tunnel had to be a tight fit; it was secured with some hazel pegs to counter the upward force that the bender stick would place on it prior to the mole releasing it.

This is the difficult part of setting these snares in place, because if it is not carried out correctly, it could fail to catch the mole. Thus if the mumble pin is pushed too hard into the central hole, it will make it difficult for the mole to release it – hence the collar on the mumble pin. Without a collar, and if the mumble pin is too tight a fit in the centre hole, it would be possible for the mole to push round it – so getting this accurate is important. Hence my own style of probe to hold the bender stick and locate the tunnel.

I have to admit that as a young lad I did not fully fathom out this solution without some help from my dad, who could put his hand to any problem. I'm not sure if my method of setting the snare was the same as those old mole catchers before me, but it worked. They possibly just had another stick, which was hooked in shape to counter the pressure of the bender stick until they were ready for it to be taken away, and the pegs holding the block of wood in position held the full force of the bender stick.

Having located the mole's tunnel, I would have everything ready. The bender stick had to be positioned first, so it was laid down so the end to which the snares were to be fixed was over the point where the hole was to be made into the tunnel. At the bender stick's other end, a long-handled spade with a spike, called a spud, was used to drive a hole into the ground. The point of the bender was then pushed firmly into this hole; it did not have to be precise, but just enough to ensure that when the stick was bent, the other end would be directly over where the snare would be set.

My adapted probe was then pushed into the ground alongside the bent stick, and the small sprig on the probe was used to hold the bender stick down. As mentioned before, a simple hooked stick could possibly have been used. Having made sure that the bender stick was over the trap site, and that the sprig would hold it under the force it applied, it could be released from the sprig and allowed to straighten up and rest in its hole.

The bender stick having indicated where the trap should be positioned, and now up and out of the way, I would then carefully make a hole into the tunnel with a trowel, ensuring the hole was no bigger than the size of the wood block, which had to be a tight fit. To start with I used another block of wood as a template, the same size as those with the snares, until I got proficient at it – and even later on the template block was often a welcome friend.

With the snares held in the hazel loops and the cord through the centre hole, I would push up the mumble pin with one hand and at the same time apply pressure by lightly pulling the central cord up with the other. I maintained the pressure by pulling the central cord as I pushed the wood block down again into the tunnel; I then held it down with a peg on each side. This could get fiddly, but by holding the central cord with the teeth – yes, teeth – rather than the hand, it is possible to maintain the pressure on the cord to hold the mumble pin in place, leaving both hands free to position and push in the pegs to hold the block in place.

Keeping the pressure again with the hand on the central cord, the bender stick is now pulled over and located on the sprig on the probe. You can then tie the central cord to the bender stick using either a loop or a clove-hitch knot. The clove-hitch knot was perfect for this job as it can be adjusted to maintain the pressure on the stick before the probe was removed.

The ground over the snares still required covering, and in shallow, light soil conditions a sprinkling of dry soil was sufficient; but in the deeper tunnels, pieces of turf were used to make a roof, with just a small gap to let the cord pull through, and then sprinkled with soil. The probe or the hooked stick could now be removed, and if all had been carried out correctly, the bender stick could be left to apply the upward pressure resisted by the pegs holding down the block of wood until the target mole released the mumble pin. It sounds complicated, but as with anything, if you do it often you become conversant with it.

The snares and blocks were all hand made by the mole catcher from materials sourced from woodland, copse, stable and hedgerow – indeed, collecting materials from nature seemed fitting for use against one of nature's mammals. This type of snare was also in the better interests of the mole whilst it was in man's control, compared with drowning it in a pot, because once the snares were set and in place, the long bender sticks enabled a quick response by the mole catcher when a snare was sprung by a mole. The sudden release of the strain on the bender stick was immediately obvious compared to previous snares that were just pegged down.

Furthermore the mole catcher could see from some distance away whether the bender sticks were up or down – that is, whether they held a mole or not. The tips of the bender sticks were possibly painted, or coloured ribbons were tied on like flags, to help identify any snare that had been sprung. Once sprung, the strain from the bender stick on the snare around the mole's body would hold the mole fast, so the mole catcher had more time to respond, and remove and despatch it. Mole catchers may perhaps not have considered the humane aspect of this working practice, being more anxious to recover every mole caught and claim the bounty payment, but it did mean they recovered moles that previously may have been lost, because if there was undue delay in recovering the mole there was a risk it would drag the snare away down the tunnel or chew its way to freedom. Indeed the humane aspect of this method even improved because increasingly the mole catcher remained and kept a watchful eye over his snares when working the fields, and thereby reduced any unnecessary suffering.

In comparison to the attacks made by vermin killers on other wildlife, the mole catcher was undoubtedly at the forefront of the provision of new standards of welfare in relation to pest control. Their ingenuity in the control of moles was just the beginning, and it was their inventiveness as the years progressed that has developed the methods available to us today. As a boy I, too, captured moles in this way – like those mole catchers so long ago I also sat in the shade of a tree watching all round me until the swift straightening of one of my bent willows sent me scurrying over for my prize. Once the moles were captured and the day was done, the snares were removed for the next day, for another contest with another mole.

These snares and bender sticks were never left in place because any snares that were sprung when the mole catcher wasn't present would be empty after any lengthy period of time. Also once darkness fell the bender sticks risked being trodden on or disrupted by domestic livestock or animals such as deer, fox or badger, rendering them useless. In addition, the mole catcher needed to retain the secret of his carefully constructed snares, and any left overnight might be of interest to those curious as to the mystery of the mole catcher's skills; and there might be others who would readily remove a mole, should the opportunity arise, and take a payment for themselves.

The simple bender stick originally provided the power for home-made clay and wooden barrels. The strength in the horsehair cords can clearly be seen.

The use of snares in this way was the main method of catching moles for hundreds of years. In the construction and use of these snares the mole catcher would have been constantly obtaining a greater understanding of the moles – how they lived and the problems he had to overcome in order to remain one to one with this secretive foe. The way the mole catchers controlled the moles with these snares changed very little, but we need to call upon every small scrap of information recorded to piece together the lives of these personalities. Those who made reference to the mole catcher in those days may not have realized just how important these snippets of information would be to us when they wrote them. Poets, authors and songwriters rarely wrote about the mole catcher, but when they did, we can, from reading these works, find important points and historical dates, which widens our understanding of these characters of our countryside. For example, the renowned poet John Clare (1793–1864) wrote a poem he called *The Mole Catcher* and its lines provide an insight into the mole catcher's methods:

With spuds and traps and horsehair string supplied
He potters out to seek each fresh made hill
Pricking the greensward where they love to hide
He sets his treacherous snares, resolved to kill
And on the willow sticks bent to the grass
That such as touched jerk up in bouncing springs
Soon the little hermit tries to pass
His carcass on the gibbet hings

THE MOLE SPUD

John Clare obviously witnessed the use of the bender stick and horsehair snares, but he also refers to the spud. This was another weapon in the mole catcher's armoury: the mole spud, mentioned earlier. It was a simple, long-handled spade, sharpened to a spike at one end, with a small 6 × 4in (150 × 100mm) spade on the other. The mole catchers would work the fields from morning until night, setting their snares and bender sticks early in the morning and then removing them all again just before dusk. As they prowled the fields watching and waiting for, as John Clare wrote, 'bouncing springs', these spuds were also used to flick a mole out of the soil when it was observed working in the shallow tunnels or loose soil.

Willow trees can often be seen in strange locations, many from discarded bender sticks, which have sprouted due to the willow's ready ability to root, the new trees 'planted' by the mole spud when the mole catcher has omitted to pull the benders from the ground. Rabbit catchers adapted the mole spud, because although its small spade was of little use in digging out a lost ferret, the slightly stouter spike was perfect for locating the larger tunnels of burrowing rabbits. This is possibly where many comments or beliefs originated, that the spud

The mole catcher used the spike of the mole spud to drive a hole in the ground, into which he would set the bender stick.

was used to locate mole tunnels. However, the spike on the end of the spud handle was not used for the placement of snares or for locating the moles' tunnels. The spike was just used to thrust into the ground to make a hole for the bender sticks, so it was easier to push them down into the earth if the ground was hard or difficult, before they were bent over in order to power the snares.

We know that this method was still being used centuries after the Tudor mole catchers and well into the early nineteenth century when John Clare wrote his poem.

Another tool in the mole catcher's bag would have been a five-pronged hand fork, often embossed with the words 'mole catcher'. The five tines were close enough to scoop out any unsuspecting mole from its tunnel without damaging its valuable pelt.

CLAY BARREL TRAPS

The ingenuity of the mole catcher was remarkable, and the need to better and simplify their methods was ever on their mind. At some time during the early 1800s mole catchers began to use a new tool in the control of moles: this was a clay barrel to hold the snare, and I have been kindly given some original clay barrels by the grandson of an infamous mole catcher from Preston Bissett in Buckinghamshire, Thomas Turner. Thomas reputedly caught enough moles in one year to buy his cottage, and these barrels have what are thought to be his initials pressed into the clay.

I have researched this a little more deeply, however, as the clay barrel traps must have originated from some local source; but these clay barrel traps that bear the initials 'TT' may not, as was previously thought, be those of Thomas of Preston Bissett, but those of earlier mole catchers in the Turner family. Thomas Turner of Preston Bissett was born in 1863, and it was not until after the death of his father William, when Thomas was in his mid to late twenties, that mole-catching work took over from his usual work of agricultural labouring.

Thomas began catching moles in the late 1880s; he continued to catch moles in Preston Bissett and the surrounding areas, and can be identified in records as residing in Gawcott, Buckinghamshire in the latter part of his life – still as a mole catcher. Thomas would certainly have employed the more modern metal traps of that time, so where do these old clay barrels originate? As well as the barrel with the initials TT, I was also given a barrel with the initials RT, and it was this that inspired me to investigate further. The Turner family have other mole catchers in their family tree, and coincidently at the time when these clay barrels began to appear in the countryside, and the Turner family may hold the key to the first use for a clay barrel. Head of the household Richard Turner lived in Goddington, in Oxfordshire, and one of his sons, William, later the father of Thomas of Preston Bissett, was to become a mole catcher.

During 1830–40 William's elder brother, Thomas, was working as a brick maker at the local brickyard, and would certainly have been producing clay drainage pipes, tiles and bricks for the area. If we look closely at the clay barrels that bear the initials TT and RT, they are distinctly different to those that were to be mass produced in the years to come. Firstly, they have only three holes in the top, as opposed to the five of the factory-made barrels. These holes allowed the positioning of the snares and the mumble pin when the trap was in use. It is quite possible from these dates that the concept of clay barrels for mole catching came from the Turner family. Thomas may well have considered with his father and his brother William that small changes to the drainage pipes could assist the work of a mole catcher.

Richard and son William were at that time, as so many, employed in work on the land as agricultural labourers, and clearly had identified the need for a mole catcher in their area. Thomas may have supplied the barrels, and would possibly have made them for his father and brother, with RT pressed into the clay to identify his father's barrels, and maybe a WT for his brother, although none of these have survived the years. The initials TT are not such a mystery, as William was not alone in his mole-catching career, as his younger brother

Timothy Turner also appears working as a mole catcher. Of course, over the years the story may have been distorted slightly, and in fact Thomas Turner brick-maker may be the Thomas who earned enough from his trap making to pay for his cottage in a year, and it was his custom to mark all his traps TT.

I truly hope it was the Turner family that was responsible for the changes to mole catching: it seems only fitting that such a character as Thomas Turner, whether mole catcher or brick maker, should be remembered – he is still spoken of today, and should hold the key to this piece of history.

The idea of constructing or adapting a piece of pipe that could be placed in a mole's tunnel so that it would maintain the structure and enable an effective but easier method of presenting the catcher's snares, soon caught on. Brickworks were abundant, producing bricks and tiles, and in the mid- to late nineteenth century they were also making clay pipes for waste water and field drainage. The smaller clay drainage pipes were approximately 11in (25cm) long, with an internal diameter of about 2½in (50mm), therefore a perfect fit for a mole tunnel. By reducing the length these clay barrels were the solution to presenting snares in a more effective way.

The idea of using such a device for mole control must have come from someone who was working as a mole catcher, and it is quite possible that the Turner family was the source of this innovative addition to the mole catcher's armoury. The clay barrels soon became commercially available; they varied slightly in size according to each supplier, and were made from moulds approximately 6in (150mm) in length with an internal diameter of 2in (50mm). A groove was made just in from each end of the barrel on the inside to hold the snares, which were passed down through a hole in the top of the barrel above each groove, and a centre hole was made for the insertion of the mumble pin. It was a clay copy in principle to the mole catch-

The original Turner clay barrel alongside a manufactured barrel trap.

ers' home-made trap, and again was triggered with the bender stick.

Making traps isn't easy and is time-consuming, and possibly at that time, in the mid-1800s, many of the new breed of mole catchers preferred to pay someone else to make the tools of their trade – like many of today's tradesmen. But to others who were looking at moving in on the gains to be had from mole catching, it opened the door for them to compete with those who until then had kept the secrets of the trade close to their chest. These clay barrels were often purchased from large production factories, as opposed to the local potter – for example, W. Meeds & Sons was a company based in Burgess Hill, Sussex, which during the 1800s manufactured many brick and tile products, including clay barrels. The factory closed in 1930. William Meeds took over the company in 1848, which enables us to date the use of these clay barrels to hold mole snares. By this time snares were made of wire, rather than horsehair. In the photograph you can see the difference in design between the factory-produced clay barrel, which had five holes in the top, two at each end for threading in the snare, as opposed to the Turner family clay barrel which had three holes.

WOODEN BARREL TRAPS

Clay is a porous substance, with the propensity to crack in frost, be broken by carts and crushed under hoof, and the trap itself still relied on the simple stick of bent willow for its motivating force. In short, clay was not up to the task, and was soon replaced by elm, the wood from which wheel hubs were made. Elm was moisture resistant and strong, and therefore offered a long life; furthermore replicas of the clay barrels could be sourced from any wheelwright, green-stick worker or bodger.

Made to the same specifications as the clay barrel, it was discovered that because of its strength, the new elm barrel could be powered by a spring made of wire. The new age of wire works, and the production of iron and steel, may have just begun to influence the tools used by the mole catcher – already brass snare wire had largely replaced plaited horsehair snares, thus saving the mole catcher the time it took for him to make the plaited cords. The stronger elm barrel also meant that a wire spring could be attached to the body to power the wire snare loops, so the bender stick was no longer needed – though the mole still had to displace the now legendary mumble pin to release the spring.

No longer were mumble pins made from sprigs of hazel or thorn: they were paddles tied to the trap with a small cord to avoid loss. Be-cause of the demand for a self-contained trap these wooden barrels, like the early clay barrels, also went into mass production; they were sold under the retail name as the 'Perfection'. The need for a full barrel was questioned, and soon the barrels were cut in half lengthways to produce two bodies, and therefore make two traps from one. I personally would say that this was because elm barrels brought various problems if they were not positioned correctly, as did clay barrels previously, and that full barrels could be detected by the moles and therefore avoided, filled with soil and rendered inoperative.

This highlights the fact that if these barrel traps were to be effective they needed to be positioned correctly, which required the experience and proficiency of someone competent; this gave the mole catchers a breathing space to consider their next move in order to outmanoeuvre those seeking to usurp their revenue.

As with the Turners' clay barrels, many also chose to stamp their mark on their own wooden full and now half-barrels; as an example I have a trap once owned by James Bassett, a mole catcher in Suffolk, who stamped his initials 'JB' on his traps, possibly to identify that they were his. James lived in Mildenhall in 1881 with his wife Sarah, and plied his trade with traps made of a wood half-barrel body with a wire spring attached.

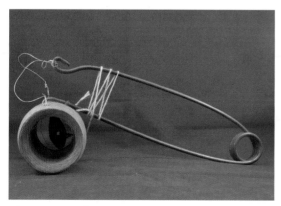

The wooden Perfection mole trap showing the attached spring, making it a self-powered device.

Wooden barrel trap marked JB (James Bassett) with attached spring.

These wooden barrels can still be found to-day in collections, and as with James Bassett's trap, they show the influence of the changes in the nineteenth century. Thus steel loops as opposed to the old whippy sticks supported the half-barrel in the tunnel, brass wire was preferred to horsehair for snares, and three, rather than five holes were made in the barrels. These changes in the mole catchers' ways were just the start of a progression, but it seems clear that they were the result of specific requests by the mole catchers themselves. It was also clear that the change from clay to wood resulted from the experience of those who used the barrel method for mole catching.

Cutting the full barrel in half also led to the mole catchers learning that they could replace the roof of the tunnel with a minimum of disturbance. Their home-made blocks of wood created a flat roof, unlike the smooth, crafted barrel shape, which now was a better fit in the tunnel. With the full barrels, whether wooden or clay, it was important that the tubular shape of the barrel lined up perfectly with the tunnel to avoid detection, which was no easy task, as each mole tunnel would have been slightly different according to the individual mole. The half-barrels supported on metal loops meant they could make adjustments in aligning the

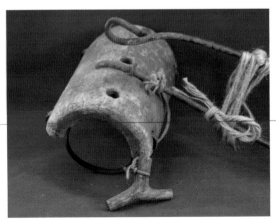

The wooden half-barrel traps were fitted with wire loops to support the trap.

top of their half-barrel with the roof more easily, by simply pushing the metal loop into the tunnel floor.

The changes to these barrels as devised by the mole catchers to make their work easier was a step forward, but they still had to combine this with understanding the quarry and placing the barrels correctly in order to obtain the results that would confirm their position as the local or trusted mole catcher. These wooden half-barrels had disadvantages in that they were bulky, and the springs, like the bender sticks before them, were still visible when in use. Also their cost cut into the income of the agreements.

They also remained a capture trap, in that the mole was still held in the snare loop against the roof by the force of the attached wire spring. Thus the use of these new traps had little effect on the mole catcher's working practice, even though they were now powered by the smaller metal spring as opposed to the bender stick. They still were placed in the morning, checked during the day, and then removed before the mole catcher returned home. This ensured a better working practice, in that any trap that had captured was repositioned, and any trap that had been sprung without a capture was reset.

Working the land in this way meant that the mole catcher provided the service required by the agreements that he had signed up for; it also prevented the theft of these treasured tools. Remaining in Suffolk, in Blaxhall, it is alleged that in 1879 another mole catcher by the name of James (Sparrowhawk) Smith caught 654 moles in thirty-two days with such traps — evidence, even in those days, of the success to be had from the mole catcher working the traps, as opposed to just leaving them in the hope that they would still be there upon his return, with or without a mole contained inside.

The size and weight of these barrels and half-barrels, and the complexity of transporting them, meant the mole catchers had to consider ways of hauling their bits and pieces from home to the fields of work. Much of this was accomplished on foot, possibly with a handcart or with a child alongside to share the load.

CHANGES IN THE VICTORIAN AGE

It is clear that during the 1800s many changes in mole control took place, including changes to how the snares were presented in the ground, as more people discovered the income to be had from catching moles. Until then the closed-door agreements had protected the mole catchers from any external interest, but the Victorian age was a huge turning point in British history, and this was to impact upon the mole catchers in many ways. For years they had quietly gone about their business, keeping their knowledge secret so as not to have to share or lose an income, but things were about to change. The agricultural revolution brought crop rotation and a new opportunity to grow winter crops, and new cultivation methods that increased the productivity of light soils for fodder crops meant an increase in livestock. Produce was plentiful, and this growth resulted in an increase in the human population, which almost doubled.

New processes were not confined to agriculture, and new manufacturing methods improved the efficiency with which factories could produce new inventions and ideas. Machines could now do the work of men in the fields as mechanical power replaced human muscle. The rural population decreased as the urban population increased, the labour force changed, and many who once worked the soil were now forced to work in factories producing the changes that had torn them from their way of life. Those who did not comply with change found themselves at the mercy of the workhouses, and many references can be found in the workhouse logs to 'ag. lab.', meaning 'agricultural labourer'.

Progress, as it was termed, quickly altered the face of the countryside, and it also impacted on the mole catchers, as this large-scale manufacture of inventions, tools and chemicals made mole catching available to almost anyone. It was to become known as the industrial revolution, because as well as changes in manufacture, new forms of transport, such as the steam train, became readily available, which enabled people to travel more cheaply and faster than ever before. New goods and products never before seen, appeared in every store and shop, making choice an option – and it was choice that was to bring changes in the ways that moles were controlled, and new levels of suffering to any mole that fell victim to them. Vermin killers had new implements to their arsenal, and the Victorians produced a vast array of new metal tools for 'bird and animal control', as it was termed in the many marketing catalogues and pamphlets of that time.

These new metal instruments were given the name 'trap' from the old English 'treppe', which means to step, as the designs of the new mechanical traps required the target to step in or on to the trap to operate it. These new engines were powered by manufactured springs, so required no human effort to make them work. The industry of trap making spread across the central and northern parts of England, in the industrial towns where steel was being produced, and patent applications for traps of every kind were submitted. Traps shaped for every known animal and bird appeared, placing an immense pressure on the wildlife of Britain. The Vermin Act of 1566 was still in force, but it was not until 1863 that it was finally revoked. The flood of traps by then available might have been a significant factor in the decision to repeal this Act, because anyone could obtain an array of traps and generate a good income from claiming the bounty.

THE SCISSOR TRAP

The trap makers soon produced a trap especially for the mole, placing both the mole and the

The scissor trap enabled all to embark on mole catching.

power was supplied by different types of spring, in the form of bow, flat or wire springs. Many old scissor traps may still be found with these different types of spring, in museums, collections, books and, disturbingly, garden sheds.

This readily available form of mole control, where no skill was required of making snares and carefully placing them, allowed the vermin killers to compete with the mole catchers. These metal mole grips could be purchased in bulk or individually, opening the door to anyone and everyone who wanted to 'have a go' at the mole. These small traps could be put in position and, unlike bender sticks, would not so easily be seen or disturbed. They were left for long periods between their placement and the mole catcher's return, because it was thought that since the springs were metal and had some level of strength, they would hold the mole until the trapper returned. There was also no possible chance of a captured mole chewing its way to freedom.

However, this resulted in moles being subject to a lesser degree of concern in relation to any possible suffering, compared to those mole catchers who used snares, and remained close by so they could respond to the operation by quickly despatching the mole and keeping its suffering to a minimum. It was thought these new scissor traps would kill the mole, but in fact they were only ever a restraint trap, like the horsehair snares, as the energy in the springs is only enough to hold the struggling animal until it expires from stress, exhaustion, starvation or dehydration. As with anything that is almost completely out of direct sight, there was no consideration as to the distress caused.

As today, scissor traps could only be set in relatively shallow tunnels or runs, so the arms, like the bender sticks, were visible above ground. Although not as prominent as bender sticks, scissor traps could also be seen to have operated if these arms were spread apart. Arms that remained in the set position were not checked by the trap user, but very often the

mole catchers under pressure. The mole trap they produced was the scissor trap, so named after the way it operated. Classifying it as a mole 'trap' could be questioned, since the mole doesn't step into or on to any part of it for it to operate. The scissor trap was located in the tunnel, so when the mole passed along the run, it was obstructed by a metal plate in the centre of the trap, which held the jaws apart. When this plate was dislodged by the mole, the jaws then closed around its body under the pressure of the springs. As all other traps manufactured, mole would have tunnelled under, around or through them and rendered them useless. Only when the user removed and properly inspected the trap would this have been discovered, thus delaying the full success of the service he was meant to be providing, and therefore prolonging the damage to the land caused by the mole's efforts.

Sticks and horsehair snares now had to compete with the new generation of mole trappers. The vermin killers plied their trade on all and any target that brought them a bounty payment, and although they may have lost the easy income under the withdrawn Vermin Act, they now had manufacturers producing traps for every living creature, whether fin, fur or feather. Species that were once not available to them suddenly became of interest, and the mole was one of them. But although they might be equipped with all the new apparatus, the old mole catchers had one advantage that those new to mole catching could not procure quickly: knowledge of moles and their habits. Such knowledge was infallible, and the old mole catchers had retained it and kept it close to their chest – and they too, now, had the option to use the small metal scissor traps, rather than making their own.

Scissor traps varied slightly in design, and most trap manufacturers produced them, but the mole catchers soon realized that these traps had a limited use, as they were ineffective in the deeper runs, requiring a shaft deeper than the total length of the trap to access them. Correct placement of the scissor trap is hampered in slightly deeper tunnels, because the shaft required to permit the spread of arms of any scissor trap in the lower tunnels would be wide enough to alert the mole to the change to its environment. The mole catchers knew from their experience of setting snares that the tunnels in which they needed to locate the scissor traps would be at varying depths, and not just the shallow runs. So the real mole catchers continued to set snares, staying ahead of the latest

influx of would-be mole catchers, who were limited to working the shallow tunnels.

So predominant was the scissor trap in all its guises that it was produced by nearly every wire works or trap manufacturer in the industry of the time. This intensification was clearly justified, as the requests to remove moles were increasing rapidly with the demand for increased agricultural productivity and the transformation of the countryside into larger fields. The new mole engines also found their way into households, as they offered an immediate do-it-yourself solution to many with a mole problem, who then no longer needed to employ the services of the local mole catcher. The scissor trap is still manufactured and sold today, but although not the first choice of many who control moles, these were once considered the perfect solution to any mole problem, and to many people remain so today.

The scissor trap of today remains as it was manufactured then, with only small changes – in fact the alterations made today are individual to the supplier, as were those made back in the 1800s. Whether the change is legal or not is a point for further discussion. Some may have serrations cut into the jaws or single spikes on each jaw, which personally I believe is illegal, although those in positions of more authority than myself consider them permissible.

At the height of the Victorian trap boom many of the traps were hand made with hand-operated presses, and with manufacturers in competition, many applications for patents were made. The changes back then consisted mainly of modification to the springs; an example was the change in 1884 from a bow spring to flat springs, made by Henry Lane, a principal manufacturer of traps in the village of Wednesfield in the Midlands. Henry Lane later made a further change, advertising new, deep curved jaws. Wednesfield was the trap-making capital of Britain during the Victorian era, with the population of this small working village growing from just over 1,000 in 1801 to over 14,000 in 1881. This situation was soon to change, however, because with the introduction of powered tools, under the turn of phrase called progress, the population dropped to just over 4,000 by the start of 1900.

Other Mole Traps

Other trap makers in the same village released their own style of scissor mole traps, but in 1874 James Roberts devised a mole trap that may have been inspired by the old mole catchers' wooden flat-top home-made trap and snares, as it was visually similar. It consisted of two metal plates, three metal loops, a bow spring or two flat springs, and a wheel. One of the plates could freely move up and down the loops via holes drilled in it, while the other plate forms the top and has the springs fixed to it and the loops. The bottom plate when raised was placed under the resistant force of the spring, and was held up by a centrally positioned pin with a wheel on the end. The concept was that when the mole passed under the plates and pushed the pin, the wheel would move freely and allow the force from the spring to thrust the plate downwards to strike the mole, and allegedly crush it.

When this trap was placed in the tunnel there was therefore no need for a bender stick to provide the power, unlike the old mole catchers' home-made trap. It was as the scissor trap – self-powered, but had the added advantage that it could be set in both deeper and shallow tunnels and still remain completely out of sight. Many would consider this a disadvantage, however, as you would need to mark or remember where the traps had been placed, and would have to physically uncover the traps in order to inspect them, rather than just walk by and glimpse over to see if they had been sprung. To the professional mole catcher, inspecting such traps would have been routine and without issue had he opted to use them, but cast iron and steel traps were heavier items to transport, which was a disadvantage since he operated predominately on foot.

THE POISON STRYCHNINE

Earlier in the century, another method of control was being developed in France, which would lay further pressure on the continued existence of the mole catchers. Two scientists, Joseph Bienaime Caventou and Pierre-Joseph Pelletier, were working on producing a substance that would combine with the scissor traps or replace them, and allow all vermin killers to offer a cheap service – but as it turned out, one that caused suffering and distress to the pests involved. It was the poison strychnine, an alkaline-based poison made from an extract from a tree found in India called the *Strychnos nu-vomica* or strychnine tree. The powdered poison was sold under licence, thus providing an income to the authority, and it was closely monitored, because it could be, and often was, used for foul deeds, as related in the files and journals of crime of that time.

The changes to the transport system enabled urban vermin killers to enter the fray, armed with a jar of poison-coated worms. Possessing no skill, they were nevertheless quick to be employed by farmers, who were grubbing out hedges and incorporating their smaller fields, including many of those once included in the enclosure act, to create large fields for grazing sheep to feed the increasing population. This was a time when landowners could earn a healthy income from farming the land. It was an opportunity to become wealthy, and any way to increase their profits was adopted, and the new breed of vermin killers exploited these changes. Fodder crops needed to be protected from mole activity, because the degeneration of pastureland carried the risk of listeria, the bacteria found in the soil that can be harmful and sometimes fatal to livestock, and which notably can be potent in a winter feed of hay or silage. Every mound of soil thrown up by the mole had the potential to pass on these bacteria, so moles everywhere came to be considered a target pest.

These new mole killers were cheap, and they spread devastation under the soil. Administering poison-coated worms was of no concern to most people – after all, no one witnessed the true pain and suffering caused to the mole: it was a classic example of the out of sight, out of mind attitude that came to prevail. But the truth was, that below the soil the moles suffered painful convulsions, and it took an estimated thirty minutes to an hour for the mole to expire. Claims that the poison was humane had no substantiated evidence. It is known that a mole carefully cleans the dirt from a worm it is going to eat using its front paws, but in so doing it is likely to remove a proportion of the poison from a poison-coated worm, thereby compromising the strength of the dosage, so that it doesn't kill the mole quickly, as the correct administration would do.

Country folk came to call this poison 'strike nine', as they believed it would pass from one

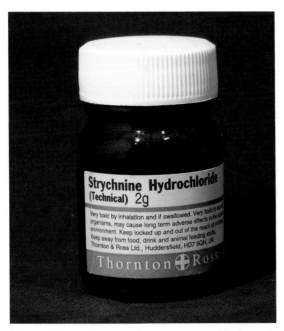

Now withdrawn from use, the poison responsible for much suffering.

target to another nine times before it lost its potency to kill. So any worm that killed a mole that was grubbed up or died on the surface could be consumed by a bird, maybe a prey species, which would die and might be eaten by a fox, which would also die. This was the true potency of strychnine, which thankfully was withdrawn from legal use in the United Kingdom in 2006.

With poison there was no substantiated evidence to any success, only the word of those who administered it, that they had got rid of the moles. Unlike the traditional mole catchers who continued to produce their captured moles and display them for the landowners and farmers to see, these mole killers had no proof of any completed task – but the crucial factor in their method was the cost to the mole, as causing unnecessary suffering didn't concern them at all, a situation that was to continue with the further changes that took place.

THE ANGLO IMPASSABLE

Later in the nineteenth century the traditional mole catcher's traps made from sourced materials and his reluctance for change maintained the divide between him and the vermin killer. Those now offering their services for the control of all species of animals and birds had every trap maker designing new devices. People actively involved in vermin control submitted ideas to the manufacturers of pest control apparatus indicating changes that would better suit their needs, and ways that would make their job easier. Mole control was included, and further traps appeared – but like those already available, all had limitations. However, a guillotine trap invented in 1888 by James Lawry and William Reed, two Cornishmen, and sold under the name of the Anglo Impassable, was more successful.

A modern version sold under the name of the 'plunger trap' surprisingly remains available, and is popular in the United States of America

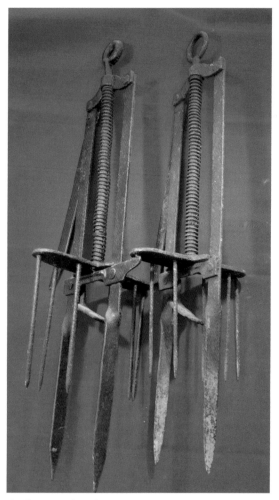

Guillotine-style mole traps.

These traps as used in the late nineteenth to early twentieth centuries would have rendered any fur from a caught mole useless, which was a serious disadvantage at a time when animal fur was commanding high prices.

The Anglo Impassable came in different models, with a Mark 1, Mark 2 and a Mark 2(a), the main differences being the ring on the top of the trap. The Mark 1 has a ring welded to the top of the spring rod, the Mark 2 has the ring formed from the spring rod, and the Mark 2(a) is just a smaller model of the Mark 2.

James Lawry was a farmer, and why he combined with the ironworks of William Reed to produce this trap may never be entirely known, as like other traps, producing them commercially for mole control would not have been practical. As a farmer he may have wanted to produce a trap that anyone could use, a trap that was simple to set, and one where it was obvious when it had operated in comparison to others. What we can learn from this time is that the real mole catchers remained faithful to their trusted snares, sticks, and knowledge of the mole. They needed to find a better, more efficient way to capture the mole, but the modern traps in all their guises were yet to offer anything better.

Thus a smaller, more compact trap or more effective snare was required – though very of-

The difference in the models was clear in the rings on the top.

as a way of controlling moles. These traps rely upon the mole passing directly under the trap in a shallow tunnel. Prior to the trap being set the tunnel roof had to be slightly compressed, so the target mole had to push up the roof to pass through. This action releases the spring, which thrusts a small plate down, which has six spikes that impale the mole. Obviously the humane aspect of this trap is questionable, since the force may be inadequate to penetrate the soil and strike the mole a lethal blow. Any obstruction in the soil that might have impeded its operation, such as stones, would not be detected, and the trap would be clearly visible.

ten a well thought out concept would fail when put to work as a result of the harsh environment it had to endure, or because the mole detected it easily. The mole catchers had good experience of these two considerations from their daily contact with the moles and their preferred environment, and they needed to deliberate this conundrum – but they were still reluctant to modify what would have been suitable, and to share their ideas, because they still felt they were at risk of losing an income.

TRADITIONAL MOLE CATCHER VERSUS VERMIN KILLER

The mole catchers were caught in a predicament: did they continue with the visible and cumbersome bender sticks they had worked productively for so long, or should they make the change? It would cost them, whichever choice they made, because with the new metal scissor traps now readily available to the vermin killers, they still faced the pressure to continue, as it meant that all could now enter the arena of mole control. The agreements for removing or destroying moles were now highly sought after, and many a mole catcher lost the work that had provided their earnings to those vermin killers who had suddenly appeared, and who were considered to be as good as any experienced mole catcher. After all, wasn't it just a simple matter of inserting a machine-manufactured gadget into a tunnel – what could possibly be all the fuss about; surely there was no mystery to catching a mole – or was there?

The production of metal traps for moles plunged a divide between the traditional mole catchers and the new opportunists, who in fact were no longer called 'vermin killers' after the revoked Vermin Act in 1863, but who now called themselves by the rather flamboyant title of 'controllers of pests'. The specialists appeared, such as the rat catchers offering exceptional services with new methods from newly manufactured traps designed to get rid of all rats, and pamphlets of others that would enable them to be proficient in the control of all pests – and of course, with the deadly poison strychnine they could take on moles, too. The lost income to vermin killers from the capture and killing of all species for easy financial gain under the now removed bounty payments for vermin directed them to consider every living pest that people were prepared to pay to have removed.

Supported by the growth of industry, and fuelled by the availability of so many new devices – the result of competition between manufacturers to prove the efficiency of their products – these controllers of pests fought between themselves for any available work. With an armoury of devices and the new selection of scissor traps, what the mole catchers considered as a secure income was often lost to those who could destroy moles more cheaply. Furthermore the man with the jar of poisoned worms and some scissor traps could also offer other services, such as rat removal.

The traditional mole catchers were clearly under threat, and to survive, many were forced to offer reduced terms of payment and shorter periods for contracts. Where once an agreement ensured many years of income, now it became a single year or short-term agreement, and with so many now competing for the same employment, those landowners requiring their services could negotiate new terms. The competition forced the mole catchers to operate even more secretively, and to make sure they kept the knowledge they had gleaned over so many years even closer to their chest.

From old photos we know that even with the scissor-action traps flooding the British countryside, the traditional mole catchers were still using their home-made wooden traps and bender sticks. Many new to the mole destroying trade probably considered they were wilfully ignoring progress, and ridiculed them for refusing to abandon such primitive methods – but the old mole catchers worked year in, year out, and they knew that capturing moles at times required placing their traps in tunnels where the new scissor traps could not be deployed because the runs were too deep.

The new generation with their new attitudes sought the moles in the spring, when they were working shallow tunnels, and they would have seen the mole catchers at this time working the new drilled land armed with sticks and spuds. The mole catchers must certainly have used scissor traps, but these were still useless in tunnels that were deeper than the total length of the trap. The mole catchers who used both the new and the old methods continued to offer the ultimate service when and where they could, and stepped in when those multi-tasking their pest services were unable to provide results due to their lack of understanding of their quarry, or if they chose to go after that other, more immediate harbinger of gain, the rat.

It was an advantage they could call upon at any time, but one that also worked against them as they continued to conceal their knowledge of the mole's habits from others. Those that make the most noise do so to disguise what they are not in possession of – and it is noise that people listen to when they should be listening to silence! The solitary old mole catchers were victims of this, as progress stamped its feet and banged upon doors, claiming to be the new generation in animal control that extended from coast to coast.

The mole catchers were not alone in this pressure brought to bear on their livelihood. As the pest controllers invaded the countryside, armed with their mass-produced engines for the capture of every living thing rolling off the production lines, other custodians of the countryside felt the force of development. Gamekeepers found that every opportunity to take what was considered game for one was also game for all. Poachers also worked under a cloak, the affable rogue, or the romantic rascal who preyed upon the livelihoods of these other rustic employees. The engines that brought pain, suffering and chaos to wildlife soon appeared in larger form to entrap those who stepped over the line, and mantraps soon lurked in woodlands, in wait for their victims. Those like the mole catchers and gamekeepers felt the full impact of what some would refer to as progress, as more people turned to the income suddenly made available by the new designs of animal trap.

The fashion for fur garments, and because it was so easy to supply food from trap use, impacted not just on the people of the countryside, but even more intensely on the numbers of animals and birds. Anyone could purchase the engines or traps and seek payment for pelts, or for removing a pest, or sell what they caught for food – and not always lawfully. I feel that the abolishment of bounty payments under the Vermin Act was influenced by the proliferation of metal traps, as more considered it an easy income. Also the mass production of traps must have caused a huge increase in suffering, as many not familiar with trapping were working traps, and often on an occasional basis.

It also became clear that new laws were needed, and were introduced, to protect landowners against the unlawful taking of game by those driven by greed or desperation. In 1816 a game law had been passed that prevented the taking of game by anyone other than landowners, with a punishment of deportation for possibly seven years if anyone was caught poaching. The battle between poachers and gamekeepers was bloody and desperate, at a time when the country was in turmoil from bad harvests and high costs. The combination of the game law, the rescinding of the Vermin Act, and the changes that reduced the number of those working on the land, must have made the Victorian countryside a distressing place in which to live during these times.

By the end of the century the mole catchers who still survived were feeling the full pressure of competition from this easy availability of metal scissor traps, cheap mole killers with their jar of poisoned worms, and claims of new specialists in the field of mole control. But the old mole catchers managed to exist because they kept the way they worked clandestine, which was so different to the self-aggrandisement expressed by rival pest controllers. Meetings between landowners, parish clerks and farmers to negotiate agreements were even more acrimonious as the values of the industrial world clashed with those of the traditional countryside.

But although many agreements may have been lost to cheaper options, the traditional mole catchers, with their close understanding of their target species, never failed to produce proof of their efforts, by comparison with those who used poison and who could only offer a verbal claim as to the number of moles removed, never actually producing physical evidence like the rows of moles tied to fences and posts by the old mole catchers.

Also, the growing belief that strychnine was causing the indiscriminate killing of wildlife, and that it was often the substance of human murder, was placing doubt in the minds of some of those with more years to live. There were also claims that the new metal traps were impregnated with the smell of progress in the process of manufacture, and that this would alarm any mole – therefore all such traps would need burying in the ground for weeks prior to use. So to employ another mole catcher with new devices would be a waste of time, as moles would return to plunder fields and lawns.

Of course much of this conjecture was untrue, but such declarations, bolstered by the traditional mole catcher's reputation and supported by his previous success rate, was often enough to regain the trust of many who had previously supported him. When new agreements came to be finalized for another term of employment, or for any lucrative new contract, the mole catcher relied on swift thinking and his enigmatic skill in keeping himself in contention.

Further pressure came from gardeners, who also acquired a few metal traps for use not just in their own garden, but in their employer's property, too. Mole traps could be purchased in garden catalogues, and the gardeners who worked in the large estates, like my own grandfather, were required to set these out, so there was no need to call the mole catcher. Scissor traps appeared in seed supplements, as did the guillotine-style trap, the Anglo Impassable of Lawry and Reed creating an interest in the do-it-yourself mole catcher.

The mole catcher's way of life therefore came under threat again from all sides, even from the landowners who once supported them, but who were looking for cheaper options, and insisting on reduced contract terms and conditions. With the competition from the flood of would-be pest controllers and their bucket of traps, and the do-it-yourself contingent, all baying from what is today considered progress, it is truly amazing that any mole catchers ever survived at all. But survive they did, and continued in their struggle to resist the hardship of the time – the threat of 'working the spike', a term used for the workhouse where men had to break oakum with a hammer and spike, ironically for use in other industries.

Such factors, combined with all the other pressures, caused many mole catchers to leave their villages and hamlets and to travel to new areas, to become travelling mole catchers. This trek took mole catching everywhere, and spread not just the tradition of the mole catcher but its mystery, too. In remote areas, where industry had yet to touch the trouble-free and slow pace of life that prevailed there, mole catchers were made welcome, and many of these villages were resistant to the changes that would follow.

Again, it is from uncovering these pockets of tradition that we can trace the existence of these people, and experience their lives and their unrelenting desire to catch the mole. Of course, the desire to catch moles was driven by the need to earn an income, and a good strike rate was undeniably made easier with metal traps – but it was knowledge of the quarry that was paramount for success. The mole catchers understood that the mole had a unique way of life, and this experience was obtained from daily contact with the moles and their environment. It only takes one trap to catch a mole, but it must be placed in the correct location, and precisely so that the mole will not detect it.

Mole catchers had the option of metal scissor traps, or the wooden barrels for shallow tunnels and the old home-made hazel loop snares, powered by the bent stick for the deeper tunnels preferred by the moles – preferred, because these are used to journey from place to place, as they are not disturbed and are more secure. However, a single and simple method of removing moles from any tunnel was clearly required.

For many years the mole traps released by trap manufacturers varied only in the type of springs or shape of the jaws, and it took until 1920 for the step forward to be made that was effectively to change mole control definitively – a step that, to this day, has never been bettered, and one which I personally think has been improved.

Chapter 2

Mole Catching Today

John Newton Duffus – or Jake to his family – was a Scottish shepherd/mole catcher from Eassie; his sons, John Junior and Henry, were also mole catchers. John and John Junior designed a compact and unique method whereby self-powered snares could be set in any depth of tunnel. They had previously used the heavy, clumsy wooden barrel-type trap, and realized its limitations. John considered any options that might be better, possibly in the same way that brick-maker Thomas Turner experimented from methods available to him. These changes in the historical journey of mole traps had to have been made by someone proficient in mole catching, which is why John, like Thomas, puzzled over a way to improve the device for controlling moles.

THE DUFFUS MOLE TRAP

John played around with various ideas and prototypes before he patented the Duffus mole trap. No longer was the obvious bent stick required, and the depth limitation of the scissor trap was a thing of the past: the new trap was a combination of everything that mole catchers had been using previously. Together with their knowledge of where traps were required, the design could, and can still be, used anywhere and in any tunnel. In September 1923 patent no. 21,309/22 became patent no. 203,484, which was the final design, and is still the half-barrel trap we see today. A prototype made from a full wooden barrel with small springs attached inspired the final design.

The Final Design

John and John Junior made a metal half-barrel, rather than one from timber, because small springs could be fixed to the top. These provided the power, and wire shape springs were used, which on release rose upwards. They returned to the use of snares, as opposed to jaws as on the scissor traps, though a more rigid wire snare loop was used than in previous designs. These loops, like the horsehair or brass snares, were also set through slots in the metal body and then attached to the springs. The firmer loop when in the down position acted as a support for holding the trap level in the tunnel, so there was no need for the hazel loops.

In addition, the rigid metal half-barrel shape made a replacement roof should any part of the mole's tunnel be disturbed as it was put in

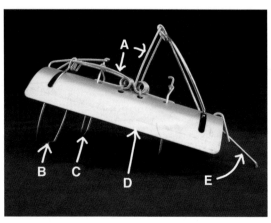

The parts of the half-barrel trap: A: trap springs, B: trap loop, C: mumble pin, D: trap body, E: retaining bar.

place. The springs were held down until the point of release by two small retaining bars. These were looped on each end of the trap body, which, when in the horizontal position and with the springs down and under pressure, located with another hook on the mumble pin. The mumble pins were no longer a wooden peg or paddle, but were now a loop of wire, with one for each spring, allowing the trap to operate independently each side. Thus two moles could be captured at any one time, or in the event of just one side being sprung, the other remained operational.

John Duffus hand made these traps himself, and sold them around the world until he was in his nineties, when he decided it was time to pass the whole business to his son John. The process was entirely 'hands on', with the steel sheet cut by hand shears and the wire springs laboriously wound by hand.

The Duffus Trap Cottage Industry is Sold

In 1958 John Junior also decided it was time to pass on the family cottage industry, and turned to an old friend David Jolly, asking him to take it on, under the condition that he would continue to make the traps himself. John did not wish for the trap to be taken over by a large operator who would mass produce it and sell it at a high price, but produce an inferior product.

David Jolly agreed; he bought the patent and manufacturing rights and continued to construct the traps, but he stepped up the process by using some new machines. Notably he purchased a second-hand 49in guillotine from a bookbinding firm for cutting the metal sheets, replacing the use of hand shears, and the guillotine enabled a whole afternoon's work to be completed in just fifteen minutes. There was always a demand for mole traps, and David was fortunate in that he continued to furnish all the previous suppliers' needs, many of which were just verbal orders, as nothing was ever written down. It was the same with his orders for the materials to make the traps: David would just send a message to 'continue order', and the materials would arrive on time.

The metal for the trap body arrived in 6 × 3ft (1.8 × 0.9m) galvanized sheets, and rolls of wire were supplied for the other components. Fifteen-gauge, 172 tons-per-square-inch strength wire made the springs, and thirteen-gauge, 40 tons-per-square-inch strength made the retaining bars and the mumble pins. Everything was measured, cut and constructed in a wooden shed in the garden of the family home, and often all the family were 'hands on', Frances, David's wife, wiring the springs to the loops, and the children lending a hand when they could be persuaded.

Such was the interest in the making of these mole traps that many visitors came knocking on the Jollys' door to see the fascinating manufacture of a simple device that revolutionized mole catching around the world. Even the local schoolchildren made visits to the Jolly household industry, and Frances was always keen to pass on as much information about moles as she could. When I spoke to David and Frances, it was clear they had the same enthusiasm and passion for the mole trap, even after so many years.

The original David Jolly half-barrel trap.

Improving the Duffus Design

Personally I only ever use the half-barrel trap, but over the years manufacturers and suppliers have opted for – as John Newton Duffus himself feared – the mass production of an inferior product that they sell for a high price, and in my experience the modern equivalent has become exactly that.

My personal study of moles had inspired me to look closely at the half-barrel trap and to consider if it could be improved. I worked with a top veterinary surgeon, and with his knowledge of animal anatomy, we came up with some very simple changes to the Duffus design of the half-barrel mole trap. The method of capture in any trap or snare is dependent upon the force that can be applied either by the target species in the struggle of capture, or the power in the spring. The half-barrel – often referred to as a 'tunnel' trap – employs two double torsion springs, which upon release raise the wire snare loops, pulling the mole upwards and against the underside of the trap body.

Many believe that this operation breaks the spine of the target mole, but in fact this is not true. The springs do not provide enough velocity to do any more than retain a mole within the loop until it expires from stress, exhaustion, starvation or dehydration. With mole traps placed below ground the mole's plight is out of sight, out of mind, so of little concern.

Ensuring a Humane Trap

However, today there is an obligation to ensure that unnecessary suffering does not occur to any animal, even under the terms of pest control, and the key to reducing any possible suffering is correct working practice and the right tools for the task. The largest moles are the males, which reach on average 100–120g in weight, so the springs must have the force to impart enough velocity to this weight to be effective in their operation. It was calculated that a minimum spring force of 6–6.5kg is required to achieve this, and like many traps available today, John's springs did not produce sufficient force, with the springs producing no more than 4kg.

Traps used for animal control are nowadays required to meet certain criteria to be humane, and notably must inflict a force that imparts irreversible unconsciousness. If we are required to undergo surgery as a patient, we are put to sleep or rendered unconscious. In this state we feel no pain, and it is the same for the animal if, when the snare is sprung, it is rendered unconscious – it, too, will feel no pain. By inflicting an irreversible unconsciousness, that is, one that the animal will not wake from, it will feel no pain and will expire from any severe injury or trauma.

In relation to the mole, I considered that the force from 6kg springs was sufficient, but the termination also had to be sudden, so the trap body had to be made from thicker 2mm steel, so that the mole is forced into it hard. The shock from this action would render the mole unconscious, providing the trap is placed correctly in the mole's tunnel. During my testing it was discovered that often a mole caught in an incorrectly positioned or weaker powered trap was left only unconscious, and in a state that it would actually wake from.

Another discovery was that the mole might only be paralysed, an injury that no trap should inflict. Many of the half-barrel traps today have a round-shaped base to the snare loop, which means that when the loop is released, the mole's body will roll into the bottom of the loop, reducing the force of the lift, and losing an important percentage of the velocity. John Duffus had a flat bottom on his loops, and this was correct for an efficient lift, as a flat base to the loop will allow the velocity to spread evenly across the body and achieve an even lift. Therefore I included a flat base to the loop, as John Duffus had in 1920.

These changes imparted improved velocity and a more effective strike; the next stage

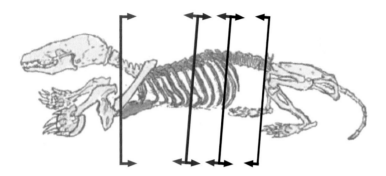

It is important to strike the target mole correctly. It is important that the mole is struck cleanly and in the part of its body that will do most damage. From the anatomy of the mole, it has been considered that this strike is best made from below and in the upper part of the body as indicated in red on the diagram. The blue area is the second point of strike but the black area should be avoided at all times.

was to ensure that the point of contact with the snare loop and the mole's body was always the same, and in the most effective position. The half-barrel loops would normally, upon release, strike the body in the lower abdomen, but here the body is soft and the force of the strike is absorbed. This was because the position of the mumble pins was slightly too far from the snare loop, so I moved them closer to the loop, so that when a large male mole or a smaller female caused the release of the spring, the loop would strike the mole in the upper chest area. This imparts the force across the heart and lungs, and the shock will render the mole unconscious; also the increased force of the springs will cause cardiac arrest, or haemophorax or tension pneumothorax injuries, which would be fatal.

Haemophorax injury relies upon the fact that the mole's blood will not clot, as they are haemophiliacs; therefore a blunt strike to the chest area will cause the blood to collect in the plural cavity, the space between the chest wall and the lung, placing pressure on the lungs and preventing breathing. Tension pneumothorax injury is the rupture of a lung from trauma such as a strike to the chest area, which results in a rib puncture; or air enters the chest cavity

and cannot escape, which places pressure on the pleural space, causing the lungs to collapse.

Many people believe that you can bend the mumble pin towards the snare loop to achieve this; however, this will depend on the bend that the operator places on the pin, whereas setting the mumble pin vertically in the correct downward position removes any discrepancies. In the modern world, any traps used for animal control should not have to be tweaked or bent, but should be fit for purpose at the point of sale.

These changes were the result of many hours of discussion and field trials using different alterations, but our findings established that John Duffus had the half-barrel design correct, and that with these changes it had the potential to be the most humane mole trap currently available. Whether it should be referred to as a trap is debatable, however, as it still employs wire loops or snares at the point of capture.

Manufacturing the Improved Trap

One of the United Kingdom's longest established manufacturing companies of steel products, Procter Brothers, considered these changes. Established in 1740, in 1897 the company manufactured the famous 'little nipper' mousetrap, which everyone still associates with rodent control today. This was the beginning of a new and complete range of traps for animal control sold under the name of 'Pest Stop', which they manufactured and supplied up until 2012, when the range and name was sold.

Prior to the sale Jeremy Procter, the then owner, agreed to consider these changes for the half-barrel or tunnel trap that they supplied, and subsequently decided to go ahead in making the small but vitally important modifications to the half-barrel traps in the Pest Stop range. However, when the Pest Stop product range was sold, making these modifications was left to the discretion of the new owner, so despite the altered half-barrel being the most humane form of mole control available, the future of the improved half-barrel trap still lies in the hands of progress – just as the future of mole catching always has done.

NEW ENGINES

Mole catchers during the early twentieth century had new engines, and the name 'trap' became a common term of use when referring to any device used for catching a mole. The half-barrel and scissor trap found new competition as newly devised alterations appeared. Variations to the scissor trap continued to emerge, and not just in the type of spring fitted to power the jaws.

The Fenn Traps

New manufacturer Fenn released a scissor trap in 1955 with a new style of trap body, which they claimed could be set in deeper mole tunnels. It is shorter in overall length than the traditional scissor trap, and employs a wire shaped spring but of little strength. The shape of the arms did allow for a setting in a deeper tunnel as they don't open as wide as other scissor traps. The arms are pivoted higher up so the fulcrum is improved, the bends in the arms providing a smaller movement in the upper arm and a wider span in the lower part of the arm.

They also produced a double-catch mole trap that in effect was a flat-top copy of the Duffus half-barrel. Another Fenn mole trap much later in the 1980s was their loop trap, which again had a flat top with two loops that rise up through the top upon release; however, these loops did not operate independently, and from the design, the trap was limited in its placement.

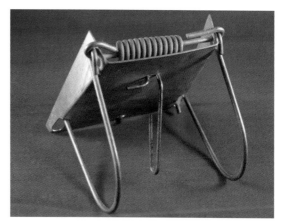

The flat-top Fenn loop mole trap.

The Gripper Mole Trap

During the earlier 1900s Gripper Manufacturing in Leicester produced a larger scissor trap. It was the length of the half-barrel, and had a spring that spanned its entire measurement lengthways. The Gripper mole trap was exported to the United States of America, and remained there after the closure of the company in 1969. It has made its reappearance in a slightly different shape under the manufactured trade name of Talpex, after crossing to Europe and back to our shores.

This Talpex version of the Gripper trap is becoming popular because it is easier to set, as it can be trodden on with the foot, while some have extended arms which makes closing it easier for those with a weaker wrist or grip. Supporters of the Talpex trap claim that is equal to any other trap as regards humaneness, because of the power in the 7kg spring used to operate it. However, this power is necessary because on release the trap jaws must be strong enough to force their way through soil prior to contact with the target mole.

The trap is set in a mole's tunnel and the soil is then placed back around it, so it relies on the mole pushing or digging through the soil for it to be released. Furthermore any resistance or obstruction to its operation will compromise its ability to strike cleanly and effectively. (The modern traps currently available are discussed later and in more detail.)

THE MOLE CATCHER TODAY

As you have learnt, this secret world of mutual understanding between man and mole has for years been thought of by many as a form of magic, a craft carried out by those with an uncanny perception of knowing where moles are to be found. Carefully placing a simple trap, and producing proof of the completed task in the form of a small, soft, warm mammal, is often seen as a strange science.

For the mole catcher the relationship between man and mole was then, and still is today, a friendship rather than an extreme dislike for each other: any hatred towards the mole is felt by those on whose land it has chosen to take up residence. However, we must accept that these creatures have lived beneath us in their secret world long before we walked upon it, and as in many cases of intrusion or infestation, it is man who has been the violator, providing the opportunity for such exploitation.

It has been estimated that here in the United Kingdom there is one mole for every two humans, and as with both species, these numbers are constantly increasing. It may be hard for some to fully comprehend the need to control the mole, but to reduce the mole population will enhance the species and actually provide for its improved development, as this creature has always demanded its own personal space. By reducing the competition for what is fast becoming limited space in the mole's ever-decreasing habitat on this island also reduces its fight for life with others of the same species.

Putting the Myths to Bed

So what are these mysteries of mole catching today – this secrecy that wordsmiths have failed to reveal, that musicians have failed to enchant, and painters have failed to produce? It is simple: there are no mysteries, no magical gift, only in the imagination of those who have created the many myths, including those of the wanters themselves in their desire to protect the animal to which they owe so much.

It will be clear from these pages, that in order to fully appreciate the mole you will need to feel respect towards the velvet-coated little creature, and to understand the knowledge that has passed from mole to man, in one of the strangest relationships that has led so many others to want to be a mole catcher.

I have always said that you cannot call yourself a mole catcher until a mole has bitten you, and having been nipped on a few occasions, I know the pain the mole can inflict. However, the bite that I refer to inflicts a far greater pain, as it produces a strange infection, one that grows inside you and demands the answers to so many questions. The 'bite' is in fact the obsession that will take hold of you as you begin to understand and enjoy the partnership that comes from contact with these fantastic creatures. You may be taking the life of a remarkable animal, but the challenges, pleasures, successes and memories, combined with the feelings of sorrow and compassion, will remain with you for a lifetime.

The relationship begins as the mole intrigues us, by allowing us to see the evidence of its existence, but never letting us glance into its private world. However, let me open a window into that world, and allow you to observe the amazing and strange relationship that calls so many to want to become a mole catcher! To help you achieve this aim, I would like to take you on a journey that will last a single year: you will learn of the mole, its habits, its needs and the demands placed upon it from its subterranean quarters in the soil. There will be life and there will be death, conflict and pleasure. Information both new and old will be gained, and you, too, will be for ever affected by its infectious bite.

Chapter 3

The Mole Catcher's Year

To catch a mole it is important to understand not just the animal itself, but also the environment in which it lives, and the influences that this environment imposes upon it. You will need to learn how it lives, and the best way to remove it humanely. There is a vast amount of information on how to control moles on internet web sites, provided by many experts from the comfort of their armchair. Here I offer my contribution to that immense volume of wisdom, which I trust the reader will find truthful, practical and honest, as to the best way to catch the humble mole.

As always, I am writing this guide to mole control from personal practical experience, gleaned from daily contact with moles and their environment. Professional mole catchers work all year round, which is essential as the mole also works every day of every month just to survive: so if mole catchers are to survive, they must do the same as their industrious quarry. To assist those undertaking this journey into mole catching, in the next two chapters I will try to provide solutions to the many problems that can and will be experienced in the course of the year. These are presented month by month, but you will need to read the whole account in order fully to appreciate all you need to know in your quest to be successful. And having experienced this journey through the year, you can then refer back to any particular month should the velveteen tutor trouble you with any further problem. Your teacher awaits your attendance. I can only provide a base for you to work from.

JANUARY

It may seem strange to begin the mole-catching year in January, as so many accounts irrefutably describe it as running from October to April. This was born of the fact that long ago, much of the mole catcher's work revolved around the agricultural calendar, which can still be the case in certain areas today. By October the harvest had been cut, and the fields were once again ploughed and drilled, and at the mercy of the new invasion of young moles from the previous season's breeding. In October, the mole catcher could access the battlefields, and it was a continuing contest, as autumn-drilled seedlings struggled in their first stages of life against the ravages of enthusiastic juvenile moles exploiting the opportunities provided by this new, now workable haven.

There is more on this later, as our modern journey is an all-year affair influenced by the many changes that will become apparent as the months pass by. Moles, like other subterranean animals, have no knowledge of the division between days, weeks and months; rather, their lives are dictated by the temperature of each returning day, and whether it places a warm, or a cold hand on the soil, and their behaviour will be influenced by nature's touch, whether this is a longer and warmer spell of weather, or a shorter and colder one.

Weather and Its Influence

Weather is very important to the mole catcher, as it is the normal or sudden changes in weather patterns that will dictate the rules of engagement. It may not be necessary to feel the moisture of a piece of seaweed or to observe which way the sheep are facing to learn what this playing field will be, but it is nevertheless important to scrutinize harsh weather and dramatic changes when embarking on mole control. Average seasonal weather conditions on a day-to-day basis have little impact on the mole, and nor do sudden short variations such as unpredicted rainfall or a slight frost. Moles will take these conditions in their stride and are often prepared for them, as the food they depend on reacts accordingly. However, prolonged cold, dry or wet spells are a different problem to deal with, and the mole catcher will need to call on every small piece of his or her experience.

To catch a mole it is necessary to think like a mole, and to react and present your trap/s where they will be most effective, and the impact of the weather plays a vital part in that presentation. Unlike the old mole catchers, predicting today's weather is not so much of a problem, as we have the national weather forecast, which will inform us of fronts and the weather to be expected across the country. However, from a mole catcher's point of view this is often of little use, even when the meteorological office happens to be correct, because it is what is happening locally, in the areas where the moles are to be targeted, that is important. Furthermore the ground and air temperatures and the levels of rainfall will be dissimilar even locally due to the geographical location. Therefore any information supplied from a national metrological office must be accepted for what it is – a general forecast.

When considering the influence of climate changes in relation to mole control, information needs to be evaluated locally and then compared with the mole catcher's experiences, and any previous measures he has taken, both successful and unsuccessful. This builds up a knowledge of how the weather is influencing the moles locally – and 'locally' can of-

ten be a considerable distance, such as within a county; but it is also important to consider the geographical terrain. I have a home weather station that provides vital information, such as barometric pressure with a daily record of change four times within the hour, and alarms for dramatic changes such as a sudden drop in air and ground temperatures. The recording of rainfall levels over certain periods provides information as to the levels of saturation in the ground, and this will indicate where the mole's food supplies may be found, and in what quantity. Armed with such information, we will still need to consider such climate details in conjunction with other matters in the complex structure of the mole's life – its anatomy, life cycle, habitat, and all the other information that combines to challenge the traditional skills of the modern mole catcher.

Working in Cold Conditions

Many mole catchers will choose the comfort of the fire when winter takes hold, and January can be a hostile month. With the festive season over, the whole country may be gripped in nature's cold grasp, with temperatures dropping to minus double figures, and many days not reaching above zero. If the ground is hard it will be difficult to locate the moles' tunnels below the surface, and under these conditions many employed in mole control may choose to sit the winter out – but still the molehills appear. In fact the molehills may be larger, as more and more soil is excavated and deposited above ground, from a depth that many mole catchers have yet to explore.

This visual evidence to the fact that moles do not hibernate frustrates many gardeners and landowners, as this industrious creature works to obtain the necessary two-thirds of its bodyweight in food each day, and probably more under harsh conditions! It is often difficult for many to accept that even under normal conditions the damage they see is the work of just a single mole – and in winter these moles need to work hard at all available levels and locations to source their food. Worms are their main diet, and these will be deep in the warmer and softer soil levels, depending on the soil layers available in that location. Moreover worms will not be multiplying at these low temperatures, and so more effort is required on the part of the mole to locate and source sufficient food, activity that is evidenced by the moles creating wider or larger areas of damage.

In these colder conditions I have a set routine, as feeling and mobility in the hands soon fail in the winter chill. Mole catchers generally never wear gloves, and I find they are more of a hindrance than a help. But hands soon become battle hardened in the wet and cold, and there is no quicker way for the skin to crack than under the drying effect of soil – indeed it was once said that the hands of a mole catcher soon resembled those of the mole, larger than normal and impervious to the elements, which must be an advantage. In this level of chill, I set the traps before considering exactly where they will be placed – I always know where I will position them in the moles' locations generally, as I fully understand the moles, and hope that you will too.

On these cold days, you will probably have no more than about fifteen to twenty minutes before numbness sets in and all feeling is lost. This may seem a short period, but in fact is longer than you need to set a few traps. The number of traps you use will always be determined by the location and the various features that impact on it, but on most occasions, three is plenty – after all, it only takes one trap to catch a mole, you just need to put it in the correct place.

The feeling of pain if a mole trap bites a cold finger or knuckle is indescribable, so care and a little more respect must be given to the traps when working in such conditions. My personal choice for all my mole catching is the half-barrel trap, as it is the most versatile. However,

half-barrel mole traps are like a horse – dangerous at both ends and very uncomfortable in the middle! Often the middle claims most victims from careless handling, as those who have experienced this will know all too well as an unexpected release strikes a knuckle.

Hard, Frozen Soil

Some will say that cold, frozen ground does not permit trap use, but how wrong they are! It takes experience to locate mole runs and tunnels, and mole catchers use a probe, a simple tool consisting of a strong metal bar with a handle; this is the only contact the mole catcher will have with the mole's environment from above ground. Everyone will have their favourite, but the thicker the probe, the more damage it will do, and the more damage you do to the mole's environment, the more damage the mole will do to yours or your client's. Normally I use an 8mm-diameter bar, but in hard or wet ground I will use one of 10mm diameter, as it provides a little more detection without causing too much damage or disturbance.

I use a probe with a wooden handle in a cold January, because it is kinder on the hands than the metal T-bars that many in the pest control industry employ; these come in the mole control kit used for administering gas for moles, or sold commercially as a 'mole dibber'.

To use the probe, simply push down through the ground where you consider the tunnel to be. A mole's run is located when the roof of the tunnel is penetrated: when this happens the mole catcher feels a sudden change in speed in the probe's travel, from the careful and steady push as it goes through the ground, to a sudden 'give' as it enters the tunnel.

As mentioned above, the thicker the probe, the more damage that is caused; some use a probe with a larger point, maybe as thick as 22mm, as found on the rods used for the application of gas. But again, although the thicker point will possibly detect runs more easily, it

The Japanese trowel is perfect for use in hard, solid ground.

years, and although it has been touched by the welder on a number of occasions, hopefully it will last for another twenty. (More on trowels later, as these are vital to any mole catcher's array of tools.)

I have the perfect answer to this problem of hard, frozen soil: it is a Japanese garden trowel, ideal for many mole trap locations, and which really shows its ability to perform in these hard soils of the colder months. It resembles a sheath knife: it has a thick, fixed blade that is concave in shape, with small serrations and a long edge. Its strength and design make it an excellent tool, as it will work in the hardest of ground and accepts the amount of leverage necessary to achieve the task. Therefore, no excuse to stay inside this month!

Waterlogged Soil

January is also a month when snowfall may occur, and again the armchair mole catcher may feel that the moles can wait; but those who rely on the services of a mole catcher will still be calling as the soil is raised in molehills all across the white landscape. However, often January weather changes for the better overnight: winds will raise the air temperature, and even the slightest increase in ground temperature can cause a thaw. With it comes soil saturation, and this changes things for the moles. The ground can rapidly turn to a wet sponge, and the moles' main food source, the worms, will quickly move away from the quantity of water draining down through the soil, and will burrow upwards or to higher ground. Worms breathe by absorbing oxygen through their skin and releasing carbon dioxide, so they may struggle to survive in oxygen-deficient waterlogged soils.

The moles respond quickly to this rush to the surface by using existing shallow tunnel complexes, or creating new tunnels or runs just below the surface. The evidence of this looks like a badly fitted carpet, ridges where the mole

will also cause extensive damage to the tunnel roof, which will alert the mole to the activity above and therefore should be avoided. If using gas, however, then the amount of damage caused to the tunnel is of no importance, though when placing the trap it is vital to ensure that everything is carried out correctly and precisely from start to finish.

In some winters the ground has been so hard that I actually bent the tip of my trowel, which is not a modern grade tool, and is damage I would not expect to happen, as you would with many products produced today. My current trowel has served me well for over twenty

The mole when working just under the surface is said to be 'running spooked', 'jigging' or 'scribbling'.

has pushed up the soil or grass – I refer to it simply as 'ripples in the sea of green' – and this is not the only occasion when this phenomenon may be experienced. Mole catchers have various names for it according to where they are; I call it 'running spooked' because it looks as if the mole has been frightened by something – there is no particular pattern, it is just a confusion of raised tunnels.

Joking, jigging and scribbling are other names given to this behaviour (I will refer to this again as the year progresses). The moles know that by creating tunnels in the upper layer of the soil they will attract the worms, which will find pockets of oxygen there, enabling them to breathe, either by lying in the runs or just holding a part of their body in them. This ingenuity on the part of the mole provides a whole new feeding opportunity as it prowls along the tunnels. The mole is in effect trapping the worms, a situation brought about by the change in the environmental conditions.

Some mole catchers try to trap the moles in these shallow winter runs, but often without success. The feeding mole is very cautious, and moves slowly while seeking and identifying its food – and this wary mole will often discover a badly placed trap in its feeding grounds. The mole at this time of the year has created a

network of shallow tunnels to exploit the situation created by the change in soil conditions, and every available source of food is important. This methodical way of hunting will leave no quarter ignored, and the mole's foraging will be slow and particular, so as not to exert unnecessary energy. However, the catcher should note that the mole may have travelled up through the soil from the deeper tunnels where it was originally feeding, following its food source, the worms. It will therefore still be using the original tunnel or tunnels to enter the feeding grounds, and mole catchers should still place their traps in these locations.

Many a trap will be found packed with soil when set in some shallow runs, but sometimes there is no alternative but to set them here (the placement of traps in shallow runs is covered in more detail later on, in the months when this is more relevant). If you do need to trap shallow runs in the winter, it is imperative to consider the night-time temperature, because if you have to cover a trap to protect it from the effects of the cold you need to do this carefully so as not to impede its operation.

Also remember that any moisture in the soil may freeze, and if a trap is covered or sprinkled with earth, even a light amount could result in a solid lid being frozen into position. This in turn could prevent, or worse, compromise its operation and only partially restrain the mole, causing a considerable level of suffering until the trapper returns. A half-barrel trap in a shallow position in frozen temperatures must be covered with an igloo of turf: to do this, shape pieces of turf to form a roof over the trap, and at a height and angle to allow the springs to operate freely. Having constructed the roof of turf, sprinkle soil over it to prevent the elements influencing the trap site.

On days of no ground frost and even if it feels cold, the moles will settle down to normal living – or as normal as they can, given the pressures of that location. Mole catching on such days is standard, as for any other day, as the food source – the worms – will also be leading an almost typical existence. Thus the moles will clear out the normal feeding tunnels as the shallow upper runs become redundant, until the next sudden change in soil conditions. If there is no change, these shallow tunnels will sink as a result of natural soil subsidence, or from disturbances above the ground. Oddly, many people seem to have a compulsive urge to tread over these tunnels, and heel them down in an almost ritualistic manner.

The moles' return to normal activity indicates to the mole catcher that he can return to putting his traps in the normal tunnels, as at other times during the year.

Many people find it hard to understand how moles live, and enter into the world of mole catching thinking that traps should be placed in amongst the molehills, as they assume that this is where the mole lives. But they are so wrong, because under normal circumstances, molehills are nothing more than fly tipping, the rubbish that needs to be removed – waste soil, stones, sand, and anything else that needs to be thrown up and out of the way in the construction of the network of tunnels where the mole will obtain its food. So these areas of molehills are the mole's feeding areas, its kitchen, where it finds its food – it does not sleep here. It sleeps somewhere dry, in a purpose-built nest lined with grass or leaves, maybe under a large tree, in a raised area, or beneath a patio, but it will travel along a tunnel it has made specifically to access the feeding area. And this tunnel will never change, because the mole will have made it at a depth ideal to that location. These main tunnels are used constantly to travel between these two locations the sleeping place and the feeding area – and come from somewhere on the perimeter of the chosen location. So it is in this tunnel that you place your mole trap, not in amongst the molehills!

Many of those who place mole traps are observed working amongst the molehills, and especially the fresh ones – but this is playing right into the mole's hands, because in the new tunnels the mole will be looking for food, and being cautious, will possibly discover a trap, especially if it is positioned badly.

You should always be one step ahead of the mole, so avoid setting traps in places where the mole will apprehend them. Certainly there will be times when it is a good idea to place a trap in an area of new molehills, or when it is the only place available, and this will be discussed later. Moles can move at a phenomenal speed for their size, almost two and a half miles per hour in this network of tunnels, but when it is feeding, it is slow-moving and inquisitive.

As well as catching moles for their removal, I also catch them for media and filming purposes, and enjoy studying them with surveillance cameras. It has been whilst filming them that I have been privileged to have this close and personal insight into their private life and habits, and have gained an additional awareness of how they live. Thus I have learned that in any tunnel used to travel from its place of sleep to where it obtains its food, the mole will be travelling fast enough to enter any positioned trap and will be struck cleanly, and therefore humanely.

Thus it is a good idea to locate a trap in these tunnels, as tests have shown that if a mole is moving slowly when it is caught in a trap, then it will take longer for it to lapse into irreversible unconsciousness – moreover the mole, full of adrenalin, is often aware of the presence of the trap prior to its release. However, if the mole is moving at speed when it enters a trap, there will be more of a jolt when the trap is sprung, and the shock of impact can cause immediate unconsciousness, leading almost straightaway to death.

Frost and Winter Sun

When catching moles during times of frost, the mole catcher must rely on every natural influence that will affect that location, and a winter sun may turn out to be his helpmate and friend.

The habits/actions of moles are dictated by their food, which in turn responds to any weather impact.

The sun obviously melts the frost from any areas it can touch, and those areas that it can't reach remain white, hard and cold. Nature will always respond to the elements and the demands of climate, and something will take advantage of even the slightest increase in ground temperature in spells of hard weather. Where a garden, field or paddock is bathed in winter sunlight for even a short length of time, there the moles will be found, as the food on which they depend also seeks the comfort of a degree or two above the daily freeze. Often molehills are confined to a particular area or corner – but remember, the mole will have tunnelled there from the perimeter of its living area.

A classic example of how the winter sun may influence the activity of moles is on a woodland golf course. The low winter sun will leave a patchwork of white frost and deep green turf as it passes across the sky, its warmth blocked by trees designed to guide the golf club members around the path of play. These pockets of green, whether on a golf course or the corner of a garden, will be exploited by any moles present. This area of feeding may be just one of many such locations that the resident mole may need to exploit under such conditions. To obtain the daily intake of food it needs in order to survive, it may travel along adjoining runs linking other feeding grounds, so consider the area closely, and how the weather has impacted on the ground conditions both currently and previously – but most importantly, consider how as a mole catcher you will respond to these conditions.

Many will choose to remain inside when the snow arrives.

FEBRUARY

February will often bring infrastructure problems, travel chaos and closed schools, when children, many for the first time, enjoy a new sort of game, as snow can, and often does, make a more persistent appearance. The United Kingdom does have a north/south divide when it comes to the weather, but February is often the month that stamps its authority across the whole country. Like the previous month, it can also be cold with continuing frosts, but in particular I would advise of the problems relating to snow. But although nature sleeps beneath this white blanket, from a mole-catching point of view nothing in fact really changes, except you must remember to mark your trap sites properly.

I will exchange the white-topped trap markers that I normally use, for red tops, to help locate trap sites when further snowfall swathes the ground and foils even the best of attempts

This red top marker is clearly visible, to help locate and recover the trap after a night's snowfall.

to remember where you have put them. What many mole catchers fail to consider is that the ground beneath the snow is often not affected by the conditions, especially during the day when it is protected by this covering, evidence of which lies in the production of dark, fresh molehills scattered about above the latest fall.

However, an overnight drop in temperature can cause the soil of these molehills to freeze, thus making it hard work for the mole to excavate further soil to the surface because it will be moving the weight of the whole spoil heap as it pushes out new waste soil from below – but it has ways around this. First, the soil may be moved into existing tunnels until it can be moved later; moles may also do this in times of severe drought when tunnels are deep and the journey to the surface may also be an effort.

Generally, moles are moving around normally and at normal depths under the snow, going about their day almost undetected until a thaw exposes the extent of their labours. Heavy snowfall hides the full picture, and the mole may have been working tirelessly under this cover. Evidence of this activity can be seen in the form of smooth, round-topped molehills resembling freshly baked muffins, shaped in this way because as the fresh soil is worked up from the ground, it is compressed against the blanket of snow.

Trapping in snow is not difficult, and the tunnels are located in the usual way with the probe. However, locating the correct tunnel is now a slightly different task than it is to find it under normal conditions, as you will have to locate the tunnels that the mole is showing as being in use. Evidence of the normal main tunnels that mole catchers strive to find will possibly be obscured by the snow, so often it may be necessary to investigate the labyrinth of feeding tunnels. These tunnels are normally avoided, as the mole will be hunting, searching for any available food – and being without doubt a cautious animal, when hunting it will be even more aware of any changes to its environment.

Snow does not prevent the mole from working.

If you need to remove a mole from below the snow, you will see where it is working from the presence of fresh soil above the snow, as explained. Ideally you will place your trap where there is some distance between the new molehills that are showing. You may see molehills butting up to each other, which is common when the moles are constructing new feeding areas. They may have found a source of food that is plentiful and need to work to extract it before it evades capture, or they may have had to work around a sunken object that is causing the soil to be slightly warmer, and the reason for this increase in food supply.

These grouped molehills should be avoided, as here you will rarely locate a tunnel suitable for trap placement without the mole detecting the disturbance. You are looking for a distance between the molehills of over 18in (45cm), as this will give you enough space to work with if you can locate the tunnel and it is suitable for placing a trap.

As with positioning any mole trap, you must look around and consider the situation, which will be different every time. With the snow and the visible molehills above the snow layer, you may only have this area to work in, but whenever you can, work as you would normally, and always seek out the main tunnels. Even in times of snow, with cautious searching and consideration you may still be able to locate the core tun-

nels. If you cannot, perhaps because the snow is too deep, when any investigative work may alarm the target mole, then you will have no choice but to locate the greatest distance between the molehills and carefully scrape away the snow to reveal the top surface of the soil layer.

This top layer is the organic layer – it may be grass or soil, and careful scraping will reveal what it is. I must emphasize that this must be carried out slowly and carefully, as the temperature may not be low enough to freeze or harden the crust, and you could open a tunnel where a mole is working just under the surface. Obviously this will not be a problem if the tunnels are under grass, but in open soil you could quite easily break into a tunnel, and this can often result in problems, which I will cover later.

To scrape away the snow you will have to kneel down – as with all aspects of mole trap placement – so welcome to the world of mole catcher's knees, often cold, always damp, and as you grow older, likely to let you down. You will read or hear of people using long-handled tools, but the reality is that you will still need to get in close to that tunnel, and so you will be working kneeling down. In snow, it is important to be close to the task, so be prepared! Once the snow is cleared, you can use the probe to locate the tunnel in the normal way: under the snow the ground will be as normal, proof of which you have already seen in the very presence and activity of the mole.

As I recommended earlier, always set the trap beforehand and have it ready to put in place, or set it now as quickly as you can. It is vital to minimize the length of time that your trap site is exposed to the colder air, because air of low temperature entering the tunnel will alarm the mole. Work as fast as you would in normal conditions, and be especially conscientious in covering the trap: this requires some attention to detail.

The colder night temperatures will have a huge effect on your trap site if you do not cover it adequately. Remember, never sprinkle loose soil on the top as this has the potential to freeze and possibly prevent but certainly impede the trap's operation: rather, you must build a protective covering from turf. Shape some turf into a roof or an igloo, ensuring that it is high enough to allow the trap to operate fully. Cover over your turf roof with loose soil from the molehills, and mark it with a trap marker, preferably one with a red top so it is easy to locate in the event of further snowfall. If the molehills surrounding your location seem frozen solid and you are wondering where to find soft soil, lever up another molehill with your trowel. Under it you will generally find a supply of soft soil, perfect for the job.

Those mole catchers who stay by the comfort of the fire will miss out on the many opportunities that winter provides to learn of the habits of moles – that is, until the next snows grace us with their beauty and their clean blanket over the countryside.

The Thaw and Waterlogging

The thaw of heavy snowfall can turn fields into lakes, and causes rising water to flow through field drains in torrents. This is another demand the mole must adapt to, and it does so very well. Moles are competent swimmers, and they take rising water from a thaw, or heavy and prolonged rainfall, in their stride; furthermore very often moles respond to the change in water levels before it challenges their need to survive, by moving to areas not influenced by such conditions. Waterlogged urban areas are no different, and higher levels in the water table are of little concern to the mole.

However, if the mole has not moved because of the change in weather conditions, the pressure on the available food source will motivate the mole to work flooded tunnels: it is not perturbed by high levels of water in its tunnels. It could be that the water in the tunnel is providing a ready supply of food, the reason being

that water travelling down brings worms up, because waterlogging will reduce their oxygen levels, or put them at risk of drowning.

Moles are happy to paddle or swim through tunnels, and I have caught moles in tunnels that have been completely flooded from floor to roof. I have also set traps in flooded tunnels because I considered that when the water level dropped they would be in the tunnel that that particular mole would be using. Often when I returned to inspect the trap the next day, and despite finding the tunnel still full of water, the trap had caught the mole. On many occasions I have caught moles in flooded tunnels, so do consider this when in times of prolonged wet weather you question your decision whether to use a tunnel that would be the favoured choice under other or normal conditions.

It is accepted that moles are solitary animals, and they will take extreme measures to avoid conflict with each other – but under any excessive circumstances, as with the saturation of the ground following any reasonably prolonged period of snow, things are slightly different. Moles will need to find any available food source, and often a garden where moles have always been active on its perimeter is subject to mole damage for the very first time. The landowner may never before have experienced any direct mole activity, but this dramatic change and call for food has brought moles into their garden or on to the land. I say 'moles' because this is often the case, as more than one mole may be searching out the food in this area. This will be apparent when the mole catcher catches two moles overnight, either in a single trap or in two traps placed only a few metres apart: this is because the moles are forced to venture into a shared environment to be able to survive.

In the same week I caught two moles in traps just a short distance apart in a small lawn, and at another location, having caught one mole, was called back a week later because there was further activity. The traps placed, the next morning I returned to find two moles in one trap. It was obvious when I set these traps that something was unusual, as I pointed out to the customer. Some of the tunnels had been blocked: these were main tunnels leading around the garden, so at first I thought that maybe the mole was aware that its main predator, the weasel, was in the vicinity. Moles will do this to create a safer area: by simply creating soil doors, they will prevent confrontation; however, on this occasion it was evidently to avoid possible confrontation from another mole that had come into the area to obtain enough food. Again, I removed two moles from this small area in one night, indicating that the moles seemed happy to share, but were still wary of possible confrontation.

Catching a small number of moles in a garden is not a regular occurrence, but nor is it a rare one: it is all down to the pressure that the area is placing on the resident moles. Claims of catching dozens of moles from a garden over a short period are posted on the internet as proof of a catcher's skill in his search for further commissions – but in reality, the number of moles taken in one place will never exceed more than can be counted on one hand. If you are fortunate enough to experience a multi catch at a small location, take a look around and study the reason why, and if you are reading it online, then again ask yourself why.

When the thaw does come and nature's white covering slowly dissolves, many people will see the extent of the damage caused during these times. Many molehills that had not broken through the surface of the snow suddenly become visible to all. Everywhere there are cries of a mole population boom, and that moles must be taking over the country, as molehills strangely appear everywhere. However, every mole catcher knows differently, as the picture now exposed simply indicates the demands of living under such conditions. If the mole was excavating just prior to the thaw, then the tunnels will have been shallow because food was drawn up as the water drained down, evident in small molehills, or even in moles 'running

spooked'. If the snow was quite deep, the now visible molehills, although still large, may not have broken through the snow surface.

All this devastation to lawns, paddocks and fields brings many calls to the mole catcher. It is a time when mole catchers are faced with numbers of molehills, but many inexperienced in winter mole control have difficulty in deciphering the clues these offer. The secret is the shape of the molehill: when soil pushed up from below comes into contact with the weight of the snow layer, but is unable to break through it, it will form a dome shape like a muffin, as described before. Waste soil that was pushed up and through the snow, breaking the surface, will conform to the normal shape of any molehill. The smooth domes tell the mole catcher when the mole was present, and more importantly, whether it is still there. If the molehills are all domed, then the mole has possibly left; if it was still present then the chances are, that due to the influences of the weather and the soil conditions, its digging will have produced normal evidence of activity.

The Mole's Breeding Season

The only thing on a mole catcher's mind will be if weather conditions in the month of February have an impact on the start of the moles' breeding season. Moles normally breed just once a year, and those females born the previous season will now be sexually mature and ready to breed. It all begins when the soil starts to warm up; down in the south it can begin as early as late February to early March, while the moles further north begin as late as April/May. It is dependent upon the changes in the soil: as it warms, the moles' food supply – worms – will also begin to multiply, which works almost as a stimulant to the moles to begin the task of reproduction. With food now becoming more plentiful, the moles know that their young will have the best possible start to life's arduous journey.

The female mole, known as a doe, only comes into season once a year and for a short period of time, approximately twenty-four hours, and in that period she will only accept the amorous advances of a buck or male mole for a few hours. Therefore the male mole gets one chance with a female just once a year! With this limited window, moles change their habits and abandon the barrier of seclusion in the interests of the continuation of their numbers: the male mole will leave his current home range, his normal territory, and go off in search of available females. Although the male mole's testes will contain spermatozoa all year round, the increased level caused by the production of testosterone can cause the testes to increase in size by almost thirty times.

Another country myth was that the moles were all males from birth, and that they divided into males and females the following spring. Now that may sound a bit bizarre, but I can understand why so many rustic storytellers have held this strange belief. It is very difficult to distinguish between the males and females apart from the fact that males will be a little larger in overall size at the point of being fully mature. If two moles of equal size are placed side by side, even with close examination the difference is difficult to determine.

The female mole in season.

The real difference is in fact just one millimetre, the distance between the anus and the penis being 5 millimetres in a male mole, and that between the anus and the urinary papilla being under 4 millimetres in the female; furthermore these intimate parts of any mole are concealed beneath the coat and are therefore difficult to observe. Moreover in the female mole the opening to the vagina remains sealed until each spring, when during the preparation for breeding a slit appears, which opens, allowing access for the male – so it is very easy to understand why the sex of a mole has baffled so many, for so long.

Many people have also continued to believe the myth that female moles dig in circles and that males always dig in straight lines! So many myths, but again claims that are made by those who have only occasionally observed the private life of a creature they have little contact with. So what is the truth behind such claims – do males dig in straight lines, and females go in circles?

Of course, moles do not dig in patterns according to their sex, but it is simple to see why such claims have been made. The male mole has only one chance to breed, once a year, so it is easy to understand that he will have just one thing on his mind. Many gardeners and landowners will have seen a line of molehills across their lawn, and this is the male mole passing through on a voyage of passion that will take him to an available female where he will present her with his eternal devotion – well, for a couple of minutes anyway.

To locate a female the male must search through existing complexes of tunnels that may not have been used for some time. These amorous moles may remember from previous seasons each and every one of these interlinking tunnels, while the new generation of males from the previous breeding season will be exploring not just a further new world, but a fresh experience. All this activity clearing out tunnels long blocked with soil subsidence produces

There is only one thing on the mind of this mole at this time of the year.

an explosion of molehills within a short period of time, which clearly fuels enthusiastic claims of a mole population boom.

Evidence that the breeding season is about to take off may be a single large molehill, a row of molehills, or a raised surface, but at the end of February, if the weather is mild, it is the first indication of the start to a whole new generation of moles.

I have always kept an open mind regarding the claim that moles breed more than once a year, and my study into the lives of the old mole catchers, from their travels and stories, has revealed how such a belief came to be. We know that the male mole, following the reduction in size of the testis, does retain spermatozoa for a few months after the spring, so should a female mole, for whatever reason, experience a later or second oestrus she could produce a second or later litter if she were to have contact with a male mole retaining spermatozoa. The chance of a second oestrus is minimal, though a later oestrus could occur as a result of bad weather impacting on an area and delaying the start of the female's breeding cycle. I have

constant contact with mole catchers across the United Kingdom, when talk of moles is top of the conversation, their influences and experiences, and there has been no definitive proof of a second litter from any female moles, but there is confirmed evidence of later litters, as a result of climate changes in certain areas. I therefore feel that claims to second litters are made by those who have little contact with the mole, or familiarity with its habits.

It is in early spring that these myths and claims of foolproof cures to get rid of moles are likely to appear, as this is often when people have their first experience of a mole, when opening their curtains in the morning reveals the damage to their lawn. Confronted with this strange intrusion and desperate for a solution, this distraught individual seeks the comforting advice of every 'expert' in mole catching, and is deluged with all sorts of strange advice as to mole control. However, the mole is probably long gone.

The male mole in search of does will liberally mate with any female he can find that does not greet him with aggression. Any female not ready for this amorous confrontation will force-fully expel the male, and the normally larger aggressor will heed the sign. Moles will fight fiercely, and fatal injuries can ensue from such brawls – though not at this time of the year, which is nature's way of ensuring the continuing existence of her reclusive species. The male mole will seek out and mate with an available female, and then move on to the next, and this continues until their levels of testosterone diminish. The male mole will not stay and help in the rearing of any of the young in the litters they produce.

With the breeding duties of spring accomplished, and testosterone levels now on empty – which is another reason to doubt a second litter – the life of the male moles returns to normality. They will look to return to their home range unless they discover a more suitable dwelling – possibly another male's home range that has become vacant. Many moles will fall victim to natural predation in the course of this moving around, so again it is easy to see how all those tales of what you must do to be rid of that mole are believed to work, as gardens remain damage free. However, with returning moles it is also possible to see why in the early part of the year people can and do experience moles twice. As the returning mole once again crosses the lawn, more soil is fly tipped on its prize turf, which calls for more drastic measures and professional advice! Convinced the mole has returned to wreak further havoc on the green baize, our householder calls on the smiling garden centre manager, who advises on an array of repellents. Once again, the garden is turned into an adventure playground as buzzers break the stillness of the night, and biodegradable smokes form a fog bank that any horror film would be proud of. At one time chemicals were permitted in mole control, but because of environmental issues and their lack of success, the liquids, powders and granules once sprinkled over and around the garden are no longer legal. Besides, even before the householder has returned from stocking up with long-life lithium rechargeable cells that would power the international space station for a week, the male mole is probably happily tucked up in its own nest sleeping off what may have been an adventure to remember for another year.

For the female, things are quite different, and when contemplating that other myth, that females dig in circles, you have to consider just what the female has been subjected to, with this onslaught of potential suitors to father the next litter of moles. Female moles have to conceive, give birth to, wean and raise the new moles alone, and they, too, similar to the males, undergo a biological change. As already stated, the opening to the vagina in female moles is sealed for most of the year, but a change occurs internally that causes a slit to appear, which opens to allow a male access. The uterus enlarges, and the follicles develop and mature, and soon the female is willing for the male to mate with her.

With all this happening, the female mole will need to increase the availability of the food source in preparation for the forthcoming weeks. To do this she creates a larger, wider or deeper feeding ground, where she will find the increasing volumes of food that will be necessary for herself and her litter. Larger molehills, and more of them, appear, because she must be constantly working to provide more tunnels in a tangle of directions in order to fully exploit any available food. Spoils of soil form clusters in every imaginable part of the garden, paddock or field, and it is this practice that has given rise to the claims that the females go in circles.

Normally the mole needs to consume two-thirds of its bodyweight per day, but these females will require even more, with the demands placed upon their bodies as the young moles grow inside them. In addition the young will require life-giving milk, and then solid food, which the female provides by constructing various chambers – first a larger one with a nest for the young to sleep in, then smaller ones where worms are stored, having received a calming bite. In these small chambers, known as worm larders, the worms will lie until they are required – many are stored to provide for the gestation period of approximately twenty-eight days, with the worms requiring the same period of time to recover. Thus the mole is providing for both herself and her young.

The latter days of a mild February will more often than not produce the first double catch of the year; as mentioned above, I prefer half-barrel traps, and these will pick up two moles at a time. As well as catching two moles in a trap face to face, you may sometimes find a mole which is the wrong way around in the trap – caught in the trap backwards. This can often happen at this time of the year, as a more aggressive mole pushes another mole back along a tunnel as they confront each other. For those who may have had this experience, this is a reason why! This can be a male-to-male or even a male-to-female confrontation as their solitary worlds explode in breeding frenzy!

MARCH

With the breeding season well under way, especially in the south of the country, the calls for help with moles will come from a wide cross-section of people, varying from those with moles crossing through gardens, or with an eruption of new molehills that up until a couple of weeks ago had seemed to be acceptable, as the mole was just in the corner of the field, orchard or lawn. Now with piles of soil spread all over the garden, or in areas where they had never been before, those who were once of the 'leave it alone and it might go away' club, suddenly have a different perspective on the ability of the mole to destroy a location in a matter of hours or days.

One male mole I studied over a period of two days whilst walking my dogs travelled a direct line from a small copse in the centre of a field to the headlands where other moles dwell. It was

Mole on a mission.

obviously a mole on a mission, as the distance was in excess of a hundred metres, but he got there leaving a straight row of small molehills in his wake. It is common for male moles to 'run spooked' to cross land, but even with the protection of the thin layer of soil above them they may still be a target for predators. Foxes, loose domestic pets and birds of prey, especially owls, now threaten the mole's journeys along such shallow runs, which some folk have called 'the tunnels of love' when they are visible at this time of the year.

So how do moles find each other? The answer is simple – first by scent, and then because they communicate. As an animal that insists on a solitary life it is important to be able to converse with your neighbours to ensure that any possible confrontation is avoided, and a mole does this by twittering. Emitting a sound alerts other moles to your presence, thus reducing the chance of having to resort to aggression.

Social networking is nothing new to moles: they have been twittering for millions of years in order to communicate with others. Like the speaking tubes once used on ships to transfer information from bridge to engine room, the sounds they produce will bounce along the complex networks of runs informing all and everything that can hear this clandestine language of the presence of the resident moles.

The Mole, Digging Machine

To a fossorial animal like the mole, digging is vital to every aspect of its whole life – travelling about, finding food and breeding – in fact to its very survival, and it is perfectly designed for the purpose. The spring breeding activity demonstrates all these aspects of behaviour at once, if you look hard enough.

The mole digs in a very particular way: it scrapes away at the ground using its huge front feet, which we all recognize as its most distinguishing feature. Like us, it has five fingers, each tipped with a strong nail, but it also has a bone that resembles a sixth finger, called the sesamoid, or some refer to it as a falciform bone. This does not extend away from the forefoot as the other bones to form a finger, but remains under the skin creating a wider palm, which the mole uses like a spade to push the soil aside and along the tunnels.

The mole is extremely strong, as anyone who has held a live mole will endorse. As already mentioned, I am asked to catch moles alive for film or media work (something not recommended unless you really have to). On one occasion it was for a photographic advertisement for a well-known children's drink. 'Hold it still!' they said, as the photographers' shutters clicked away from every conceivable angle – but have you ever tried to hold a mole still? The power in the upper body enables it to force its way into the ground, and its neck and shoulders are used to gain any possible advantage from any available point.

This leverage is how the mole digs, and at all levels – though I may have led some people to believe that they use their heads to dig with, in a dipping and lifting action. In the early 1990s I hosted an instructional film on mole trapping, which was released on the old VHS video and then DVD formats. During the filming, I was again asked to produce a live mole to be filmed running around so that the viewers could see what was for many, a live mole for the first time.

The obvious problem was that the mole would immediately seek the sanctuary of the soil and be lost forever, but this was overcome by the mole being filmed in light soil at a depth of a few inches. The mole was filmed scurrying along in the soil, and was seen to be moving the soil and pushing it aside and lifting it upwards with its head as it dipped in a bid to submerge. The truth is that the mole was filmed on a large board so it could not escape down and out of shot. It desperately tried to plunge below the soil but was prevented from doing so by the board; if you viewed this footage, then yet another myth would have been explained.

Working with programme makers means that I am fortunate in being able to study moles from the film rushes. The producers work hard to obtain the best angles and effects, and to a mole catcher watching in the wings, this is a

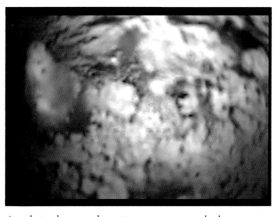

A mole in the tunnel moving at pace towards the camera; the mole's shape can be seen on the left.

priceless opportunity to analyse what a mole actually does in its own secret world. I have extended this fascination and used my own filming to look into the world of moles, and it has been from this process of filming moles in their own environment that I have improved my own skill in controlling moles, and have brought that information to you in these pages.

The rate at which the mole can construct tunnels depends upon the condition of the soil in which it is digging. Light soil is easier to work than a heavy, wet soil. Under ideal soil conditions, the mole can easily tunnel 18 feet (5m) in an hour – and remember this is not always in a straight line, but can be a collection of tunnels in different directions and depths – a Herculean feat. When most people look at a series of molehills scattered over an area, they imagine these indicate just a flat, level tunnel. They accept there must be a tunnel, but they compare it to that of the London Underground train system, linking one point to another. It is nothing like this, as the mole has to cope with different soil conditions, various obstructions, and most importantly, according to the demands of that all-important food source.

The mole is perfectly designed for digging in confined spaces, as the shoulders have evolved over the years to allow for a different movement. The humerus bone is short and broad, and the muscles surrounding it are extremely strong; furthermore it rotates, which determines the height of the digging. This movement therefore dictates the overall diameter of the tunnel in relation to the size of the mole itself. It scrapes the soil and throws it backwards, and it can achieve this because the shoulder blades – the scapula bones – are long and thin, and they run parallel to each other: if we try to rotate our arms back or behind us, we are prevented from doing so, because our shoulder blades lie across our back.

It should now be unmistakably clear just why the mole needs such a large intake of food, as the calories required by its whole body in order to sustain such a high metabolism, necessary to function in such an environment, are of titanic proportions.

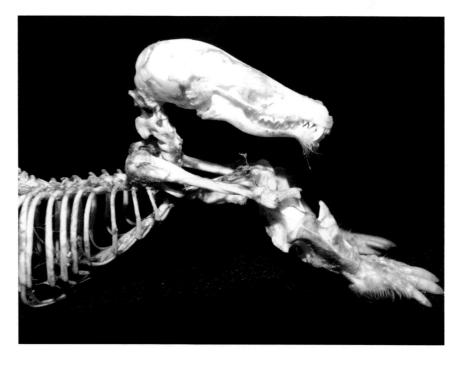

The mole's skeleton is perfectly adapted for its life below ground.

Having thrown the soil behind it, the mole actually moves most of this waste away with its rear feet; it can, and does move soil with its large front paws, but it does so more efficiently using its back legs. When filming moles I have seen them do this: one moment they are gazing into the camera lens, the next they have turned around, and as if from nowhere backfill the tunnel and camera with soil in a matter of seconds.

There are often occasions when you are called to investigate mole activity, and the mole has already left; this is understandable, as many see a molehill and assume this must mean they have a mole. The breeding season is a prime time for receiving false calls, but it is important that the mole catcher attends in order to assess the situation and calm the frantic landowner, and makes the most of the opportunity to understand mole movement. If you, as a mole catcher, do decide to undertake this investigation process even over a short period, you will absorb vital information concerning the life of the mole.

Touch of Velvet

In the latter part of March, temperatures can be quite mild in comparison to how it begins, and this is evident when female moles are caught that are clearly in oestrus, or pregnant, and showing evidence of a spring moult.

Moles moult twice a year to change their pelage, and the month the moult begins varies from one region to another according to climate differences. The mole's fur is renowned for its smooth touch, and this is because it has no lay in it: 'lay' is the direction in which it lies – with most animals the lay is from head to tail, but the mole's fur stands up vertically and may be stroked in any direction with no resistance: a touch of velvet.

Ever since man began capturing moles, this touch of velvet has been a sought-after commodity. As long ago as the Roman Empire, the skins of moles have had a use, ranging from items of clothing to objects of utility: caps, uniforms and tobacco pouches, to a simple cloth to wipe plumbers' joints, moleskins have been gathered in their millions. The clears – the winter coats – held the highest commercial value, as they are thicker than the summer coat, between 11 and 12mm, while the summer coats are slightly thinner, at 9–10mm. As I said, the spring and autumn moult can begin at any time in their respective seasons, and will depend on the individual mole.

It was thought the female's moult was achieved more quickly than the male's; however, this is of little concern to a mole catcher today, as there is very little call for moleskins other than from those who use them in the art of fly tying.

Mole Parasites

Occasionally a bald mole may be caught: this is nothing strange, but the effect of a parasite called the Demodex mite. Humans can also be

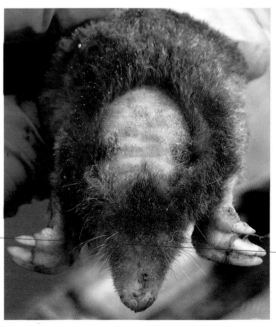

The Demodex mite will attack the hair follicles, causing hair loss. J. NOBLETT

infested by a mite from this family, a condition known as 'demodicosis'. The Demodex mite attacks the hair follicles, and the mole contracts a form of mange and suffers body hair loss. (More on moleskin later.)

If the mole in your hands has some additional guests, look more closely, as it may not necessarily be the Demodex mite, but fleas. The mole flea *Hystrichopsylla talpae* is the largest flea to be found in the United Kingdom, and at ⅛in (5mm) in length is not difficult to see. This flea is also found on other tunnel inhabitants, such as voles and mice, and probably infests the mole's environment by dropping off these other rodents.

Moles and Listeriosis

Agriculture welcomes a drier March because it is then possible for heavy machinery to access the silage and hay fields – but many farmers become – to put it politely – disgruntled when mole spoil appears all over the grass crop, which is an important commodity for the following winter. Soil-contaminated hay or silage has potentially fatal consequences to livestock if it is used as feed, because it could cause listeriosis. The bacterium that causes listeriosis is called *Listeria monocytogenes*, and it is found in soil, mud, dust, silage and sewage, and in fact in most of the animals that are tested. Incidentally, it is also found in the gut of a small percentage of healthy people, so exposure to this bacterium is unavoidable. The organism can be killed by proper cooking or pasteurization, but some products, such as certain cheeses, may still contain traces of it.

To address this problem, the farming industry – as we have learnt for hundreds of years – has always employed authentic mole catchers to control the moles, so I consider myself fortunate, like many others, that I continue to be indispensable to British farming. With the changes made to our modern methods for mole control, together with the use of poisons being made illegal in 2006, and the increased costs incurred as a result of new regulations that require multi-operator gas application, I have trust in the future of the methods used by those old mole catchers, who laid the foundations for their use all those years before me.

Mole Control in Large Fields

Mole control in fields is 'bread and butter' to mole catchers, and large numbers of moles frequently need to be removed, often from large acreages of land. But there is little difference between setting traps in large areas and setting them in small areas: they still need to be placed in the correct tunnels, and the number of these tunnels will depend upon how many moles are present. Some people feel that controlling moles in large fields is a mammoth task, but in fact this is not so. A common mistake is to misconstrue the number of moles present because of the number of molehills in the fields, often scattered around or in clusters, and which many see as the obvious place to put their trap.

Another error is to flood the area with traps in the hope of catching the mole or moles! I was approached at a mole show (an educational entertainment show I perform at agricultural, horticultural and county shows around the United Kingdom) by a farmer who exclaimed that traps didn't work – he had set thirty in his field and not caught a single mole. However, you can't blame the traps for your own mistakes, and in the case of this farmer, he had set too many. Furthermore, not conversant with the way a mole lives and how the environment constantly influences it, the farmer had set his traps in the wrong locations – and I would question whether he had the skill to place a trap in the ground correctly once, let alone thirty times.

It is important to stand and look over the ground when dealing with large fields. Treat each area of damage in the field as an individual task, and concentrate on ascertaining the influences this field places upon those individual areas of damage. The following features should be considered: does the field slope, and if so, to what degree, and would it have an effect on the water table? Is the natural water table high or low, or is there natural or artificial drainage? What borders the field? Are there areas that will provide dry shelter for nest building, such as areas of woodlands and banks, and most importantly, are there boundaries such as hedgerows and fences? Are there molehills in clusters on the headlands of the field, or are they generally scattered about? And do these clusters seem to be linked by a few single molehills? There is a great deal of information to consider, and combined with how the field is used, you should be able to figure out a system for how best to work your traps, and how to obtain the best results in the shortest possible time.

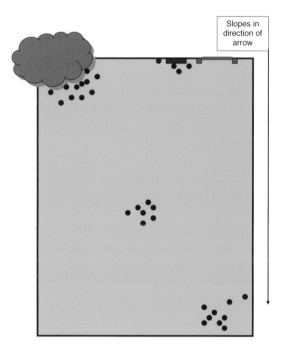

Slopes in direction of arrow

The following is a scenario from a typical agricultural situation: a 10-acre field of grass with quite a steep slope (*see* diagram). At the top end of the field there is a large oak tree, and also a water trough, as the field is used for livestock; it is completely bordered by a post-and-rail fence, and has gate access on two sides. The field adjoining is smaller, and provides a strip of grass that meets with small woodlands. The field you are concerned with has three main areas of molehills: the first are a short distance out from the large oak tree, the second are in the centre of the field half-way down the slope, and the last are in the bottom corner of the field. So how many moles do you think there are here? The obvious answer may be three, but it could actually be just one: even in a field of this size, it could be a single mole. I am using this scenario to explain why you should never assume how many or how few moles may be present.

It is important to reflect on how the field will influence the mole in its everyday life, and the first consideration is, where will it sleep? Somewhere dry, probably under the oak tree where a large quantity of water will be drawn

from the ground by the tree roots, leaving a dry location and an opportunity to build a nest. The scattering of molehills around the oak tree will normally begin directly under the outer fringe of the maximum span of the tree. From this point, they will spread out from the canopy provided by the leaves. It will be the natural drip from this umbrella of flora from any rainfall or dew drop that will create a higher level of moisture in the soil beneath.

This is where the mole will generate a feeding area – look for yourself next time you see mole activity under a large tree! Stand amongst the molehills, and then look up and you will find yourself on the outer edge of the tree's canopy.

Incidentally, it will not be uncommon to find that a tree or shrub root confronts you when you open up that perfect trap site. The location is just right for the trap, but you discover that a root bridges the tunnel. Under no circumstances should you pull it, as it will possibly break the tunnel structure in some way, either the walls or the base, and the disturbance will alert the mole: you must cut it. To do this, use a good sturdy knife, one with a good handle and a locked blade to prevent it possibly closing back on your fingers; your knife will be used in wet, muddy and slippery conditions, so big is best to ensure a good grip. Secateurs or small pruning shears could be used to snip it, but in deeper tunnels, the knife will prove best to get the cut as close to the side walls as possible.

Returning to our example field and the circumstances, when drier weather arrives, water will naturally drain in the direction of the slope, and the moles' food source will also naturally follow this movement according to the moisture levels in the soil. I said that you have an area of molehills in the middle of the field, and half-way down. The question is, why here? And the answer is simple: this is the preferred location of the food. So in such a large enclosure, why would the food be in this particular location? The field may now be used for cereal or grass products, and possibly livestock, but if we go back and find out how it was used previously, we can find the reason. It may be further back in years than you think, and it is all to do with the condition of the soil.

The field at one time may have been divided into smaller plots – remember when men owned an acre of land to provide for their own families, and some plots would have been tended well and others would not, and what was planted and grew in these smaller plots had an influential impact on that area of land. As is still the case in today's modern usage, the pH (potential of hydrogen) value of soil changes in relation to what is planted, or according to what additives are mixed into the land to condition it. In times gone by, the use of quicklime was a favoured soil conditioner, and although once a common material, it was highly dangerous to produce. Some fields or plots would have been treated with quicklime, while others would not, and the enriched soils attracted the sources of nutrients for the moles. Worms are also an influential part of the cycle, and because

they must process the soil for nutrients for their own survival they will congregate in preferred areas. This is why we witness pockets of mole damage in some areas, and not others.

Incidentally, on this matter modern farming now has the benefit of global satellites, which can manage machines to work the land without human input at the controls. One use of this system is to plot the soil condition of the soil, and to apply products to determine an even balance across an entire field, whatever its size, so there will be an even yield from the whole acreage at harvest. This has to be good news for the moles and bad news for farmers, because what is currently a field with just pockets or oases of opportunity will become uniformly productive, a vast haven that will provide for a considerable increase in mole numbers where previously there was only a limited problem. Farmers, you have been warned!

The bottom corner of our field is the area where the mole will feed in times of drought or reduced rainfall, as food will be found in the wetter areas.

There may be molehills around the water trough, and these will be associated with the spillage from use by livestock or that sticky ball valve. The damp area created encourages the worms to the moist soil, and is the explanation as to why moles tunnel around such field furniture – not to find a drink, as many have claimed.

Always consider the location of molehills, and reflect on why they are there; here in the photograph the molehills are below the natural drip of the trees and in the shade from the sun, both of which circumstances promote the retention of moisture.

This example is just a means to get you thinking, and to show you, as an aspiring mole catcher, how to decipher the information presented to you, and how to work such a location – and yes, you would always place a trap under the post and rail fence lines, and the reason will be explained in the next chapter.

Fortresses and Raised Nests

Large fields may be flat, and due to the formation of the soil layers, they become waterlogged in wetter periods or months; in these circumstances a mole may build a fortress. This is a remarkable construction, created by a mole when it needs to build a dry nesting area; it is a frequent feature in regions where probably the water table is higher, and on land at, or below sea level. It can be quite a feat of achievement, reaching 60 centimetres and more in height, with a complex of tunnels winding through it, providing for a quick exit when required. It may, however, only resemble a molehill that is slightly larger than others in the area, or occasionally it may resemble a small soil bank that will soon become covered in grass and weeds, thus providing further protection against discovery.

Moles will sometimes build a raised nest in areas that have a level of shallow top soil, for instance in some areas where I catch moles on the

The moles do not want to lie in a cold damp bed so natural materials will be taken for comfort.

chalk downs. Here they create a raised mound of soil, as they cannot find a suitable area for a nest. The hard chalk prevents any working at depth, and they are forced to survive in a nest located in a mound of soil constructed from the gathered workings of the tunnels. The soil taken from the tunnels is collected to form a dome, which will contain a nest lined with grass or leaves to insulate the resident mole from the cold.

Whether the mole has a nest in a location that is naturally dry, or in an artificially constructed one in the form of a fortress, it is completely protected from a harsh environment, from damp or cold.

If you do find a fortress in a field from which you have been requested to remove the mole, do not open up the fortress until you have removed the mole! Use the fortress as a central point and work out from it, looking for the tunnels leading away from it and to the feeding grounds, and place your trap in one of these. Having removed the mole, take a closer look into the fortress: it is a remarkable sight. In construction it is not just a pile of soil, far from it: rather, it is a calculated and carefully planned affair, requiring a huge effort on the part of the mole to tunnel and remove the soil from various areas, and to collate and collect it to one given point. As the tunnels are extended and the fortress gets taller, then the inside is hollowed out with another complex of tunnels or chambers, and the structure is complete. Obviously the soil will act as an insulator, but the central core chamber is lined with gathered grass or leaves, increasing the thermal capability considerably and making for a cosy, comfortable home.

APRIL

A request I receive on a regular basis is from a renowned local equine veterinary hospital: the first signs of mole activity in any of the paddocks and the phone will ring. The fragile legs of a foal can be damaged beyond repair from stumbling in a shallow mole run or tripping on a molehill, which has generated an intense dislike of moles in the hospital staff.

Setting Traps in Fields and Paddocks

Equine paddocks are often a mole haven, and the hospital's 100 acres are no exception, as they are bordered and divided by post and rail fencing. Where moles are present, a main mole run is likely to follow the line of this type of structure, whether natural or manmade. Again, as with the canopy of a tree, this is because early morning dew and any amount of rainfall will drip from the fence and cause a damp line below it, creating a permanent area of moisture, and soil conditions that are perfect for a tunnel.

To demonstrate this, take a handful of damp, moist soil and push a finger into it; then remove your finger, and you have created a tube. There is no waste to remove, nor will any soil stick to your finger because you will have compressed the soil into a pipe; and this is exactly what the moles do, because under this drip, at an ideal depth and distance from the main drip area, the moisture content will be perfect for this task. The moles do not need to deposit any waste soil on the surface, which is the first consideration of many inexperienced mole catchers in locating the presence of moles. These main run systems may have been under these locations

of natural drip for many years. Only the occasional disturbance from a heavy hoof or piece of machinery, which necessitates a repair, may expose this hidden tunnel, as a certain amount of debris will need to be deposited at surface level.

These tunnels are a prime location from which to remove moles, as they often share them, to access their home ranges, to locate females or to source new areas. In the situation relating to the veterinary paddocks mentioned above, the moles do not actually have their nests in the paddocks, but in the woodlands and hedgerows surrounding them. They must travel some considerable distance to locate their feeding areas, but they cover it quickly, with the speed they are capable of travelling even in the confines of the tunnels. The compacted tubes make travelling easy, and the clue is to open the tunnels and take a look at the inner surface – a polished surface is a sure sign of regular use. Our example field discussed earlier was bordered by a post and rail fence, and below it would have been the tunnel the moles used to travel round the field to gain access to the different feeding areas.

The best position for any trap in this situation is in the tunnel under the fence line, with the next best trapping location being in any of the tunnels that lead out into the paddocks

Post-and-rail fences provide an easily accessible route around the countryside.

towards any of the areas of molehills. Any trapping in a field location needs to be carried out in a methodical way: you need a plan to work to. I will begin at a gate and move round the field or paddock in a clockwise direction, seeking out the tunnels that journey out into the centre where the feeding grounds are.

Having removed the moles from these tunnels, I then concentrate on any central activity, looking for a possible fortress. If I identify this larger molehill, I will use it as a reference point and work out from it, towards the feeding grounds. If you consider the situation carefully, you will soon be able to pick out the linking tunnels that run to areas with clusters of mole damage, which indicate the feeding grounds. When I am working the field centre, I have time to check for moles coming in again from any perimeter, and remove these at the same time.

If you are working a large field, always consider what the field use and size may have been, as moles will have been present for many years. The discovery of molehills in the centre of a field is often a mystery to some, who wonder how they got there. To the mole catcher, the answer is often quite simple, in that the moles are using existing tunnels that quite possibly were once located under old hedgerows and fencing now grubbed out to increase the size of the field. These tunnels will be deep enough so as not to be influenced by any level of traffic, nor will they be damaged by machinery working that area, such as the plough, so remain in situ and available for constant use.

It is important not to use traps unnecessarily in any location you are requested to remove moles from, particularly in large areas where you might put down a number of traps, when you must ensure you pick them all up again. However, do not get drawn into the belief of many amateurs that the more traps you set in a location, the better the chance of a catch. On the contrary, it is a fact that the more traps you put down, the more disturbance you cause to

the mole's territory, and in doing so you can generate more problems for yourself because you alert the mole to your presence. Remember, you only have to find the correct tunnel – the staircase or corridor that the mole will be using to access its feeding grounds – and put a trap there. Putting down a large number of traps displays a lack of understanding and skill in the profession of mole catching.

Trap Markers

When trapping moles in any large location it is imperative that you remember exactly where you have positioned the traps, and retrieve

Under some circumstances it is important to mark traps so they can be retrieved, and so that other users may be aware of their presence; prominent markers can be seen from the tractor cab.

them all. Furthermore if the land is still in agricultural use when you are asked to remove the moles, it is also important to ensure that the trap sites are marked clearly. I use two options in such a situation: hazel sticks with white-painted tops, or white nylon rods with red-painted tops, which show up well in a snow-covered landscape. The 50cm long sticks or rods are clearly visible to machinery operators, who will steer clear of the areas and thus avoid destroying or damaging traps. Nylon rods are preferable to hazel in situations where there may be animals – sheep, deer and rabbits will chew hazel and pull markers from the ground, but they shy away from those made of nylon.

It is also important to consider the safety of livestock and machinery. Some catchers use thinner wire markers with plastic builders' warning tape tied to them to mark trap sites, but in my opinion these are best avoided, as the wire may tangle with machinery, and the plastic presents a possible choke risk to other animals. Using rods as trap markers provides a professional, uncomplicated way of remembering the number of traps used, and where they are. If you have twenty traps in your bag, then also carry twenty rods: as the traps are placed and individually marked with a rod, it is easy to know how many traps have been used by the number of rods left in the bag when you finish trap setting. It is then just simple mathematics to subtract the number of rods left in your bag from the number you started with, to know how many traps have been used. The easy-to-view trap markers are collected along with the traps when these are inspected at the end of the day, and therefore all traps can be accounted for.

Landscaping and Extensions

April is a time for landscaping and extensions. I was once asked to remove the moles from a new grass area to the front of a large house; it was quite a long frontage, and there was a cen-tral driveway up to the house, which had undergone renovation and some new build. The builders had decided to become landscapers and had carried out what increasingly seems to be a trend, of spreading the rubbish and rubble, and then covering it over with soil. When I first attended there were clues that contractors had attempted to create some sort of grassed presentation: there were tufts of dry turf scattered around, with dead wood, broken house bricks and plastic bags and cable. The owner claimed that the area had been ploughed and drilled, but the probe revealed the truth, which was that soil had been taken possibly from the foundations of the building works, mixed with a few loads of topsoil, then scraped and raked around over the area to create a level field.

For mole catching this had the undesirable effect of creating twin layers. Covering the original grass with soil may have given the impression of a good job done, but it had in fact hidden the truth of what was going on beneath ground level, where the moles were still working undisturbed in the original levels. These levels contained tunnels that addressed the influences placed on the mole and its source of food prior to the change. In fact the inclusion of another layer of soil had little initial impact on these moles, as the ground was over clay and with a high water table. The new top layer of soil was never more than 6in (150mm) deep over the original grass, so the water soaked down quite quickly to the now decaying original organic layer, where it slowed down before continuing on its journey.

This decaying organic level provided an opportunity that the moles' food source also exploited: it produced an increase in food for worms, which in turn dwelled at a basic level. This created the problem that the moles' tunnels were also created within the decaying, buried grass level. This meant that the tunnel was literally amongst decaying grass matter, a mass of compacted material that required careful attention to detail when placing traps. To describe it better I would say it was like placing a mole trap in a bowl of cold spaghetti. More than ever it was necessary to ensure the trowel cut just enough of a hole to fit the trap. In this situation, the half-barrel trap is ideal as it provides support to what can be a fragile tunnel.

Ensure that when cutting into the tunnel the trap fits extra tight; in fact any trap site requires cutting slightly smaller to provide the trap with a tight fit, and this cannot be emphasized enough. In a situation such as this, it is to allow for the almost false support of the decomposing grass layer. It has lost its strength as it has decayed, so cutting the hole smaller all round allows the trap to hold up the tunnel where it contacts both ends of the trap and sides. If you do not reduce the trap site, the tunnel roof will slowly sink down and around into the tunnel and the mole will be alerted by these changes. You must take your time with this type of location, ensuring that you change the tunnel as little as you can.

Covering the trap site is no different from other situations of covering a trap at this depth. The simple solution for any person or contractor is to remove the moles before the changes are made to the land, or for the land to be managed better – both of which choices are often out of the hands of the mole catcher! If the moles had been dealt with prior to the works, then the damage to the new landscaping would have been avoided. Many mole catchers will face this problem, as this trend, of developing areas on a budget, is spreading across the country.

The Effects of April Showers

April can be quite warm, but also damp with its seasonal showers, and normally these conditions will cause the ground to soften and food supplies to become more readily available, which especially in the south makes the return journey for many male moles after their breeding exploits that little bit easier. When April showers do fall, they can often be sudden and heavy, which is welcomed by much of the mole's food, while the mole itself will be on the cusp of seeking to breed. The bugs and grubs, and especially the worms, will take advantage of this rainfall by working their way up the soil as the water soaks down – and this is not just because they seek life-giving oxygen, but because they, too, are looking to increase their numbers. Worms will use the spring warmth and any wet spells to move across the ground surface more quickly, so as to inhabit new areas faster, and to mate.

Evidence of this can be seen from the moles' immediate response, which is to run spooked and to create shallow tunnels so they can make the most of this opportunity to harvest such a bountiful supply. For the female mole it will be a welcome feast, as her litter may now be demanding that vital life source, her milk, to begin their life journey.

Litter Numbers

The size of a mole's litter may be worthy of further investigation, and the mole catcher is in the best position to pursue this information: his daily contact with moles will, over the years, expose secrets that no laboratory study can reveal, nor global positioning system monitor. The rivalry amongst any litter of animals for life in the early stages is intense, as they will all struggle and battle for life, and moles are no exception. Any species that shares a nursery will be in constant competition to feed, and if the number of siblings exceeds the number of teats, then many will fail to feed sufficiently or possibly at all, and the consequences can be fatal. Even in circumstances where there are fewer young than there are teats available, fatalities can occur, the fact being that once attached, many siblings will remain there until the teat is depleted, so denying any of the others the opportunity to feed. Due to the confined space in the nest it may not always be possible for the

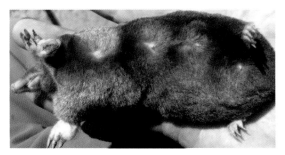

The mole's milk is high in protein but all siblings must be able to suckle to survive.

young to feed from both sides of their mother, and this will become more difficult as the young themselves increase in size.

Further investigation is needed for us to understand fully the early lives of moles, from evidence obtained in this everyday contact of catching moles during their breeding season. Controlling moles in their breeding period could be controversial, as the indiscriminate removal of a female could possibly cause a litter unnecessary suffering, and often death. Indeed, the death of any single parental creature either from natural causes or from predation will have devastating consequences, not just in the mole's world but with any species.

Sibling rivalry is something that stimulated my personal thoughts regarding mole survival, and in relation to weaning I began to wonder if the number of teats on a female was of any significance regarding the number of offspring in the litter. If a female had eight teats – four on each side – and four kits in her litter, then when feeding, all four would be provided for, and even in the confinement of a small nest, all could feed without compromise. If she had only six teats – so three on each side – then the best litter size would be three; and if she had only four teats, then two would be best provided for.

This is only a theory, which those more educated in the world of moles may possibly research in the future; but the reason for my interest in this conjecture is the mole's ability to maintain numbers under any circum-

stances. Females caught showing signs of early pregnancy have therefore been dissected to see how many foetuses they were carrying. Varying numbers have been present, but rarely large numbers in the latter stages; on occasions I have seen more than four foetuses, and sometimes as many as six – but could this be the abnormal as opposed to the normal, given that with any species, more than expected have sometimes been born to ensure the survival rate of the species? And could the opposite be happening, that mole litters are decreasing in numbers because of unfavourable environmental changes? It is only a theory, but if the mole is able to maintain its numbers even under harsh and competitive circumstances, this could be a part of their success.

Survival of the Young Moles

The new litter would have been born red in colour, changing through pink to a bluish tint at approximately nine to ten days, before achieving their full covering of black fur at seventeen days; their eyes open to their world at twenty-two days. The milk of a lactating mole is obviously high in proteins and nutrients, as the young at five to six weeks are fully grown, and begin their individual journeys of life.

A mole nest if discovered would be an easy meal for a marauding fox or badger, and the adult female is no match for a predator of this size. Smaller predators are weasels, not actually

Born red, the baby moles will soon be covered in the distinctive velvet jacket.

a prime natural enemy of the mole, and under normal circumstances the mole can avoid this ferocious foe. However, it would not be possible to carry all her litter to safety in the event of an attack, and many, if not all, would be lost. When the female mole starts to wean her litter, she will move the young to another chamber if she feels threatened; any disturbance will alert her to protect her offspring, and this could be the beginning of the new moles' natural instinct for interpreting the dangers of life.

My assertion that the weasel is not a prime natural enemy of the mole is the result of my studying moles with a video camera in their environment. This fascinating look into their world has revealed many secrets, and one is that they are not alone in these labyrinths: these are shared with other small animals, mainly field voles and mice. Often the film footage exposes the presence of these squatters of the moles' world, exploiting what may be considered tunnels of safety. However, the natural enemy of these rodents is the weasel.

The weasel is small enough to get into the tunnels and travel around in them in search of its preferred repast: it likes nothing more than a small rodent, and it knows the tunnels will provide for that need. Not being a sight predator, it hunts 'on the nose': it tracks its prey by its

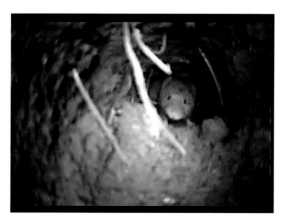

In a mole tunnel, showing they are not alone in the subterranean world.

scent and may pick up the odour of another animal, so may locate a nest of new mole kits. The weasel is an opportunist predator, and one that will take any unsuspecting mole for its meal, but normally the mole can escape its attentions as it has a unique ability to evade the hunter, which I will explain later.

Before the juvenile moles begin their personal quest to survive on their own, they will start to venture out on small excursions away from the sanctuary and safety of the close quarters of their mother. These investigations into the new world will be made in tunnels that are close to the nest, where they will instinctively hunt and consume any food they discover, food their mother had previously sourced and stored in her worm larders. Exploring the tunnels in this way gives them the confidence to follow their instincts in locating food. These short trips will increase in the distance and time spent away from the nest, and eventually they will not return. Squabbling amongst the youngsters as the solitary instinct begins to grow within them may be another step towards the intolerance shown to each other later in life.

The new litter will remain close to the home range of their mothers' territory for some weeks, even after leaving. Evidence of this can be found when numerous juvenile moles are caught in and around the known range of a female mole. The extra range or territory she created before giving birth was to provide for her litter in the weeks before they could fend for themselves, but now it has more moles than it can provide for, which will place further strain upon the youngsters, and again will drive them to disperse to other vicinities.

Once the mother leaves her brood she will have abandoned all maternal feelings, and any of her offspring who encroach into her territory will be greeted with aggression. This aggressive reception, and the need to find food, will send the new moles on their solitary existence, and drive them to clean out and create further tunnels in order to avoid conflict and survive.

Those that fail to move on will lose bodyweight and possibly die, especially if the range or area doesn't have enough food to support so many moles: only the strongest will survive. The litter will eventually disperse and go their separate ways, but many will fail to see the following spring.

Understanding the Mole

In a subterranean world, instinct is the key to survival, and as a mole catcher it is important to understand fully how a mole experiences his environment in the earth.

It could be said that one of the greatest mysteries of moles and mole catching is why a mole catcher always manages to catch his mole, even in a small garden, where others have failed. The answer is a simple one – he understands the mole completely, and from this knowledge competes on a level playing field. Those who are not so conversant with moles will use waffle and excuses to justify their failures and their delay in achieving success. The mole is a complex animal specifically designed for the world it lives in. If you understand this, it is quite simple to apply your knowledge of the mole with the circumstances that prevail at the time, and obtain results not just quickly and efficiently, but humanely, too.

The important factor in any form of animal management is disposing of the pest humanely, yet many often disregard this when dealing with moles in favour of convenience and profit, when the truth of the matter is that recognized humane working practices in fact speed up the process. Some will always reject such claims, but the decision is always down to the trapper, despite any regulations that may or may not apply.

Therefore as a mole catcher, what do you need to know about a mole? The easiest answer is absolutely everything, including what might be considered unnecessary or irrelevant, despite what so many may claim. In fact many who

claim to be mole catchers often make mistakes because of their lack of knowledge of the mole, which is the reason for their failure. But at one time, established mole catchers would refuse to educate those who wished to learn this skill of controlling moles, because to do so might have led to them having to share the spoils within a parish. As we now know, it was a sure way to secure an income – but where there is any opportunity for financial gain, others will always seek to take advantage of it.

A good example was when the poison strychnine was easily available in 1818, which saw many others giving themselves the title of mole catcher, be it under somewhat false pretences! These mole killers armed themselves with a jar of poisoned worms and offered a cheap service, but without any guarantee of positive results; furthermore they could never produce the mole or moles as evidence of carrying out the requested task. Yet today in our modern world, we still witness such claims and occurrences, and also neglected practice.

The use of any explosive other than ammunition for the purpose of killing or taking any wild animal is currently prohibited under section 11(1) of the Wildlife and Countryside Act 1981. However, the practice of administering a mixture of gas and air into the tunnels of moles and other ground-burrowing animals is permitted; the volatile combination is then detonated, to blast and collapse the tunnels to prevent them being reinhabited. It is clearly not permitted to take an animal's life with this practice and all living creatures must be removed from any tunnel prior to such work. Many will declare that they have removed the mole or moles from an area before they carry out this discharge, but it is often questionable whether all animals really have been removed. Significantly, has consideration been given to the removing of any other proven tunnel-dwelling inhabitants, such as the field rodents or the opportunist weasel, if this work is carried out according to current legislation?

April will start to draw to a close, and many in mole control will be surprised to receive calls to new locations towards the end of the month, especially to the gardens of people who had never before experienced mole damage in any way. Most of this damage will be made by males on their journey home, as they stumble into new areas in search of food. Many of these moles will have no intention of staying, but it highlights how moles will exploit a situation, and the fact that they can appear anywhere, at any time, and in any place. Over the course of time moles seem almost to have learnt that during this month man will respond to a strange urge – that of gardening. Even the smallest of garden plots will become the topic of attention, like some spring ritual; to some it will be only a whim, to others an obsession.

This is an excellent time for moles, as rested soil is turned, broken, raked and enriched in preparation for that other rush in May, when bedding plants become available and are squeezed into every available space. Aided by the ease of working primed raised beds for vegetables, the mole can venture around old tunnels and deposit soil randomly on lawns and under shrubs, evidence that many consider indicates a veritable army or new epidemic of moles. Early planted onions are pushed out, and shallow runs bore along border edges. To the owner it is devastation, to the mole it is an adventure, and to the mole catcher, it is another lesson.

MAY

For a mole catcher, with the arrival of the month of May, farming work for the beginning of the year is almost complete. The agricultural growing season is now under way, with fields left to the dictates of nature as to what the yield will be. Farmers now watch and wait, just keeping a close eye on their crops, occasionally feeding and weeding. This month the mole catcher transfers his attention from agri-

culture to horticulture, apart from occasional paddocks and any late sowings that a foraging mole may decide to investigate – but otherwise the character of his work is quite changed, because now many moles decide to venture out into gardens and allotments.

The soil is tunnelled for the first time as moles divert their tender loving care to areas that were somewhat neglected over the colder season. This perfectly coincides with gardeners starting to make new plans for their borders, bringing out trays of bedding plants and shrubs – and of course May heralds a task that for the mole is also a favourite pastime: lawn care. Out come the lawn mowers, and combined with feeding, spiking and watering, the gardeners compete to create the perfect lawn, complete with stripes – while under the organic layers that over the next few months will become the pride of the street, the moles are on the prowl!

This attention to detail by professional and amateur gardeners alike is to some moles often literally a lifeline. Any disturbance to the soil, also aerating and the application of manure, means that moles will find new sources of food. To many male moles returning to their home ranges this could be the difference between life and death, and they will exploit the opportunity, often at the expense of the landowner who, alarmed at the emergence of even a single molehill, will once again be found browsing the shelves at the garden centre.

Many of the items sold to repel moles work by exploiting what is considered must be annoying to the mole. In fact many of these items do the complete opposite, and encourage new or further mole activity in an area. For the reader to understand completely the reason for this assertion, and why it is imperative for trap use to be carried out correctly, it is important to know more about the mole. I have already explained where the trap needs to be placed, and which tunnel you will find the mole using daily to go about its business. Now a mole catcher must think like the mole, imagine he is in that tunnel, and experience how the environment influences every mole that uses it. If you can identify with this amazing subterranean world as a mole, then your success in their control will greatly improve.

May is a good month to talk about the mole in more detail, as during this month the new young moles in the south of the country, where I control moles, will also be experiencing this secret underground domain for the first time, as their natural instincts flow through their body.

The Mole's Eyes and Sight

Moles are not blind, as many believe: they have two perfectly formed eyes the same as you and I, but having lived in an almost permanently dark world for millions of years throughout their evolution, their eyes have developed in a specialized way, to provide their brain with the information it requires for the mole to survive in such an environment.

A mole's eyes are very small, measuring approximately 1 millimetre across. The retina of any eye is a vitally important part as this is where information relating to the surroundings will be received, supplying the brain with a vision of the backdrop. The light-sensitive retina consists of both rods and cones: rods are used to see in the dark but only in black and white, whereas the cones allow light to enter and can distinguish colour. The mole's eye contains considerably more rods than cones – between 100,000 and 130,00 rods in relation to just 10,000–15,000 cones – so it is clear that its eye has developed to process information perceived in the dark, although it still retains some ability to distinguish images in the light, or to determine the difference between light and dark.

New information on the mole is constantly being discovered, with the advantage of new technology and interest from the scientific world, and information about moles recorded in earlier books is now being superseded by

these new discoveries. However, the knowledge of those former researchers has been of immense value in providing a base to compare the details of what we once thought comprised the life of the mole, to the one we are beginning to understand today.

From a mole catcher's point of view this wealth of comparative information provides him with new direction as to how best to adapt trap use and improve welfare prospects for the mole, and offer a better service to the client. Moreover modern technology has enabled us to look even more closely into this strange secretive world, and to build on this new knowledge. I personally use an endoscope camera to study the different mole tunnels and environments to better my own knowledge, and as a result of intricate examination of a mole's eye, we have been able to change and improve our approach to mole control using traps. One change has been brought about by the discovery that the structure of the cones in a mole's eye is such that it is sensitive to ultraviolet light (UV): evidence shows the presence of a UV cone photo pigment consistent to that found in the eyes of other species such as rodents, which also have the ability to use UV light in their everyday lives.

For example, such gathered facts immediately alert the mole catcher to the problems of

A mole in its tunnel before it blocks out the light.

tunnel disturbance from stimulating light signals, because as well as being able to see UV light, moles can also without doubt see infrared light. To film moles in the ground the cameras must be able to 'see' the images the photographer is seeking, and he uses infrared light to illuminate the area – invisible to us humans, but certainly not to the mole, because at the first sign of the infrared light, they turn round and close down the source and the filming with a shower of soil!

The longer days of May often mean a greater amount of sunlight: the sun's journey is higher in the sky, and it is stronger and warmer to promote growth. This is also a reminder to the mole catcher that the covering of any trap site needs to be appropriate to these changing conditions, if successful removal is to be quick and efficient – more on this later. In the darker months, this consideration may not have been so important, as the more overcast conditions and darker skies helped to mask any mistakes made.

The Mole's Ears and Hearing

Moles have inner ears, in that no part of them is visible outside the body. We have an external ear that channels the sound waves into our head, where they can be processed by the internal organs that enable us to interpret sounds. Some animals depend on their hearing to warn them in advance of impending danger, and have large ears that rotate, scanning for the slightest sound that will alert them to alarm calls, or to the presence of a predator. Moles live in and around a complex of tunnels, where any sound will travel along a tube providing information by way of an echo in a normally silent world. Sound moves in waves, and in certain conditions can travel either faster or further, and the way the mole has evolved has enabled it to use and interpret sounds in another way.

Sound is a form of energy that is created when an object moves or strikes another: it will vibrate or collide, which will produce this energy. The energy will push the air molecules next to it, and as the air molecules are compressed they form waves as they transfer from one molecule to the next, until the energy is exhausted; this is why sounds become softer the further away they are. The waves or vibrations created by sound actually travel faster through liquids or solids because the molecules are packed together more tightly, and therefore able to travel more quickly. The pitch or frequency of sound is the term used to identify the speed at which an object vibrates. High frequency is fast, low frequency is slow, and the frequency is measured in hertz (Hz), at the rate of how many times it vibrates per second. For example, if it vibrates ten times per second, it would have a measurement of 10 hertz.

So why is a mole catcher talking about the measurement and frequency of sounds? This is because moles are more reliant on the vibrations of energy than on sounds. In the soil, which can be saturated with water, or dry and hard, or frozen solid, the energy created from a sound will, through vibrations, provide information to the mole both faster and more accurately than the noise itself.

How the Mole Senses his Environment

For the mole, outer ears would be a clear hindrance under such confined conditions, and instead they have strategically located stiff hairs called 'vibrissae'. These are found in various places on the mole: there are four in front of the eye and three behind it, and the chin, rear feet and tail also have these hairs. The hairs located on the tail are important, as not only are they used to detect vibrations, but they are also a gauge as to the dimensions of the mole's tunnel. The mole runs with the tail held vertical and in contact with the roof of the tunnel, and information gathered from these hairs from their touch informs the mole of the shape and size of the tunnel, and helps in determining the diameter of every tunnel in relation to its own size, in the same way as the dimension is assessed by the size of the humerus bone. Therefore the mole can determine the exact size of the tunnel with these measurements of its own body.

These stiff hairs are unlike other hairs that pass through the epidermis. The vibrissae are set directly into what are known as 'Merkel cells': these work alongside touch receptors, which in moles are the vibrissae. These Merkel cells amplify the signals they receive, and distribute them directly into the main nervous system, to produce a highly sophisticated means of sensing the environment.

The point to remember is that these stiff hairs are not just tactile in that they can absorb information from any form of contact, but they act as antennae that detect any vibrations passing through the ground. Vibrations as low as 5 hertz can be detected by this sensitive, finely tuned processing centre, which can alert the mole to any immediate disturbances or threats. The mole will experience any vibration and be immediately informed of movement in and above the soil, warning it of potential predators; the principle of some mole repellents is based on this response to vibrations. Battery- and solar-powered 'mole chasers' are described as devices that will scare the mole from the prized lawn, and rely on the theory that the mole will feel the vibrations emitted from these devices and will interpret them as a possible intruder, and will leave to seek an alternative home. Similarly it was assumed that windmills or bottles placed in the ground would have the same effect.

The mole will certainly respond to any disturbance, but for how long? A constant repetitive wave passing through the ground will soon become acceptable, as it will be construed as no longer a threat, and in truth will be taken to mean the opposite. In the same way a mole detects food in the ground by the vibrations it creates as it passes through the soil or moves in the

tunnels fashioned for the very purpose of trapping it as prey. Some thought that moles used scent to locate food, but this is not the case, as scent would not pass efficiently through the soil, unlike vibrations.

Tests confirmed this when a mole in a laboratory tank of soil responded to worms placed on a glass sheet set over the soil. Dead worms laid on the glass obviously didn't move so created no vibrations and were ignored by the mole; however, live worms placed on the glass produced vibrations as they moved, and were detected and identified as a source of food. So to a mole, a continuing source of vibrations will indicate a vast quantity of available food and will encourage it to the area. Similarly big birds such as gulls, rooks and crows – even the humble blackbird – will be seen to stamp on the ground, and they do this to encourage the worms to the surface. So vibrations will bring a mole to a garden near you.

The Mole's Nose: the Eimer's Organ

Our spring-born moles will now be experiencing their new world with these astute senses, but they have more characteristic features that will help them on their path to adulthood. Often those employed in mole control believe that the mole's nose is fully tactile, and that it uses it physically to find its way around its tunnels. However, this is not the case, and these mole

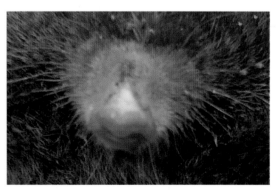

The all-important mole nose.

catchers are ill informed and misled by myths such as the mole using its nose to smell its food. In fact the mole's nose is a highly intricate organ, and far more complex and important than one just used for breathing and smelling.

The muzzle of a mole is covered in thousands of tiny receptors called papillae – another example of these can be seen in the pads of a dog's feet: its pads are covered in pimples, and these are also a form of papillae. The mole, however, can fill its papillae with blood, which increases its sensitivity. In 1871 Theodor Eimer, a German zoologist, was researching the European mole, and discovered much more about this well developed organ. It is a complex amalgam of corpuscles, axons and sensory nerves, collectively now called the Eimer's organ, after its originator. It is a composite unit that provides the mole with a different sensory modality.

From this research it became known that the mole uses this mechanosensory structure to sense temperature, humidity and airflows, and more recently further research into different species of mole has made further discoveries concerning the importance of this organ. This modern data on the mole's Eimer's organ has certainly helped me, as a mole catcher, to understand the mole better, and to instigate a higher level of control.

Although this latest research was carried out on species of mole other than our European mole, it is accepted that moles collate and respond to the information provided by the Eimer's organ in the same way. It was discovered that the receptors acted in different ways, in that some responded to compression, while others were stimulated by airflows brushing across them. We know that when the mole is foraging, it taps the ground with its nose, and we now understand that it does this to activate those receptors, which need compression to operate. This quick tap, applied at a speed of just 30–35 milliseconds, will trigger the sensory units to absorb any information when the mole is static. It is not yet established what this stimulation may detect, but as airflows and pressure would need to be monitored constantly, we may assume that it could be temperature or humidity levels in the environment.

The Eimer's organ is also compressed against objects as the mole travels along its tunnels, and this directional stimulation as it moves, informs it of surface features such as patterns of surfaces and contours, possibly as a form of assistance to tunnel mapping. This tapping of the nose on the tunnel floor to stimulate those receptors that require compression to operate, may also be a method of stimulating a function to detect seismic signals. In a mammal there are three bones in the inner ear, which if a mole were detecting seismic signals through its auditory system, would be vital to this function.

'Bone conduction' is the term given to how vibrations might be transmitted or directed to the inner ear through the skull. There has not been any substantial research into whether moles do use seismic signals, but many soil-dwelling animals do rely upon such senses, and I personally do not see why moles should not also employ some sense of seismic signal detection. Vibrations are important to moles, and we know that through their vibrissae, they can detect them to low levels, but bone conduction recognizes both high- and low-pitched sounds. High-pitched sounds would cause the segments of the skull to vibrate individually and compress the bone case of the inner ear, which in turn will stimulate the sensory cells of sound. Low-pitched sounds are detectable as these would vibrate the whole skull, but the sensory parts of the inner ear would remain at rest. Therefore, this would allow a full range of sounds to be heard, and since the mole has no outer ear, the use of seismic signals and bone conduction seems logical, as it makes the low range of the mole's communicative twitter more detectable, and reduces the chance of confrontation.

Immediately I understood this behavioural use of the Eimer's organ I made the mole runner, a small tool that helps ensure that trap location is correct; I will explain its use later.

Some of the papillae are actually directional in the way they perceive information – that is, certain cells in the Eimer's organ only respond and provide information when stimulated in one direction. This could be from airflows passing in the face of the mole, or from the side, which would be beneficial at tunnel interchanges where possibly quick and vital decisions may have to be made. When a mole is not moving in the tunnel these receptors, which are normally stimulated by movement across them, will be still utilized, so the Eimer's organ provides vital information even when moles are not actively exploring their environment. This constant monitoring of information concerning temperature, humidity and airflows must always be kept in mind by any mole catcher if he is to be successful.

When a mole moves through a tunnel that is the diameter of its body size, it will naturally create a positive pressure in front of it and a negative pressure behind. The Eimer's organ will be constantly detecting the influences of the airflows over the receptors, and sensing the pressure of the air in the tube shape of the tunnel. As the mole moves along the tunnels, the positive pressure will increase and decrease, and it will also be affected by influences from turns and junctions. The mole will use this information as part of its understanding and memory of that environment. It is therefore important that the mole catcher ensures that no changes are made to this air pressure in the way he goes about removing that target mole.

As an example, leaving the base of the tunnel irregular with large soil deposits would influence the flow of air created by the mole's movement: this could increase or decrease the pressure, and if detected by the mole would alert it to the change made in that tunnel. This is why it is so important to ensure the top or roof of a half-barrel trap and the tunnel roof are tight, and that they align perfectly, as any

gap will allow the positive pressure from the mole's movement to be lost as it approaches the trap site. A sudden change from a positive to a negative pressure would be a huge warning to any mole, resulting in a trap full of soil as the mole reinstates the tunnel to maintain the pressure.

It is the collective information from all the receptors in the Eimer's organ that provides the mole with the information it needs to survive – those receptors that require compression to be activated, those that are unidirectional, and those that are single directional – all contribute to fuel a keenly perceptive and intelligent sense. It is hard to comprehend the intricacy of this feature, but in the hard environment below ground, it has to make the mole the most adaptable animal in the earth.

The Somatosensory System

All the information gathered from sensors and receptors needs to be processed, and collectively this system is known as the somatosensory system. It is a diverse sensory system consisting of the receptors and processing centre that a mole uses to produce the sensory modalities such as touch, pressure, temperature, proprioception and pain.

The somatosensory system is spread through all major parts of a mammal's body (and other vertebrates). It consists of both sensory receptors and sensory neurons in the body's periphery (skin, muscle and organs), to deeper neurons within the central nervous system. Initiation of probably all 'somatosensation' begins with the activation of some sort of physical 'receptor'. These in the mole's nose are these receptors of the Eimer's organs activated by movement, pressure, and/or temperature – but in each case the general principle of activation is similar: the stimulus causes depolarization of the nerve ending, and then an action potential is initiated. This action potential then travels inwards towards the spinal cord and into the brain.

It is important to understand that the mole uses these senses, combined with other senses, to evaluate the environment. To explain this in a simple way, the system works when a sensory neuron is triggered by a specific stimulus; this neuron passes to an area in the brain uniquely attributed to that area on the body, and this allows the processed stimulus to be felt at the correct location. These multiple sensations are grouped into three different pathways in the spinal cord, and target the brain in different parts. The first is discriminative touch, which includes touch, pressure and vibration perception; we humans have these senses too, and they enable us to describe the shape and texture of something without actually seeing it, just from holding it in our hands or feeling it. The next is pain and temperature, two important senses that we can all relate to. The third is proprioception and includes receptors for what is happening below the skin, such as muscle stretch, joint position, and tendon tension. This information is constantly sent to the cerebellum, which needs instant feedback on what the muscles, joints and tendons are doing.

The cerebellum (Latin for little brain) is a region of the brain that plays a significant role in the integration of sensory perception and coordination, and it is important to understand proprioception to appreciate how crucial it is to the mole. The majority of us believe that we have five senses, but we do actually have six! The sixth sense is proprioception – the unconscious sense that provides us with information relating to the location, movement and posture of our bodies in physical space. We have receptors all over our bodies that help maintain our body schema; this provides an unconscious map of our body in our brain, which tells us where our body parts are. Proprioception is in constant use, and without it, movement and balance would be impossible.

Now consider the importance to a mole of these senses, which are constantly informing the mole of the environment and any changes that have occurred, or are occurring, whilst others are ensuring that its body functions are responding to that information as it moves in and around the range it knows as its home.

The Mole's Kinaesthetic Sense

The mole has another innate skill, which is finding its way around its intricate network of tunnels in the dark. This is a feat in itself, but the mole can achieve it at speeds of almost 2½mph. It uses another sense that we humans also have – for example, when you wake in the middle of the night, you can reach out and find the light switch in the darkened room. This is the 'kinaesthetic' sense, and we all have one, and it is like an imprinted pattern of memory: the brain simply sends a repeat signal to the muscles, joints and tendons to carry out the same task as previously. The brain does not require the use of the eyes to source the information, only to recall the repeated function.

The mole's kinaesthetic sense is far greater then we could ever comprehend, in that it recalls each turn, junction and change in tunnels. So as far as the mole is concerned, its kinaesthetic sense, working with its finely tuned proprioceptive sense, aided by its somatosensory system, stimulated by the amazingly sensitive abilities of its Eimer's organ, makes it a formidable opponent for any would-be mole catcher.

Earlier I stated that the mole does not actually detect its food by smell, but this is not strictly true. As you have learnt, the mole uses the vibrations in the ground to assess its environment, and it will interpret every quiver, shudder or judder in the soil, including those made by potential food. Every animal possesses a sense of smell, and for some this is incredibly acute, as the shark in water, but the mole does have a certain ability to smell and of course will utilize this sense whenever and wherever it can. It will establish the presence of food from vibrations, but it will also detect odours in the tunnels. Air in tunnels will remain static until influenced by some level of intrusive force – in the case of the mole's environment this might be movement from the mole itself, or other habitants such as rodents. Under such conditions any odours would soon be detected – we can possibly relate to this experience as when we return to a room or house which has not been aired for a while.

The mole's sense of smell has recently become of interest to the scientific world, and there is a theory that moles can actually smell in stereo. Research has been carried out in the United States of America on a species of mole known as *Scalopus aquaticus*, or the eastern mole. Although this species of mole is not found in the United Kingdom, it must be of comparative interest as it is important to consider that our native European mole might also utilize this sense. Researchers discovered that the mole would move its nose back and forth as it sniffed, and would zero in on a source of smell and then move directly to that source. This would obviously be of benefit in detecting food that was not moving, but just lying in a tunnel.

The researchers found that if they blocked one of the mole's nostrils, the mole relied on further movement to compensate for this blockage to detect the food. Blocking the left nostril forced the mole to veer further to the right, and blocking the right nostril further to the left. The mole was then subjected to a chamber test where with both nostrils open it would move directly to the positioned food source, but again with a blocked nostril it moved in the opposite direction to the blocked nostril until it located the food with the open nostril.

From this experiment, by comparing the input across the nostrils, the researchers deduced that the mole obtained directional information to source the food. Whether this is stereo is perhaps open to question – the obvious reason seems to be that to use its sense of smell the mole had to turn its head so it could use its open nostril, and if they were both open it didn't. I used to keep barn owls for a hobby and these

wonders of the night hunt by directional noise. Their ears are set so that one is slightly lower than the other. From this positioning of their ears and with head movements, it enables them to detect sound waves, to determine the exact source of that sound, and so locate their prey. Whether moles can smell in stereo would not be surprising, with so many acute senses to call upon, and it is exciting to know that science is continuing to look more closely at the humble mole.

Every Molehill Tells a Story

With each day that May progresses, moles will be putting these senses to the test as they exploit the efforts and patience of those who are working to have the perfect garden for the summer months. Thus both parties will be working the land, but for two very different reasons, the moles to enjoy the ample new source of valuable and varied food choices, and man in his bid for horticultural splendour. However, with all this activity both above and below the soil, the month of May can be a difficult month for the mole catcher. Moving from agricultural work into the minefield of domestic gardening, mole catchers are also drawn into the battle for dominance of the soil.

This feud between mole and gardeners, both professional and amateur, always results in molehill stamping. In their frustration, people insist on stamping on the molehills, but this is the worst thing anyone can do if they have a mole: never stamp down the molehills, and as a mole catcher, never ask people to do this either. The reason is simple, in that the more damage you do to a mole's environment, the more damage it will do to yours. Kicking or stamping on the molehills and flattening the shallow tunnels will result in the moles having to repair the harm done with more digging, therefore causing further damage.

Furthermore I prefer the client not to remove or rake out any mole dirt prior to my arrival, as these molehills are a huge assistance in my ascertaining what is actually going on below ground level. Assessing the spoils of soil provides clues that help me to assess what the mole is doing in relation to that location, and the impact the weather or other influences are placing upon it. Every molehill tells a story, and the different layers or seams of soil that make up the structure of that location are often revealed in the molehill as the mole works the different depths. A simple example of this would be sand in the mole spoils, because immediately you would have to consider at what level the mole would have to be working to expose a seam of sand. This may not be a natural seam, but the result of building works or landscaping, but from considering the contents or size of the molehills you can calculate at what depth the mole is working – so much information can be gleaned from examining what to some is just a pile of dirt.

May Bank Holidays seem to be a special time of molehill stamping, and it is important that people are educated that stamping on molehills will not make the mole go away. Leave them alone and wait: if the mole is only passing through, then there is a small chance that the molehills will stop; but if they do persist, then call your local mole catcher.

Without doubt, leaving molehills alone is possibly one of the most difficult things for anyone to do when they are confronted by a mole's work, but it will be even harder for gardeners to come to terms with when they are told by the mole catcher that he needs to see more molehills before he can help you. Strange as this request may seem, it can happen, and under a range of circumstances. Often in May when the male moles are returning from their final breeding forays, they will happen across a vacant mole territory that they may not necessarily, but could inhabit. However, they will often excavate the tunnels of the territory anyway, to locate food. This may result in a couple of molehills, but that will be all, as the mole will only take what it wants, and will then move on to a more suitable location. Hence at this time in the year the mole catcher will want to ensure that the mole is staying before making the visit.

Therefore if you call your mole catcher it may be that he asks you to wait if you have only a single molehill. For example, in drier times when the moles are working deeper runs, a single molehill can appear as the mole is moving soil from different depths to gain access to another location or another part of that locality. The single molehill will be quite large, as energy can be saved if all the waste can be deposited in one hill. The same could happen as the moles move through and clear out the tunnels that have collapsed because of man's work above ground. It is from these instances, where the moles create sudden eruptions of soil, that many catchers claim they have successfully got rid of the mole. However, it is important to consider the pressures of that location, and how this impacts on what the mole is doing, to realize that it may not stay. Therefore, you should also understand that when people are offered advice on how to be rid of a mole, even though at certain times and under certain circumstances such advice would be seen to work, in fact the real reason for this lack of mole activity is because the mole has moved on.

In a dry spring, a mole will possibly be coming up from a deeper level because of an obstruction, normally tree roots. This will be evident because there will only be a single molehill, and a total lack of tunnels ranging out from it – and in this instance customer relations will need to be at their best, because the mole catcher will need to see the mole create more damage before he can know where to set his trap and capture it. The customer must understand that the mole will probably throw up more molehills as it builds a tunnel from the central shaft of entry out into the lawn, but it is only when these appear that the mole catcher will know that he then has a tunnel in which to work his traps. The tunnel where he needs to locate his trap links the first molehill to appear, to the second molehill.

JUNE

June is often referred to as 'flaming June' because it is expected to be a hot and dry month – and with these conditions come mornings of heavy dew. This is because the warmer temperature causes the water from lakes and rivers, and if you are near the coast, from the sea, to evaporate, resulting in more moisture in the air. The cooler nights allow the moisture that is still present in the atmosphere to condense on the cooling ground, forming dew. In the higher day-time temperatures of high summer, or under extreme circumstances, this dew will evaporate back into the air; during June, however, the day-time temperature might not be quite hot enough for the moisture to evaporate, and so the grass from this morning dew turns to a lush green.

This can result in dry soils under a damp organic blanket: people have no reason to water their lawns because they look so green, so the moles will be feeding at a lower level, forced downwards as their food also burrows downwards into the damper soil. This means that the moles' tunnels that the mole catcher needs to locate will now be in soil that lies below the dry crust. The sight of molehills on the plush green lawn often causes many people to look for tunnels here, with the intention of catching the mole from this area; however, it is better to continue to locate traps in those tunnels that are used by the mole to travel to and fro between his feeding grounds and where he rests or sleeps. Even the new moles or the existing resident mole will still be using such tunnels, either creating new runs or clearing existing ones.

The existing tunnels could have been discovered by a mole from a new litter – maybe this is a territory once used by a previously removed mole – or by a returning male mole. Even this late in the year the male mole could have found itself under threat in a territory it had considered as a new home from a more aggressive mole, which for a number of reasons had returned. As male moles return from the spring breeding frenzy there will be much fluctuation in mole numbers until they all settle down. Inevitably some moles will locate in other moles' territories, and would stay if the territory were suitable, but a returning mole will result in an aggressive confrontation, which will end up with one having to leave, and this will cause a possible further wave of movement.

Under the demands of the environment the feeding tunnels will be found at a depth below the dry crust. The presence of new spoils of soil, dark in colour, peppered around a deep green lawn will cause many to set traps in these areas, but in doing so they run the risk of alerting the moles to their presence because they are putting their traps in the wrong place. The clue is in the colour of the soil fly-tipped on the surface: soil that is damp and dark in colour comes from a deeper level as compared to the dry light surface soil deposited previously. Many will rush to these new molehills and start prodding the ground in the hope of stumbling into a tunnel.

The Mole Catcher's Probe

The contact the mole catcher has with the mole's environment from above ground is with the probe, and it must become an extension of his hand. The texture of the soil and its moisture content can be felt as the simple metal bar passes slowly down into the ground. The information gained is processed by the mole catcher almost like the sense used by the mole to feel the same environment. Using a firm, positive push, the speed the probe travels downwards indicates the consistency and composition of each different soil of each different location. The moisture content can be determined as the ground prevents the extraction of the probe, holding it fast or sucking back as it is withdrawn.

The mole catcher subconsciously processes these simple experiences, and he will then know how that particular location will be influencing the mole's behaviour. The depth of the tunnel is immediately revealed, as the probe enters into the tunnel through the roof – therefore the length of the probe below ground determines the depth of the tunnel.

Locating mole tunnels is possibly the challenge that most people undertaking mole control, especially those new to the experience, will at first have difficulty in comprehending. Under abnormally dry soil conditions this will be even more difficult, and the mole catcher will need to concentrate as he pushes down to identify each change in the probe's movement as it passes through the dry harder soil, then the slightly moister soil, and then the 'give' that indicates the location of the tunnel – which is often mistaken for another deviation in the soil horizons.

This highlights my reason for teaching people, and I cannot stress enough that the correct runs to use are those leading into the feeding areas; remember the mole will not create new tunnels for this purpose. These tunnels will always be there, and at the same depth, whatever the effect the weather has on the soil. The moles will create these tunnels at depths that are not influenced by changes, which is why they offer the best opportunity for positioning a trap and catching the mole.

The size of a mole catcher's probe is a personal thing, but in truth size does matter. I have seen a varied selection of rods all proclaiming to be the best for the job – thick, thin, long and short – but which one is best? The answer is the one you get on best with – though remember that choosing the wrong probe can alert the mole to your presence and your intentions. I prefer just two sizes of thickness in the probes I use: the thinner is just 8mm in diameter, and thickest is 10mm. I use the 8mm probe for all normal soils, and because I have

used this size for many years I can also use it in wetter soils. Because I am accustomed to the feel of this diameter of probe from daily use, it is part of my life. I would recommend the 10mm diameter probe to those who have difficulty in locating tunnels, especially in wet soils. The slightly thicker diameter allows for a more positive definition of the probe's travel through the ground, and its entry into a tunnel is more obvious.

Some catchers use a probe with a large bullet-type head attached to it. These are approximately 22mm in diameter at the head and are sold under the guise of a mole dibber, but in fact they are supplied to the pest control industry for use with gas application equipment. The large bullet head is the same size as the plastic tube through which gas products are administered into any located mole tunnels. As well as having a larger diameter, this gas application probe is normally long and has a T-bar handle.

The longer the probe, the less control you will have over it, and its all-important feel. Now this obviously depends upon your height, but a probe needs to fit the person using it. You need to be comfortable; I personally prefer to be slightly bent over, so the ideal rule of thumb is that the probe handle should be at, or slightly above your knee height when vertical and in contact with the ground. A probe of this size and length is a guide, but with regular use you will soon adopt the probe that is right for you.

The handle must be kind to the touch, as you will have contact with it in all weathers. I use hardwood file handles, as timber is sympathetic to the touch. I stay well away from T-bar handles, especially metal, because the hand must grip the T-bar in such a way that the travel of the probe cannot be felt as accurately as when the probe is held like a poker, or a better description would be like an epée or foil sword as used in the art of fencing. Held in this way, you will have total control over the probe and therefore a more personal contact with what you are doing.

Getting up close and personal is something you have to do with the mole and its chosen environment, and it starts with your first contact, and that is the probe. Get this wrong, and it can be a downhill slide to other problems, and a failure to catch that mole. The probe requires a sure grip, and some say that a T-bar handle will not slip in wet conditions: this is quite correct, and the wet or mud could make wooden handles slippery so you lose your grip. However, a mole catcher will never rush his work: he will use a methodical approach, and all his tools must be fully prepared for the tasks in hand, and in wet conditions a simple wipe from a towel is all that is required.

The most important consideration when using a probe is that whichever diameter you choose or whatever type of handle it has, it must not cause any unnecessary damage to the tunnel. This is why I suggest using a probe with a diameter of just 8mm for normal soil, and one of 10mm for wetter soil, as anything thicker will have a considerable impact upon the mole. Certainly when the tunnel is discovered the thicker 22mm 'mole dibber' provides a feel that is more readily identifiable, as the larger rod will burst through the tunnel roof rather than breaching it in a controlled manner. However, the thicker rod will extensively damage the tunnel – though this is not that important if the entry hole is to be used for gas application equipment, since the intention is to flood the tunnel with gas, which will possibly fatally asphyxiate the mole.

However, when using traps, any extensive damage to the tunnel roof will alert the mole in many ways. A large hole punched in through the roof will allow changes in airflows, and may even allow the loss of that all-important positive pressure. Excess water from any rainfall could access these unwanted shafts and affect the humidity and moisture levels. The damaged roof will result in soil being pushed down into the tunnel, and the excess spoil under its feet will first alert the mole, and that all-important

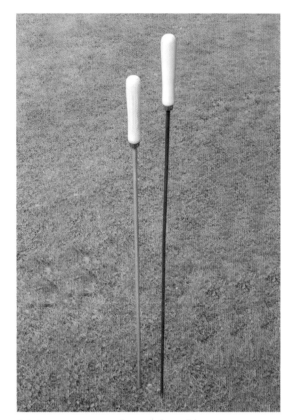

It is important not to damage the mole's environment, and probes can do just that.

tail will detect the damage to the tunnel roof. These warnings will result in the mole creating a different approach tunnel, or back filling and making alterations that will have a possibly disadvantageous effect on any trap placed in the tunnel.

Working with Wet and Dry Soils

June can always be relied upon to provide some levels of rainfall, so mole catching in the summer can involve a mixture of wet and dry soils, and sudden change from one to another. When setting a half-barrel trap it doesn't matter what the soil is like, providing you avoid simple mistakes. Some soils will be forgiving to the disturbance caused by the trapper, and to an extent will dissemble mistakes; other soils will show up these mistakes, and every part of the mole catcher's experience will be needed to ensure the mole is caught. It all depends upon the mole catcher having an intimate association with what he is doing.

Having located the mole tunnel you require, and with careful use of the probe to find the perfect position for the trap, things can still go drastically wrong in the bright sunlight of this summer month. You open up the ground and are immediately blinded by the darkness – meaning that, having opened up the ground in the bright sunlight, you look into the hole and can't see a thing! No definition of the tunnel's shape can be seen at all, it is like snow blindness. However, there is a simple solution, and that is to work in the shadow of your body.

In these conditions many placing a trap will make small mistakes because they cannot see the full features of the exposed run. These mistakes will range from failing to line up the traps correctly, to making changes to the tunnels – but such inaccuracies can be avoided with some consideration to the position of the sun. Out of tradition, the modern world I am sure will find more fashionable solutions to such a problem, with sunglasses, baseball caps and who knows, purpose-built portable mole-catching sunshades!

The Impact of Hot Weather

June can send the thermometer high into the twenties, and the moles low into the soil, very low. The problem now is that the soil bakes hard, and cracks appear in the surface. Unable to locate entry tunnels from any perimeter, molehills are sometimes the only visible evidence that a mole catcher has to work with – and remember that in extended dry conditions the mole's food source will be in the lower levels, and the mole will need to create a tunnel complex at those levels in order to find this food. The soil deposited will be from this depth, but the molehills may be of a normal size and not in

any great numbers to identify how deep this is. Under normal deep excavations, the deposited soil would obviously result in large molehills, as new digging will require a considerable amount of soil to be removed.

What the moles do under these dry conditions is create a tunnel complex at these low levels to obtain food, but to conserve energy they only remove the soil up into the higher tunnels – they may remove some soil right up to the surface, but it is only a proportion of it, and this will dissemble the fact that they are working in deeper tunnels. Many mole catchers will locate the tunnels at these normal depths because of the normal size molehills, and place traps – but on return they will find that these traps are full of soil from the mole working below and pushing spill soil along these runs. Always look at the situation closely, consider the impact of the weather on the mole's environment, and respond to that information accordingly.

Multiple Catches

In June many mole catchers find that they will often catch more than one mole in a garden. Called to remove a mole, they do so successfully, but are then called back again and remove another mole, bringing into question the claim that all moles are territorial and live singly. In fact this occurrence is not that strange if you consider what is going on in the mole's world at this particular time of the year. In the previous months, moles experienced changes that drove them to perpetuate the species, but with the breeding cycle completed, everything is returning to normal. However, this means that the young, now fully grown, are seeking a territory of their own, and a vital source of food. The males are trudging back to old haunts and territories, some rather late in the season because they have been evicted from a more desirable location by a more dominant late returning mole. With this sort of migration taking place during June, every vacant suitable location will be occupied and reoccupied as soon as it is available, and moles' lives will be altogether in some turmoil.

Considering these facts, it should be simple to realize how regular catches of two or even three moles might be removed from a garden that would normally support just a single mole. A female mole in the spring will be of interest to all the males in the area whether she is in season or not, and these rampant males would have entered – albeit carefully – into her range to test the temperature of the water, so to speak. The wrong signals or an aggressive reception would have moved them quickly on their way. Now recall that the female will have been preparing for her new litter, gathering more food and storing it in her worm larders, and could have increased her home range considerably in order to meet these demands and the possible limited sources of sustenance.

The cycle of life completed, this larger but then vacant home range plays an important role in the lives of the young moles. When fully grown at five to six weeks old, naturally they will have become inquisitive, and will be venturing out separately to make their own way in the world. Thus they will start their solitary life in the home range created by their mother. It will be a reasonably safe location, but the juvenile moles will be required to leave; they may not all go together, but may leave individually, as they are increasingly driven by their instinct to 'go it alone'.

Again, the mole catcher may make a multiple catch of moles from a single location because the young are moving off, either passing through an area, or creating molehills – evidence of their presence – because they are busy clearing out an old territory or creating new tunnels in another garden. Multiple numbers caught could be a complete litter from that spring taken by a mole catcher in a matter of days. This may seem harsh, but the life of a mole is not without risk, and new moles will bumble around in nature's

educational classroom, which to begin with comprises tunnels created by other moles. Ultimately they will learn to fend for themselves, but it will be a hard journey.

Of all the moles born, only one will normally survive to see the following spring, such is the harsh and competitive reality of their early life. Even in the confines of their mother's nursery tunnels, in the month of June the young moles will face the threat of death, if not from the mole catcher, from their own kind. Aggressive males returning to normality also seek a welcome meal from any feeding grounds, now with low testosterone levels to distract them; they will impose their strength and superiority upon these young, naive moles. It is a hard time, and many young moles will fall to predation from their own kind as well as other predators. From birth to this time of dispersal, the sibling rivalry amongst moles is intense, and from their first struggle to find a nipple to suckle, to their quest for self sufficiency and independence, for an immature mole the competition is constant.

I hope that mole catchers will now understand the reasons behind those return calls following their removal of a mole, or why they took two moles in a small area of land, and why that large old mole suddenly appeared in the midst of capturing young ones.

JULY

July can arrive almost unnoticed, just another hot day. But July in the world of mole catching has turned full circle, coming from the least demanding month for mole control to the busiest, and the warm summers are to blame. In the past, mole catchers could take a well earned rest during the summer months, whilst wheatfields turned to gold and laden hay carts toiled through the meadows; some may even have assisted in the harvest as they waited in anticipation for the calls to the same locations in the autumn, when the harvest was complete. Now, month seven is commercially booming, and the reason is the mole's exploitation of today's enthusiasm for gardens.

Gardens the Centre of Attraction

Hosepipe ban or not, that perfect lawn in neat stripes in a shade of emerald green that would grace any paint sample card is in more demand. Irrigation systems are turned on in the dead of night, and rolls of artificial mulch or the tree bark from half a forest are spread around the borders to maintain moisture in modern man's maintenance-free garden. In times of drought, when rain is not forecast, these oases of delight will be on every mole's mind. Moisture retention under the mulch provides easy soil to work, with easy access to food.

Vegetable plots are all carefully weeded and rows of root crops sit in a bed of worms, encouraged by the trend to be organic and the application of high nutrient manure. Runner beans reach to the sky as gallons of water are poured daily around their base. It has to be said that gardeners tend to over water – how much to water depends on a wide range of things, from soil type, wind, temperature, root depth and plant spacing. Whatever you have planted, flowerbeds and vegetable plots need water: cut back or over supply on this element, and the quality of the harvest will be affected.

This is good advice to pass on when the disgruntled gardener calls because the inevitable mole has arrived – as it will in a prolonged dry spell. Comfortable under the dark weed-suppressing matting or the bark beds of the borders, a mole may lurk undetected for some time. Others may brazenly announce their arrival with a row of molehills along the edge of the lawn where the borders of bedding plants occasionally conceal this evidence. It is important that the mole catcher inspects these areas as they often provide the best opportunity to remove the offending mole. Like the areas below natural drip, where grass meets borders again often holds the ideal level of moisture to allow a good tunnel to be constructed. Sometimes these tunnels are in the dip between the grass and the border, or they may be found just in from the border or under the edge of the lawn.

Wherever the moles decide to dig it will be in areas of moisture where they can find food – under the lawn, in the border, where there is dew, or sprinkler water – but the tunnels will be shallow. If in the mulch, again they will be quite shallow, and a gentle scrape to one side with a trowel will reveal them, rather than an aggressive dig. So during this month gardens are a centre of attention for moles – and as well as the enticement of any continual watering, there are the fun and frolics to be had with the provision of outdoor toys, which although designed for the enjoyment of children both young and old, are also keenly supported by moles in the summer months.

The mole has taken full advantage of the benefits arising from the presence of the trampoline.

Garden trampolines are particularly attractive, and the popular trend for having a paddling pool large enough to float a boat. Both are guilty of encouraging moles to the garden: jumping up and down on a trampoline will send out a constant stream of vibrations that alerts and attracts worms, together with the effects of any rainfall dripping from the trampoline structure, providing a ring of delight for the moles, who will celebrate this fact with their own personal ring of molehills around the circumference of the trampoline.

Splashes and spills from the paddling pool are another supply of that all-important moisture for the mole's source of food, as grass is turned to mud in a welter of splashes, slips and slides. The plastic pool itself is also an ideal feeding ground, because once filled with water it is normally left in position, whether used or not, for the duration of the summer, and only occasionally topped up and cleaned. Underneath, the plastic construction will have warmed the ground and retained the moisture, and the mole will have exploited these conditions, evidence of which is often not discovered until the arduous task of dismantling or dragging the pool to another part of the garden is undertaken. Then the damage from tunnels of various depths on the site where the pool was located becomes only too apparent. Under the noise and fun of the garden playthings, the moles have been busy taking full advantage of the means to survive the periods of drought.

Therefore, there is a lot for the mole catcher to consider in what many see as the quiet month of July. This includes placing traps in tunnels not normally used, but which are the only option for success. It is another month of learning and opportunity for the mole catcher, and definitely one not to be missed with excuses of having other commitments.

Forms of Mole Control

Honesty and respect are the two main factors when providing a mole-catching service: honesty to the client and respect for the mole, and those who offer forms of mole control other than the use of traps must look closely at the service they provide. Furthermore, when talking to customers it is often revealed that the mole catcher has been called in as a last resort. Prior to his arrival, the list of products purchased by the aggrieved customer, many of which are currently illegal, always seems to be longer than before. In the month of July many attempts fail to remove the resident mole, on the part of both amateurs and professionals, and this can be attributed to a combination of things. Moles make the rules in any confrontation, and it is because catchers fail to make the effort to understand mole behaviour that they are so often unsuccessful.

In July gardens are looking at their best, so even the slightest damage from an intruding mole is catastrophic. The problem for the landowner is even greater in times of drought or greatly reduced rainfall because moles often tolerate a degree of time-share in their territory. Every mole will be under the same pressure of needing to source food, and dry times mean hard times.

The decision as to which method to use to remove the mole now depends on many circumstances. During this month of the year, many pest controllers are more fiscally motivated by the competition from wasp control – compare the simplicity and speed with which a wasp nest can be removed, and the time and trouble it takes to remove a mole, and it is obvious why prospective clients are asked to wait until later in the year.

Although some pest controllers will offer a trapping service, several larger companies prefer gas as their form of control for moles. The gas applied is aluminium phosphide, and it is the most toxic substance currently used in the pest control industry for vertebrate control. Its use close to watercourses and buildings is prohibited. Understandably it is compulsory for an operator to hold a certificate of competence for use, which requires that two qualified operators are present and a full risk assessment is made prior to and following the application. Because of these strict health and safety regulations, and the limited permitted use of the substance, and the high cost, on a local level this service cannot compete with the traditional mole catcher.

The moles must also contend with amateur mole catchers, who arm themselves with what they are capable of obtaining and putting to some level of use. Their personal attitude towards the mole is another consideration, because in spite of the annoyance, damage and anxiety it causes, some still refuse to harm the mole in any way. The thought of despatching the offender is considered barbaric and cruel, but once attempts to scare away the mole with a variety of devices have been tried and have failed, they seek the alternative solution, which is to physically take it away.

The 'Humane Live Catch Trap'

At one time, one option was the 'humane live catch trap': thankfully now scarce, these plastic tubes of death were sold to those not wishing to harm the mole, and were once a popular choice. Mercifully, the catch rate with these traps in the hands of an amateur was low, but any mole that happened to stumble into one would have been subject to a high degree of suffering – and at this time in the year it would most likely be naive young moles.

Constructed from black plastic, the 10in (25cm) long pipe, just 2in (50mm) in diameter, would allow entry from either end via a simple one-way door. Any mole would be sheathed in this tube with no escape until the operator saw fit to return. Despite requirements to check these live traps at least twice a day, in fact they came with no instructions to that effect. Any mole unfortunate enough to be captured in one of these live traps is immediately subjected to stress, dehydration and starvation.

The live trap is possibly the most inhumane form of mole control.

The next question is, having captured a mole, what will the mole-friendly hunter do with it next? He will say he is giving it its freedom, but in reality he will be causing the mole further unnecessary suffering. The stressed, starving, thirsty mole will be driven to another location and released into another person's land. With no knowledge as to the actual carrying capacity of this chosen location, or how much food, if any, is available for the mole to survive on, it is confidently tipped from a bucket and left to fend for itself.

The mole has only approximately 3g of body fat, which it relies on to keep its vital organs and joints warm and lubricated. The calorific burn or energy required by a mole to dig is immense, and without any stored energy it cannot afford to dig for no reason – moles only dig if there is a reward, and that reward is food. Therefore to release a mole into a strange location is subjecting it to a high level of suffering, and if the area does not contain sufficient food, then that mole will probably die. So why would anyone wish to be this cruel to a mole?

I personally requested that these traps be removed from sale; Procter Brothers used to produce one design, and following consideration, fortunately they refrained from further supply. In addition, it is now displayed on HM government advice web pages that any mole captured alive must be humanely despatched.

The Month of Time-Share

Whether the gardener or landowner has live or kill traps at their disposal, they will now declare, in the light of summer, another war on the mole – or rather, in July we should say moles, because for moles, this is the month of time-share. Unlike the professional mole catcher, the overall picture created by the prevailing circumstances often confuses the amateur into believing other myths. At the very first sign of a new molehill they will arm themselves with new mole traps, which they carefully set into the ground.

Now many people, including those who are not proficient at catching moles, are capable of successfully capturing a mole at this time of year, because very often the moles they are encountering are immature and inexperienced. Flushed with success, and quick to boast about their aptitude for catching moles, they are very soon frustrated by the appearance of another molehill. In truth, removing one mole may have no effect on the situation if the moles are adopting a time-share of the area. It may be just one day, or perhaps a few days after removing the mole from what could be a small area for it to live in, that the new molehill – new evidence to another mole – appears.

Once again, this instantly questions the belief that the mole is a solitary animal; I personally would state that like us, moles will, and do, tolerate some level of permitted access. We are happy to share the roads with others providing they do not park in our space, or outside our house. It is the same for the moles, because often they will share a main tunnel to gain access to their feeding ground, their array of senses enabling them to avoid conflict as they go about their daily lives.

What is happening now is that the moles, so dependent upon finding vital sources of food to survive this possibly parched month, will exploit any opportunity. So as well as the moles that are moving around in the hunt for a possible perfect haven, there are others living maybe just a short distance away from the idyllic font of food that is the tended garden. Time-share by moles is when one or a number of moles are attracted to an area as a result of the conditions prevailing in that location – it can happen at other times in a year, but in the months of high summer when rainfall is low, moles are attracted to a garden like a moth to a light in the dark. Sprinklers, dribble pipes, mulch and garden toys may be the immediate explanation for this invasion – and what other indefinable reason could there be? Often just a single glance over the garden fence, hedge or wall is enough to reveal why the neighbourhood moles are visiting: it is tantamount to the dig-in diner.

The moles, desperate for food, venture into these areas whenever the occasion permits, communication and scent confirming the presence or not of another mole. The tunnels explored and food unearthed, they then return to their respective territories, leaving behind devastation on lawns, under runner beans and along raised beds. Return, that is, if they have a sanctuary to return to – if they don't and they choose to stay, then they run the gauntlet of capture, and in that event verify the fact that moles can share. Knowing that the mole has been removed, the landowner is very upset when the next day there is further evidence of the presence of moles.

Whether a mole that is caught is a temporary resident or a visitor exploiting the situation under the circumstances, the fact remains that in this month, multiple catches of moles can be made in a very short period of time, in a small area, and most people fail to fully understand why this should be, as it appears to contradict the accepted view of how a mole lives.

Circumstances Causing Occasional Damage

Occasional damage by moles is nothing new, and there are times when mole catchers are called, to discover the mole has already left of its own accord, spring breeding being an obvious situation. The hotter months are frequently subjected to storms and periods of sudden heavy rain. Thunder and lightning has no adverse effect on moles, but a deluge of rain on soil that absorbs the water quickly will cause the worms to rush to the surface. The moles will respond, and will quickly produce areas of damage by running spooked, creating shallow tunnels to obtain a needed meal at this time of potential hunger.

To the current year's younger moles, now venturing further afield, these conditions are a lifeline, but there are also dangers. The urgency to feed and the need to work close to the surface is a situation exploited by one of the mole's other predators: the owl. These silent hunters will pull many moles from the loose soil or mulch, and moles are a welcome source of food for young owls in need of food at this important month in the year. The increase in water that falls on hard ground will run off into land drains and ditches, creating higher water levels. The damper areas around these ditches, which during the dry times have provided a runway for the moles to tunnel and travel and find food, can change overnight as the water rises and forces the moles to move their runs to bordering fields and gardens.

Following heavy summer rains the moles will therefore be obliged to travel away from the formerly moist areas as they become uninhabitable from floodwater, and will move upwards, away from the lower ground. Water always finds its own level, and therefore will run down towards the lower levels of these ditches, and in response the moles, along with their food sources, will seek higher, less saturated and more suitable soil. The moles will then assess the situation again, and create new feeding areas. When the water level falls, then food and mole will once again return as before.

It is therefore important to consider the soil, the impact of the weather, and the different conditions in different locations in relation to how they will influence the mole, your clients, and yourself in this busiest time of the summer.

The mole has run spooked following heavy rain, seizing the opportunity of an abundant food supply.

AUGUST

The mole is without doubt a private individual that lives an isolated life – it may well time-share in an area to survive, or commute along adjoining tunnels, but generally it exists alone. Professional mole catchers will speak of multi catches in tunnels they are working without any excitement, as they are aware of the pressures of life that the mole endures, and know why such a thing occurs. Other, less knowledgeable catchers are surprised at catching more than one mole in one location, and consider it most unusual.

However, early August is when a litter will finally disperse, if it hasn't already. Those moles that have survived the first weeks of life by this time will have endeavoured to extend their range; now they face the arduous task of reaching maturity for the following spring's breeding season, when the whole cycle will begin once more. They will have discovered the linking tunnels made by other moles, previously dug and used by males to find females, by females to find food, and by all moles to travel and survive in. These linking tunnels will be busy, as these young moles set out to explore a brand new world. At first moles will be naive in life and will make many mistakes, which could be costly, but those that feel the first touch of frost should have established enough knowledge to join the ranks of all the others that continue to manipulate man's dominance of the land.

By August, these young moles will have squabbled with each other, sought to find food, slept in a small nest created by their mother, ventured around the tunnels with siblings within the safety of their mother's range, possibly dodged the threats of predation, and felt the changes of climate. These first experiences will provide the foundation to what lies ahead in their unique and unusual lives. Every mole requires its own space, and the young moles achieve this by venturing out to find an unoccupied area that offers suitable shelter and food; the size of this range will entirely depend upon what the locality can offer. This is evident to us in the amount of visual damage seen to lawns, fields and paddocks, or any area considered as rightfully ours.

It is important to understand what a young mole – or any mole, for that matter – is experiencing when it makes a claim to an area. The world of the mole has its hazards, and a vacant territory requires the incoming mole to investigate very carefully the system of tunnels. What fate befell the former mole, and how, will be of no interest to the prospective new mole occupier: its only concern is that the complex can directly, or with some alterations, provide for its needs. The mole must implement the full range of its senses in order to assess the capacity of the territory to do this.

If the newfound habitat is suitable, then its occupancy will need to be both announced and enforced through noise communication and scent passed in its urine. Moles need to advertise their presence to other moles to avoid confrontation, and this was confirmed in tests that demonstrated that moles stay away from the odours of other moles. So mole catchers who fondly consider that the smell of a recently caught mole in a trap will encourage another mole into it – think again! The mole's scent comes from two glands known as the preputial glands located beneath the skin in the urinary tract. Urine passed from the bladder is impregnated with a secretion of elements that provides the odour of identification.

This mixture of urine and gland emission is deposited at the junctions of tunnels, which is the best possible place for it to be positioned to inform other moles that the range is occupied. Evidence of this secreted preputial fluid is often detectable in the odour and light staining of the fur under the body of a mole, caused by this brushing of scent as it travels along the runs and tunnels. Worms are between 75 and 90 per cent water, so the urinary system in the mole will be constantly at work, and with this personal identification on tap there can be little doubt that a mole is in residence. If at any time this scent fades due to natural or unnatural occurrences, then the territory might soon be deemed vacant, and suitable for occupation by another.

THE MOLE'S FOOD SOURCES

Without an adequate food source the mole will not survive, and to achieve access to this, the new tunnel complex will need some work. Humans are very much the same when it comes to habitat. How many can say they built their own home? We will move into and occupy a new or vacant property, and normally will immediately decorate it, and probably put in a new bathroom to impart our own touch on the new home. In the same way the mole in a new territory will need to familiarize itself with the plan of the tunnels, their depths, and what food there is on offer, and of course it will clear out and create new tunnels.

People very often fail to understand the importance of worms, and how they determine why the mole is behaving or working in such a way. Moreover many mole catchers fail to appreciate the information provided by worms, and are therefore slow to catch their mole, because they have failed to consider the impact of this food on the target mole. The world of the worm is the same as that of the mole: sometimes dark, damp and dismal, at other times demanding, dry and desolate.

Other Food Sources

Of course, it may not be the humble worm that a mole is feeding on when people are faced with damage caused by moles. Again, shallow runs may be seen in this summer month following heavy storm rain, and the mole may be making such runs so it can feed on other bugs and grubs that are available – and leatherjackets are a source not to be missed. These are the larvae of the crane fly, which many have come to know as the 'daddy long legs'.

The Crane Fly and Leatherjackets

In the south the crane fly emerges from its pupal state normally during late July and through August, but as with all insects, its development may be dictated by the conditions prevailing: these greyish leathery pupae are sensitive to the sun and must not dry out if they are to survive. Periods of dry weather will place pressure upon them, so any wet spells are welcome, when they will move up to the surface. The mole will exploit this, and will create shallow tunnels almost in a frenzy to enable it to fill its stomach on this available food source. The leatherjackets generally stay underground during the day and move up during the night, so the mole's activity may also occur in times of average weather and rainfall, evidenced in an overnight skirmish of tunnels that leave the lawn looking like a badly fitted carpet, or in the words of the Mole Show – 'ripples in a sea of green'.

The adult crane fly will lay its eggs in the ground: when they hatch, the new larvae will start to feed on grass roots. Those people who experience damage from moles feeding on leatherjackets may well have the same problem the following year if they fail to address the presence of these insects. Yellow patches in the lawn indicate the presence of leatherjackets, as the grass is weak and may be easily pulled from the soil by hand. If you suspect the presence of leatherjackets, just water the grass and cover the area with a plastic sheet; next morning pull back the sheet and the culprits will be revealed.

Moles may also be found hunting the borders, as leatherjackets eat the roots of plants, damage that many people often blame on the mole. However, the moles are in fact seeking the leatherjackets lurking there, though because of their more obvious presence, as evidenced by the ripples of soil, the mistaken assumption is that it is the mole eating the plant roots. The mole will be alerted to the leatherjackets emerging and moving upwards in wet weather by the vibrations they cause as they move rapidly through the soil.

The Humble Worm

The mole's response to any available food must be considered by the mole catcher, but the humble worm is its prime source of food: abundant, readily available and much preferred. Therefore the better you understand the biology and ecology of the worm, the more likely you will be able to offer a better service of control. If you have an immediate knowledge of how the worm influences mole behaviour you can relate what you know to what the location reveals, and often you will find new tunnels to explore, leading to better results, more quickly. Worms demand a huge amount of study to fully understand how important they are in this unique ecosystem, but as a mole catcher, to be able to identify the influence that worms have on the mole is a clear advantage, because the humble earthworm without doubt often explains the presence of the mole.

Earthworms fall into three categories according to the levels they inhabit in the horizons or layers that make up the structure of the earth's surface: epigeic, endogeic and anecic earthworms. Epigeic earthworms are litter dwellers that live on the surface of the soil in leaf litter/grass, in the organic layer. These species tend not to make burrows, but live in and feed on the leaf litter, so the mole can be found feeding in shallow runs if this is where food is available. The practice of some gardeners to cover areas of their garden in leaf mulch is a situation the mole catcher should consider.

Endogeic earthworms are shallow dwellers that live in and feed on the soil. They create multifarious burrows to enable them to move around and to feed. Some can burrow deep into the soil, though not so far down as the deep dwellers, which are the anecic earthworms: these make permanent, deep vertical burrows in the soil. They feed on the organic matter found on the surface, such as leaves, which they drag into their burrows. Their presence is indicated by casts left on the surface. They also make piles of casts, known as middens, around the entrance to their burrows.

The anecic earthworm is the largest species of earthworm in the United Kingdom, so is a good source of food for a mole. Moles will dig to any depth as dictated by their needs, and these anecic worms may be as far down as 1.8m; however, it is not necessary for the mole to seek them at this depth, because a shallow tunnel complex amongst the middens will enable it to intercept these worms during their after-dark excursion to the surface. These large worms will keep a part of their body in their access shaft, so it is easy for the mole to intercept them.

Earthworms are thin-skinned invertebrates with little protection against the changes in temperature and moisture content, and physical chemical characteristics, that occur in soils. Water loss is a major threat to their survival, and in times when the soil is dry they must move and find an area of higher moisture – if they do not, some earthworms, such as *Lubricous terrestris*, can lose almost 70 per cent of their total body water content. This is because they have no way of maintaining a constant level of internal water content themselves, so their internal water content is completely reliant on the water content of the soil. In dry times various species of earthworm will migrate to deeper or to adjacent areas where the soil has a higher moisture content.

Some species can survive in a dry soil, but they will go into a state known as 'diapause', when their metabolism slows down, suspending their bodily development and growth. Species that diapause will not move, and therefore will not always be detected by moles. In the same way worms can survive in saturated and flooded soils, only needing to move when the oxygen levels fall – those who use worms as fish bait will know that worms can survive for a remarkably long time when submerged in water, because they absorb the oxygen from the water.

Another major factor affecting worms, and therefore moles, is the temperature of the soil, as it influences the worms' whole rate of metabolism and growth, and its capacity for respiration and reproduction. Temperature and moisture are normally related, and high surface temperatures and dry soils are more limiting to earthworms than low temperatures and waterlogged soils. Therefore in this summer month of August, the worms' response to water in any form, or the lack of it, will be relevant to the mole catcher.

The capacity of this combination of the mole and its food to work the soil may be considered by some to be of benefit to the land, as both carry out acceptable and even advantageous tasks, the worms in providing nutrients and aeration, and the mole in controlling many insects that are harmful to the garden.

It is my hope that in fully understanding this relationship between mole and worm, the mole catcher will acquire a better knowledge of the environment they both share.

Setting a Trap in Shallow Runs

When a mole creates a shallow complex of tunnels, whether in search of leatherjackets or worms, or because of the impact of the weather, it is important that the mole catcher tackles the mole at this level. Simple mistakes are often made when setting a trap in shallow runs, at any time of the year. I always prefer to use the half-barrel trap, as it immediately replaces the tunnel roof that you will have to remove when positioning the trap in the run.

How deep is a shallow tunnel in relation to other tunnel depths? This is a question I am often asked, and I have a simple rule of thumb: if the tunnel roof located with the probe is less than the overall length of a half-barrel trap below the surface, it is shallow. Therefore, less than 6in (150mm) down rates as shallow, between 6 and 12in (150 and 300mm), or two lengths of a half-barrel trap, is normal depth,

and anything deeper than this is deep. The use of a half-barrel trap as a form of guide for an aide memoire is ideal, as it will always be close to hand. This simplifies the decision as to how shallow is shallow with regard to mole tunnels.

Whether the mole is alerted to the presence of the trap at any depth relies on the mole catcher having the correct focus on the situation, and obviously every occasion will be different. The shallow run may be under a grassed area, or in a mulch in the form of bark or black matting, or just in loose soil – whichever it is, the covering must reflect the ability to mimic the same influences, whilst imparting little or no change. The shallow run found in loose soil at a depth of just 1 to 2in (30 to 50mm) from the surface to the roof of the tunnel may be covered with loose soil, but the strength in the springs of a good quality half-barrel trap will be sufficient to push up through this loose soil and still strike a fatal blow to the mole.

It is important to consider how much loose soil should be used to cover the trap under these conditions, because a tunnel at this depth in light loose soil will allow slight moisture to pass down into the tunnels – but even more important is that sunlight may also penetrate into the tunnel, and to block out either of these

The trap has operated unimpeded as it was only lightly covered with loose soil, and not the gravel as can be seen in the photo. The soil is lighter than the gravel but allowed the same influences.

elements will alert the mole. I discovered that if a mole is travelling in a shallow tunnel and you place an object or a board over the tunnel blocking the light, the mole will tunnel down slightly deeper and under the darker area. Obviously, as far as the mole is concerned, the tunnel has changed, so it reacts accordingly and tunnels out a path it knows is safe. Remember, if natural light can enter into the tunnel, then the mole expects to see it, and you should always try to leave your trap site as the mole expects to find it.

With a tunnel at the same depth but in a grassed area, many trap users will often just sprinkle a light covering of loose soil over the set and positioned trap – but this often results in the mole filling the trap with soil. This is because a sprinkling of soil is not sufficient to mimic the tunnel, as the more solid consistency of turf would block out sunlight, reduce the effect of moisture seeping down into the lower layer, and might also influence the air pressure. The mole would be alerted by such changes, since ultra-violet light in natural sunlight will possibly be filtering into the trap site, whereas before it did not, and there might be moisture, where before there was none.

The trap needs to be covered appropriately to prevent these changes, but also – and more importantly – in a manner to allow the trap to operate effectively. Turf that is 2in (50mm) thick if placed over the trap will reduce the velocity of the trap's operation, as it will have to lift the turf as well as strike the mole. Therefore the trap covering must shut out the elements but still allow the full, unhindered operation of the trap.

To do this a small igloo must be fashioned from turf, in such a way that there is enough clearance over the length of the trap site so the trap action is not impeded. To achieve this, build a wall of turf around the trap site, and then bend the tops of the walls inwards until they meet, forming an igloo over the trap with enough room for the trap springs to be able to

operate to full effect. Then sprinkle loose soil over the top of the igloo to completely cover the turf covering of soil, to ensure that any external elements are blocked out of the tunnel below.

When shallow runs are just under loose soil or mulch, the best way to expose the site for the trap position is to scrape aside the soil or covering using a trowel, in the same way an archaeologist would expose items in the soil. This is the best method, as you will not damage the tunnel too much. As you scrape away the soil, the tunnel will slowly reveal itself in the form of an oval shape.

Be careful not to expose too long a stretch of the tunnel: it is better to scrape away just a short hole and simply push the trap into the oval shape you have. A small amount of loose soil will possibly fall into the trap site, but don't worry, because in a shallow tunnel and under these conditions, the mole will expect some soil movement and loose soil to have entered the tunnel. Covering the trap needs to be with the same media, such as bark chippings or mulch, and again it must be replaced to the same thickness, as long as the trap can still operate to its full capacity.

Never cover a trap so that its effective operation is impeded: it cannot be emphasized enough how important it is to impart a humane strike on a target mole.

Remember that shallow runs may be dramatically affected by circumstances out of the mole catcher's direct control, such as sudden changes in the weather, third party intervention in the form of items placed over them, or even an impulsive episode of mole tunnel stamping. People do have this strange fascination of walking over and treading down shallow tunnels, like the compulsive popping of bubblewrap.

I would like to reiterate why traps positioned in shallow runs are often found full of soil. First of all, many catchers fail to cover the traps they have placed in shallow tunnels correctly, and often the same mistakes are made – as is the case with traps placed in any depth of tunnel, and even when other traps are used. The most important thing to consider is the air pressure created by the mole in the tunnel: as already explained, as the mole moves along the confines of the tunnel it will produce varying levels of pressure, both positive and negative, and it will monitor those pressures with the amazing organs and abilities that it has at its disposal. So the mole catcher should consider this pressure and the movement of airflows when covering a trap site, because a loss of positive pressure when the mole does not expect it will result in a soil-filled trap.

The same thing will happen if fresh air is allowed to enter into the trap site when the mole is not expecting it. Any source of fresh air would indicate to the mole that an entry had been made into the tunnel, and it would interpret this as possibly the intrusion of a predator, and shut off the source. Again, a mole would have no difficulty in sensing a fresh airflow in a tunnel.

The mole catcher must decide at what depth he will position his trap, and how best to cover it, without changing that environment. He should consider this carefully, as even some shallow runs will be deep enough to obscure the light, and a sprinkling of light soil might not be enough. A small, or even a larger igloo of turf and a covering of soil may still be required to convince the mole that no change has been made – for example, bark or mulch may be sufficiently thick to present a picture to the mole that the mole catcher may not immediately consider.

SEPTEMBER

The dry conditions of summer can continue into and throughout the whole of September, provoking shouts of warning from many environmentalists about global warming. However, September can also be a month when whole counties may be submerged under floodwater.

But as soon as the water levels drop there will be evidence of moles back in residence, which just confirms the resilience of this amazing creature. Their ability to adapt and survive in the face of whatever adversary they may be forced to confront is clearly displayed as once again the molehills rise up as the water drops.

I have caught moles on islands in the middle of the River Thames, and many will wonder just how they managed to take up residence there – but they are like little paddleboats, with tremendous swimming capabilities because of their huge shoulder muscle grouping, and front feet like two oars. Undoubtedly they arrived on these islands by accident, as I would be surprised if they had set off with the intention of risking their lives against predator fish and birds in order to establish a home range amongst the wealthy humans who reside there. These moles possibly fell into the water, and in a bid to remain afloat, paddled with and against the flows and currents until they once again touched land.

Setting Traps in Deep Runs

The main problem encountered by the mole catcher in times of prolonged dry weather in the summer months is the depth at which the moles are found. Catching moles at depth is not a problem if the correct trap is used, and once again the half-barrel trap is supreme, as it causes no more disturbance to a deep tunnel than to a shallow one. The problem is often locating the tunnel where the trap would be best placed. However, the mole catcher often overlooks the fact that the mole will be using its original tunnels to access its feeding grounds, and that these tunnels will be at the same depth as they were in normal everyday conditions. Also the feeding grounds may still be in the same area as they were previously, only the mole has moved down deeper in response to the extenuating circumstances.

If this is the case you should still locate and

use the primary tunnel, but if you do have to set traps at depth, the probe must be pushed down slowly and carefully, and in 6in stages. To explain, push down where you consider the mole's tunnel to be for approximately 6in (150mm). Withdraw the probe slightly, and then push down a further 6in; then withdraw it again slightly, and repeat the process. By withdrawing the probe slightly and probing down again, a difference in the sensation of the travel can be felt. Probing in short sections will smooth a path more sensitively through the soil, so the required tunnel can be detected. Probing at depth is more time consuming, but under some circumstances it is necessary for success.

The visible signs of a mole digging at depth can be clearly seen in the amount of deposited soil that it makes. When confronted by a series of molehills, amateur mole catchers will probably recall the childhood game of joining up the dots, and imagine a tunnel running directly between the molehills, probably in a straight line. However, when a mole is working at depth, the spoil will be greater, obviously resulting in large molehills.

The distance between the molehills and the size of the mounds is the clue. Imagine the possible length of the tunnel between the molehills in relation to the amount of soil deposited on the surface. Where did all that soil come from? The answer is from digging at depth. A group of mole mounds in a small area is another vital clue, and this may not be just because of the weather. If a mole is faced with an obstruction it must tackle in the ground, it may need to tunnel under or around it, which will result in the appearance of larger spoils, as more soil must be worked to solve the problem.

Opening a Shaft to Access the Tunnel

Having located a tunnel at depth, and having decided that it is the only appropriate position for trap placement, the next problem is to open a shaft to access the tunnel. When setting any mole trap it is essential that it is a tight fit in the

hole made by the trapper. Some make the elementary mistake of cutting a hole larger than is required, sometimes as much as 6in (150mm) square.

The importance of the trap fitting tightly cannot be stressed enough, especially when working in the complexity of this restricted realm: the least movement of the trap may alert the mole to its presence, or may compromise its capacity to strike correctly. Any trap must be a tight fit in the tunnel, and this can only be achieved with a close, 'hands on' approach. In these deeper runs, such an intimate approach is even more necessary, because if you make even a small mistake the mole will win the contest every time.

If not done with some care, digging down to expose the trap site can result in the shaft being too wide or too long. Again, in the same way as the probe work used to discover the tunnel, it is better if digging down with the probe is done in small sections. The depth of any tunnel can be gauged on the probe: having entered the tunnel roof, pinch the probe between two fingers at the surface level and remove it: the depth of the tunnel is tantamount to the distance the fingers are from the tip of the probe. With regard to tunnels at a greater depth, this information is helpful when soil must be removed in sections.

Once you know the depth of the tunnel you can calculate the best way to dig out the shaft so as to place the trap. You may consider the depth can be achieved by making small cuts and removing the soil, but it is important to remember that as the shaft enters the tunnel it must be no larger than the size of the trap. Cut a shaft as small as is practical for the hand to reach down, then feel the directional travel of the two entry points with the fingers; using small cuts the tunnel may then be opened up until the site is just large enough to accommodate the half-barrel trap comfortably.

From the mole catcher's point of view, what is considered to be a deep tunnel has to be measured in terms of how practical it is to access it, but as gravediggers often find mole tunnels, we must not underestimate the efforts of the mole itself. Having removed moles from many cemeteries I can assure you that the mole catcher would have no cause to be digging to the depths of gravediggers, and would not wish to be seen head and shoulders down in hallowed ground. We could, however, be required to place traps in tunnels deeper than the travel of a plough-share or than would be damaged by the weight of a tractor. Tunnel depths of 2ft (600mm) or over are quite accessible, though to ensure the trap is positioned in the best place it is good practice to cut a slightly larger shaft down to a point above the actual tunnel. Stop approximately 6in (150mm) above the tunnel, and then enter the run with the smaller shaft that will fit the trap.

The trap set at such a depth must be covered appropriately, so remember to pay attention to such details.

Having got this far in the book the reader could be forgiven for asking when I will actually describe how to place a trap in the ground, and how it should be presented and covered, and I will be explaining this in due course, along with the mistakes that so many catchers make. However, before I do, I want you, as the reader, to understand fully the target quarry, and what those old mole catchers before us experienced, because it is their enthusiasm, dedication and skill that is the foundation of the mole catcher's occupation.

Setting a Trap under a Molehill

One example of damage caused by a mole working at depth can often be seen on the fairways of a golf course. The machinery used on golf courses is not always heavy enough to cause the mole's tunnels to collapse and so force it downwards. The push along or small ride-on mowers keep the tees and greens tidy, but fairways are always mown by gang mowers, which constantly trundle up and down to maintain the grass at a suitable length – and if a mole crosses a fairway there will soon be a call for the mole catcher to come and remove it. The molehills are often found in a straight line as the mole leaves the longer, rough grass and ventures across to the other side, a journey that provides some extra hazards for the golfers to negotiate.

I use the golf course as an example, but in dry conditions this activity may appear anywhere. Setting a mole trap directly under a molehill is generally a practice that is laughed at, and under normal circumstances is a sure way of the trap being kicked out by the mole and landing on top of it, like the conquering flag of an intrepid climber. However, under these particular circumstances, setting the trap under a molehill is the option to use, and the secret is to ensure the trap is located under a molehill in the middle of the row. Because of the fairway traffic, the soil will be hard and compacted, and the mole will take the easiest route to the surface by making a vertical shaft. This is therefore also the easiest way down to the offending mole's path.

Scrape aside the chosen molehill, and slowly and carefully dig down the shaft that the mole has made. The shaft will not be directly vertical, it will follow a path, and this path must be meticulously traced until the tunnel is located. It is important to ensure that the path you follow is precise, and that the shaft when it enters the mole tunnel does not damage the run in any way. The half-barrel trap is then set so that its centre aligns with the centre of the shaft. This positioning is critical, and requires careful cutting and accurate fitting of the trap to ensure it is just right.

The reason for choosing a molehill in the middle of a row is that the horizontal tunnel already created by the mole is not likely to suffer subsidence due to the compaction of the soil above. Thus no further work from the mole will be needed, thus minimizing the chances of the mole bulldozing soil along it and possibly springing the placed trap. The mole will travel along this tunnel and will enter the trap unhindered, from which it can be removed.

This is possibly the only occasion that a mole trap could be placed under a molehill, despite what the armchair experts say. Setting traps at depth is a task that many catchers shy away from, in the hope that the mole will move into another area, either of its own volition or because the impact of the weather changes, but there should be only a few occasions when the mole catcher would need to work deep. Being unable to locate a tunnel that links the resting area to the feeding grounds, especially one at depth, is a disadvantage, so learning to locate it with the probe is time well spent.

Always look carefully at the location and ascertain how the whole area may be influencing the mole. And always remember that even in times of drought or prolonged heavy frost, the mole will still use the readymade tunnels – it will have made these before any changes in the weather, and will still be using them as the passageway to move around, and to journey to any areas of existing or new food sources.

Getting Close to the Action

I have referred to getting up close and personal with the moles earlier, and there are many reasons for this – the main one being success. The closer to the action you are, the better you will understand what you are doing, and this will help you avoid mistakes. Some think that this is unnecessary, and that everything can be carried out almost at arm's length. This is evident in the use of long-handled T-bar probes, converted lawn edging tools, or even purpose-made spades, all used at a distance from the actual trap location – but then you have to kneel down to place the trap, so in effect these catchers have to get close to the mole's environment sooner or later. They claim it is kinder on the knees to remain standing until the last minute, when all they need do is produce kneepads or a cushion.

If you have considered the area and studied it in relation to the presence of a mole, then use of the probe should be minimal. If you can locate the tunnel and insert the trap in the least possible amount of time you will cause minimum disturbance. Time is important, as the longer you take, the more chance there is of the mole being alerted to what you are doing, and taking alarm. Having found that all-important run, if you are already kneeling down with all your tools and trap at the ready, you can set and place the trap quickly and accurately. Poking around from above and then digging and chopping the ground somewhat at random is a poor way to do the job, and only confirms that this person doesn't fully understand what actually is a quick and simple task when carried out correctly.

When setting traps at any depth, accuracy is vital, and if the trap needs to be low in the ground, it is the skill of a mole catcher that is required, not somebody able to quarry out a grave.

The Mole's Survival Tactics

Moles are without doubt pure strength, but having only a minimal amount of stored fat in their bodies they must feed regularly to fuel this strength and to preserve this important fat level.

Fat is located in precise areas around the mole's body – the shoulders and hips to ensure ease of movement in the joints for digging and movement, and around the abdomen to protect the lower internal organs. Cold and periods of drought place tremendous pressure on this body fat to ensure the mole's survival. Because it is a warm-blooded animal, during colder months the mole will burn this fat in an effort to keep warm, and must feed to recharge the fat store.

As is the practice of female moles in the spring breeding season, moles cater for periods of hardship by providing themselves with worm

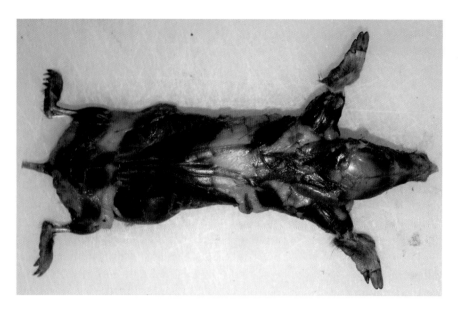

The mole has little body fat. M. PAYNE

larders, stashes of worms that are caught when available to be used in these times of need. I have discovered many worm larders at various times of the year, all the work of a particular mole making the most of the food available, and storing it; it will incapacitate a worm by injuring it, but leave it alive, so it can return later and feed when food is scarce. I know they will store food at any time of the year, in cold or dry weather, or just when food is in abundance. Moles do not dig without reason, as they cannot afford the calorific burn if the energy they expend exceeds the rewards. If a mole has detected food and tunnelled to locate it, it will store it so it can return to it later.

Many people will experience mole activity in an explosion of molehills, but then there may be no evidence of any further digging. The mole may well be thought to have left the area – but in fact, it may not have. Because of circumstances dictated by the location or the weather, or a combination of both, the mole may actually be feeding on the stocks it has built up. This enables it to conserve energy at any time of the year – but in times of shortage and hardship, worm larders are its lifeline.

This explains the observation that 'the mole comes and goes', and also why mole catchers may be advised to make a third daily inspection before the mole is caught – and don't be caught out yourself by removing traps on the second day because you feel the mole has gone. It is worth making the third visit, because if you don't, you might have to make a further two visits to investigate further mole activity, and reset and reinspect your traps at the same location. The energy a mole expends in digging out and hunting for worms, bugs and grubs obviously greatly exceeds that of feeding on stored sources and resting, but with experience you can soon decide what the circumstances are.

Depending upon how many worm larders it has, and how much weight of food it has accumulated for its personal needs, the mole may be dormant for some time. A sleeping mole uses less energy than an active one, fat is conserved, and moles do spend more hours asleep then awake.

The Mole's Patterns of Behaviour

Pick up any book written by one of the many research scientists on moles, and there is always some reference to the periods of mole activity.

Even government departments have referred to such patterns of movement, but all deviate on the findings or the interpretation of what has been termed 'mole study'. This is because the information came from captured moles in laboratory conditions, they were fed different foods, weighed, prodded and poked, and then dissected in the name of science. They produced patterns of activity that many experts claim is how moles actually live their lives. Some claim eight hours of sleep followed by eight hours of activity, others dispute this and refer to a pattern of four hours' sleeping and four of activity.

If this were correct then we would be able to choose the exact couple of hours to go mole catching – if only it were that easy! Moles are a wild animal, they are dictated by sleep and hunger, when they are tired they will rest, and when hungry they will eat. I am sure that you, like me, have seen new evidence of moles at work at random times during your day, heard tales from people of moles digging before their eyes in the morning, afternoon and evenings, and of course those who have thrown back the curtain in the morning to see the changes made to the lawn overnight.

So there are no set periods when a mole will work, or rest, or play. They are entirely independent individuals, and their lives are completely fashioned by the environment and location where they are found, so I find it very difficult to accept that set behaviour patterns could relate to all moles. Having caught live moles for various reasons I have a duty of care, and am required to maintain them and provide for their welfare, and I can confirm they will eat whenever food is offered, and will immediately curl up in a ball and sleep until it is digested.

A Month of Opportunity

September is full of opportunities for moles, in the same way that in the summer months water irrigation systems and sprinklers provided many moles with the opportunity to source food. This is because in the autumn, vegetable gardens and allotments become another prime area for moles, as the gardener, in his quest to be self-sufficient, comes to harvest the fruits of his work in the spring; despite the increase in rainfall, automated irrigation still pours water over these areas on a regular basis, as summer bedding plants are neglected, and the lawn, no longer of leisurely interest, is permitted to grow.

Root vegetables suddenly become the pride and joy of those that grow them, especially for the first time, and any sign of a mole in close proximity to their crop raises their concerns. However, moles may in fact be a friend to the vegetable garden, rather than a foe. As always, the mole will be in need of food within its dietary range, much of which will be found in the vegetable garden.

The insects it seeks are cutworms, wireworms, millipedes and other plant-loving pests. The daily temperature is dropping towards the end of this month, and the combination of possibly dry conditions and watering encourages millipedes, which will eat the roots of many vegetables planned for the festive season. Cutworms and wireworms also dwell under the soil: wireworms attack potatoes, boring into the tubers, while cutworms are normally more active in the months of July and August, eating lettuce and cabbage roots, and severing the leaves at ground level before returning under the soil.

The mole is nature's control for these garden pests, as there is no chemical control for these raiders of the vegetable plot.

OCTOBER

In days gone by, this month would have been considered the start of the mole catcher's year. With the harvest complete, agricultural workers sought employment, and many who had hung up their traps in April now returned to the fray. The parish and full-time mole catchers felt the stress of both competition and change, and this continues today, as those offering control of other pests now seek money from mole catching.

In October the canvas of the landscape will be painted a darker colour as the golds and greens turn to russets and rusts. Soil is turned in preparation for the next season's growth: it will be enriched, tilled and drilled as the countryside is prepared for the colder times ahead. The soil that is now easy to work provides a haven of enjoyment for the moles: the new surviving spring-born moles can develop the natural skills gifted to their species, and the older moles can re-acquaint themselves with the tunnel complexes they know so well. Suitable territories are investigated, and new ones created, and the now aggressively territorial moles stand ready to repel any other mole that happens to invade their range.

In October the temperature drops in comparison to the previous months as the days get shorter and the sun sits lower in the sky. Even this small change has an effect on the mole, because it produces dew, so as well as the drip provided by excessive dew as it runs off manmade structures, it can also have an effect on the land. The upper horizons or layers of the ground begin to receive constant moisture from dew formed when the ground surface cools to a temperature that is colder than the dewpoint of the air next to it.

Dew is water that has condensed from some of the water vapour contained in the air. The grass cools in the night after being warmed during the day, and a very thin layer of air next to the grass deposits some of its water vapour in the form of water on the grass. This water will soak down into the ground and moisten the soil, and heavy or prolonged periods of dew will benefit the soil inhabitants in periods that can be unusually dry. Dew can form on the ground at all times of the year, as many a camper will know, when they wake to find that

everything inside is damp as well as outside, but in the summer months this light dew is easily burnt off in the hotter sunlight.

In these early months of autumn the air temperature in the morning will be quite low so the ground will remain wet for longer. You have probably experienced this when walking on the grass, as footwear needs to be water repellent. Because of the damper conditions, October rainfall will soak into the ground, and be absorbed in the layers more quickly. Depending on the weather of the previous month, the moles may welcome being able to return to the upper soil levels, or to move to more favourable areas. It means that the mole catcher is back to working 'normal' tunnel depths and with the 'usual' trap placement, a welcome return from weeks of working dry, loose soil, or having to break through soil layers like concrete to reach the caverns below, which can so often become a tedious task.

Trap Placement

So let us finally look at trap placement, because at this point in the story of mole catchers and their traditional skills, you will now have the knowledge to appreciate the quarry and the demand that life makes upon it, which is such an important part of mole catching. Anyone can purchase a mole trap and stick in it the ground, but as with anything, there is a correct way and a wrong way to do anything, and setting a mole trap is no different. I have explained some of the problems you may encounter – now let's look at why so many catchers make mistakes.

Even normal mole trap placement has its problems for some trap users, with target moles often inducing spells of apprehension, frustration and desperation. In the same way the old mole catchers returning to the fields, and those in the pest control industry who respond to requests received for mole removal after weeks of dealing with wasps, might have made the same mistakes.

The following section explains how I present a mole trap, and although I do not shy away from those who insist I am doing it wrong, ultimately it will be up to you to decide which is the right way.

Often the first error is inappropriate probe choice, or using the probe excessively – walking around randomly poking the soil and plunging holes into mole tunnels is not a useful method, nor is prodding different molehills in the hope of finding a tunnel the mole will be using. Careful study of the location, and the impact that it places on the mole – from natural elements, the character of the soil and other physical influences – and a considered decision as to where that better run or tunnel might be, in order to catch the unsuspecting mole humanely, not only produces a result more quickly, but also removes any doubt as to whether the trap is in the correct place.

Any frustration experienced when mole catching is self induced, as the mole only reacts to environmental changes or if it is impacted by forces out of its direct control. It will be easy for the mole to avoid a trap positioned where it would expect to find it, or positioned incorrectly. Every mole trap placed in the ground to capture a mole will be subject to the same influences as the target mole: set up your trap so it fits the environment exactly, and there is no reason for it not to catch – you can't blame the trap for your own mistakes.

So what are these simple errors? Well, I can't say what mistakes are being made to cause the mole catcher frustration, but if I explain how I would carry out the task, then some of them may be exposed and they can judge for themselves.

Locating the Tunnel to Use

First of all, on surveying the area, I will look to locate the tunnel the mole is using to access the area, and decide if it is there to establish a food source. Is it obvious because of the presence of molehills, or is it using possibly shallow tunnels? Consider if the mole is in fact staying or passing through to enter another area – the perimeter of the property may reveal this tunnel under the fence line, or along a wall or hedgerow. In a smaller area such as a garden the mole may be feeding in the lawn, so locate the tunnel between the perimeter of the property and the first molehill.

Also consider the reasons why molehills would be there, by the number that you can see – though remember that even a number of molehills does not always mean the mole is still present. Are the molehills fresh, or have weeds grown through them, indicating it has been a while since the mole last moved soil to the surface in that area? Why has the mole not moved any soil? Has it left the area, or is it because of circumstances prevailing at different depths, or is it living on stored supplies? How big are the molehills, how far apart are they, and is there any change in their content, such as sand, or gravel or soil of a different colour? Just from these simple observations, you can deduce so much about the location, the reason for the mole being present there, and the depths at which it is working.

Other questions you might ask concern the flora of the area. For example trees absorb large volumes of water, and some species prefer to have their roots constantly moist, such as willows, and this will help you ascertain the possible level or movement of the water table. Are there any natural water sources such as streams or ponds that will influence the mole's available food choice? In addition, consider the activities that prevail in the location, and how seasonal activities and the weather might influence the mole's behaviour. Having evaluated all these points, you can then proceed to detecting what you would consider to be the correct tunnel or run from which to capture that particular mole.

Using the Probe

You now have to use a probe – or as I was told as a boy, a 'talking stick' – because it will tell

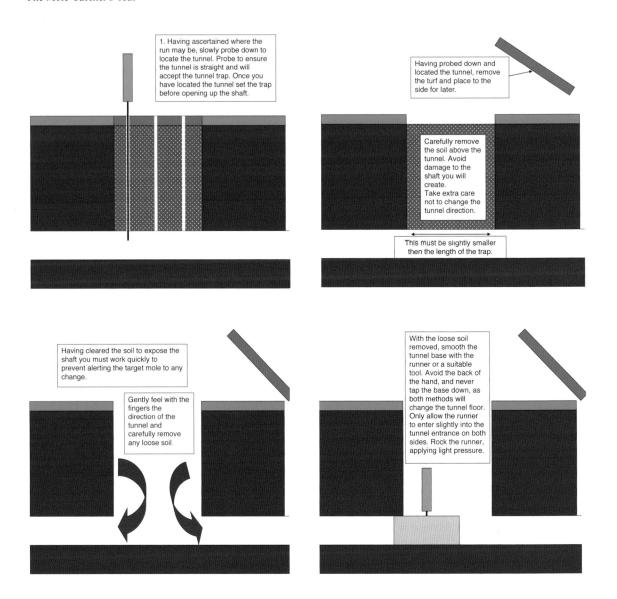

1. Having ascertained where the run may be, slowly probe down to locate the tunnel. Probe to ensure the tunnel is straight and will accept the tunnel trap. Once you have located the tunnel set the trap before opening up the shaft.

Having probed down and located the tunnel, remove the turf and place to the side for later.

Carefully remove the soil above the tunnel. Avoid damage to the shaft you will create.
Take extra care not to change the tunnel direction.

This must be slightly smaller then the length of the trap.

Having cleared the soil to expose the shaft you must work quickly to prevent alerting the target mole to any change.

Gently feel with the fingers the direction of the tunnel and carefully remove any loose soil.

With the loose soil removed, smooth the tunnel base with the runner or a suitable tool. Avoid the back of the hand, and never tap the base down, as both methods will change the tunnel floor. Only allow the runner to enter slightly into the tunnel entrance on both sides. Rock the runner, applying light pressure.

you what is going on beneath the surface. The probe will tell you the density of the soil below from the amount of pressure you need to push it downwards; it will inform you of the moisture content, according to the suction you feel; and on reaching the tunnel, it will tell you how deep it is. It can notify you of any obstructions on the way down – roots, stones and buried objects – along with marking the exact point of entry as you lay it down.

I would normally use a probe diameter of just 8mm so as not to cause unnecessary damage to the mole's tunnel and alert it to my intentions to enter its world. As already explained, I would never use a probe thicker than 10mm in diameter, and would choose one that I can hold in the same way as an Olympic fencer would present his weapon, not like a gravedigger with a shovel.

Having examined the area visually I will know where that mole is travelling from, and where it is going. I now need to pinpoint that

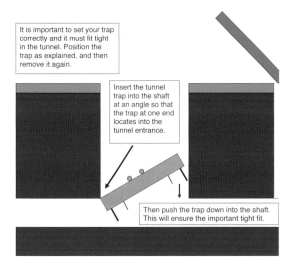

It is important to set your trap correctly and it must fit tight in the tunnel. Position the trap as explained, and then remove it again.

Insert the tunnel trap into the shaft at an angle so that the trap at one end locates into the tunnel entrance.

Then push the trap down into the shaft. This will ensure the important tight fit.

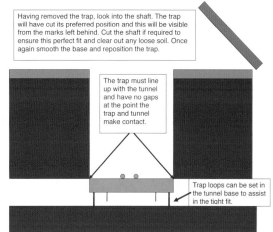

Having removed the trap, look into the shaft. The trap will have cut its preferred position and this will be visible from the marks left behind. Cut the shaft if required to ensure this perfect fit and clear out any loose soil. Once again smooth the base and reposition the trap.

The trap must line up with the tunnel and have no gaps at the point the trap and tunnel make contact.

Trap loops can be set in the tunnel base to assist in the tight fit.

OPPOSITE AND THIS PAGE: *Positioning a tunnel trap.*

tunnel, and this procedure must be carried out with precision and as little disturbance as possible so as not to alarm the mole. I say 'not to alarm the mole', but in reality it is probably fully aware of your presence above ground level if it is in the vicinity. Moles are fully aware of their surroundings, and it is quite common for the mole to be heaving up soil in the very location you are working and to be completely unworried by your activity, providing you carry it out correctly.

This means walking slowly, and never treading amongst the molehills: step over them if you need to move in or around them. Never tread down the tunnels under any circumstances, and ensure that anyone with you refrains from jumping around and flattening all around you. When you are using the probe let it do the work: you may be the force behind the pressure to send it on its journey, but then all you need do is absorb the information it provides. You need to discover the secrets below, and the probe is the first and only contact that a mole catcher has with the mole's environment from above ground. Use it correctly and understand what it tells you, and your next steps will be

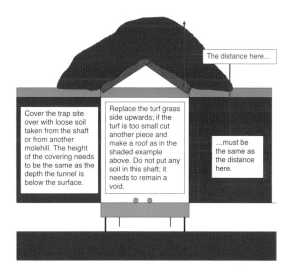

The distance here...

Cover the trap site over with loose soil taken from the shaft or from another molehill. The height of the covering needs to be the same as the depth the tunnel is below the surface.

Replace the turf grass side upwards; if the turf is too small cut another piece and make a roof as in the shaded example above. Do not put any soil in this shaft; it needs to remain a void.

...must be the same as the distance here.

made easier – get it wrong and your quest for the mole can be a long and arduous task.

If you have access to a piece of land that has resident moles, then practise using the probe. Get the feel for it, look for different runs at different depths, and feel for any obstructions – but remember that the more damage you do to the mole's environment, the more likely it is to move its activities, and thus the more damage it will do to that area. So be sure to obtain permission from the landowner.

It is only necessary to probe down a few times, as you should have decided from your observations the mole's probable route. When the probe reveals the tunnel, you will need to determine the direction in which it travels — another probe down in what you believe to be the tunnel's direction should expose it. This next probe down only needs to be 2in (50mm) or so from this first probe. If you find the tunnel, then do the same on the other side of the first probe. If you can't find it, then the tunnel may not quite be as you thought — but this can happen, so just be patient and try again. It can often help to have another probe down to the side of your now discovered tunnel to ensure that it is a straight run with no annoying side tunnels. Any other tunnel entering your chosen trap site will alert the mole, and means that you are not in the correct tunnel location.

On my training courses, I set the students the task of setting the traps in amongst the feeding ground, as there they will find tunnels without much effort, and they can feel this new strange world immediately through their probe. More important are the problems they are confronted with — bends, junctions and dead ends are all reasons not to set a trap in amongst molehills, but it is better they learn from these mistakes on the course than in the real world of mole control.

Opening the Ground

Having determined which tunnel to use to place your trap, the next important task is to open the ground and enter into the mole's world. This needs to be done with precision and accuracy, as any mistake here and the mole is likely to detect where you have placed your trap. Have everything you need ready and to hand. My canvas bag with its flap is perfect to kneel on, because despite what many authorities will tell you, you do need to work close to what you are doing in order to complete this task correctly.

Have your trap set and ready to deploy; also,

kneeling on the bag flap means you can reach into the bag easily for any tools. Having already probed down, and now you are sure that this is the right place to position the trap, a tip here is to return the probe to the middle hole and lay it down on the ground. It now points to the centre of the place in the tunnel where you will need to set the trap. If on grass or soil, you only need remove a small amount of turf to expose a shaft that is slightly smaller than the trap size.

This is very important, and I cannot stress this enough. I only use the half barrel trap, and would strongly recommend that the mole catcher who is a beginner also uses this style of trap. These half-barrels are quite easy to set, but the traps with 6kg springs can be hard to depress if your hands are frail or weak. On purchasing a half-barrel trap for the first time, handle it, but don't try and set it, just hold it and examine it. Just feeling the trap will let you become accustomed to the parts and how they move and work, and then you can fully appreciate the importance of how it will operate and despatch the captured mole.

Take note that you can take a new trap out of its box and catch a mole with it on the same night — you don't have to bury it in the ground, boil it in a pan with nuts, or present it to the first full moon. The smell of a newly manufactured trap will not alarm the mole at all, but do keep your traps away from strong and obnoxious smells such as solvents and vehicle fuels — another reason for a safe carrybag for your whole mole-catching kit. If you are an amateur, just catching your own moles at home, you could use a plastic bucket, as you will only need a few traps. From a professional point of view, a canvas bag is a better choice as it not only carries and keeps everything to hand and safe, but it does look more professional, too. To turn up with a plastic bucket might risk undermining your customer's confidence, just as you might feel if your doctor appeared with his stethoscope hanging over the side of a plastic carrier bag.

Handle the trap with confidence – it can't harm you until it is set and ready to place in the ground, and holding it will help you feel more assured in using it, and trust in its ability to complete the task for you.

Setting the Half-Barrel Trap

When setting a half-barrel trap hold the trap by its body in both hands, with the trap springs uppermost and at a slight angle down and away from you; this will allow the retaining bar furthest away from you to hang free. Place one or both thumbs on top of the spring that is also furthest away from you, and push down. This will allow the trap loop to drop down through the trap body until it reaches the correct position.

Next comes the part that many feel apprehensive about, as now the power of the spring can be felt in the hands, and instinctively you worry that you won't be able to remove your hands without the trap catching them or taking a lump from a finger. The simple answer is confidence: with confidence in the trap and in your handling of it, setting it will become second nature. With the trap held as described, push the spring down a few times to get the feel of how strong it is, and slowly let it back up – you can be sure that you are stronger than the springs, though you might not be quite as fast.

With the spring in the down position and the retaining bar hanging free, you can now hold the spring down with one thumb of one hand, and with the other hand, pull the retaining bar that is hanging free, up and over the trap loop and on to the top of the trap spring. The clue is in the name of this part of the trap – the retaining bar, as it retains the trap spring down and under pressure until its release. You may want to practise this manoeuvre a few times until you are confident that it can carry out its task. It will also confirm that you have to have the trap tilted slightly away from you, because if it is not, the retaining bar can get caught inside

the trap loop, especially if you angle it upwards.

For those new to setting this style of mole trap, it is somewhat alarming to have the spring under pressure and held down, and then suddenly find that they can't locate the retaining bar. The retaining bar must lie on top of the spring, and then locate on the hook on the top of the mumble pin.

It will take some practice to complete setting the trap, but when the spring is under pressure and the retaining bar is sitting under the hook on top of the mumble pin, you can take your hand away from restraining the spring. It is purely instinctive to move it away faster than a startled rabbit, but if the trap has been set properly then there is no reason to worry, as the trap can only release if the mumble pin is pushed from underneath, and then your hands should be nowhere near these parts.

One important point is to ensure that the retaining bar locates right in its corner of the bend, with the hook on the mumble pin. Set it in the middle and it may fire in the hands, as the springs place the retaining bar under a lot of force, and it will possibly slip and you will use words that your mother did not know you knew.

If you have strong hands, setting these half-barrel traps is no problem. Those with weak hands may have to consider the options of other traps that are available, but some of these traps do have welfare issues, so let us take a look at how to get round the problem. If you can hold the spring down with both thumbs, by holding the trap angled slightly away from you, you can flick the retaining bar over by quickly moving the trap in a circular movement downwards away from you, and then towards you. This will throw the retaining bar over, and it will lie on top of the spring and almost line up with the hook on the mumble pin. You will have to jiggle it a bit, and this can be done by using a finger underneath the trap to move the mumble pin to locate its hook on the retaining bar. Now with both hands holding the trap spring down, and having overcome the full force of the spring's initial movement, you may actually be able to hold the spring in one hand.

It all takes a little practice, which is why it is a good idea to handle the trap and get the feel of it. If you struggle even with two hands, or if you are still not fully confident in your ability to move quickly enough to set it in the way described above, then you can employ the help of a cup hook. Screw a cup hook into a strip of wood, and use it to hook on the trap loop, and then you can use this to advantage to pull the trap up, and therefore the trap loop down. Use a strip of wood long enough to hold down with a knee so your bodyweight can resist your upward pull. The trap hooked on the cup hook is easier to control and will give you some confidence until you become more proficient and can set the trap with your eyes closed. With one trap loop set, now turn the trap around and repeat the same procedure at the other end, so maybe keep one eye open for a while.

Positioning the Trap in the Ground

With your trap now set, you can proceed to the next step of positioning it in the ground, which is all about size. If you have already used traps for mole control you may be surprised by this statement, but size is important. The size of the hole you will make to set your trap in must be slightly smaller than the size of the trap, and never any larger. At school, the woodwork teacher used to say when making a joint with a chisel that you can remove wood, but you can never put it back, and this is also very true when referring to mole trap placement. Make the hole too big and the trap will never fit correctly, and will compromise the full potential of the trap operation.

You have already determined the location of the tunnel, and that you can place the trap there from your use of the probe. So don't spoil this opportunity by now entering the mole's world making all the mistakes of an enthusiastic amateur. The half-barrel trap is in fact a template of the size of the hole that you are to make. Place the trap on the ground surface where it is to be positioned, and with a sharp – and I emphasize sharp – hand trowel, cut a mark at one end of the trap and another in line with the trap loop at the other end. This will mean your hole will be approximately ½in (15mm) too small in length for the trap to fit, and this is vitally important, which I will explain later. The width is important, but should you cut the hole a little too wide, this can be rectified.

The trowel must be sharp, as it must cut a path into the mole's world, and not tear or rip its way down. Keep your trowel sharp, and work with precise movements. Slice down from one end where you made your mark – depending upon the depth, you may feel the give as the trowel enters the tunnel, as you did with the probe. Repeat at the other end, again at your mark, and then cut a line along the length between those first two cuts so you have a rectangle of the required size.

Trowel Choice

Trowel choice is important, as this tool is often the reason why so many fail to catch their mole – they have used a trowel that is inappropriate to the task. Ideally it needs to have a straight blade, rather than a curved one. Potting trowels commonly have a curved blade, so try to avoid them, as they will not have the straight edge required, especially at each end of your trap site. The trowel needs a straight tang, not a bent tang – the tang is the part that connects the blade to the handle. The bent tang is found on some trowels to make the scooping action easier. Handles are best made of wood, of course, because you will be using the trowel a lot, as you will the probe, and wood is kind on the hands.

The best modern trowel is down to personal choice, but a planting trowel is probably the best or closest you can get to what is my personal favourite, an old trowel. The planting trowel blade is straight but slightly too pointed, and comes in varying blade lengths; archaeologists often use it as their preferred tool. I find my old trowels in antique shops, and these are excellent, as the steel quality offers itself to the bench grinder, and a hand sharpening stone in the mole bag will hone and maintain its edge during the working day. Old trowels can often be found with a straight-edged blade, and I will change the original handles to a 6in (150mm) hardwood handle for comfort.

If the trap is to be set under grass, then it is important to keep the turf safe, as it will form the roof when the trap is in position. Once you have cut out your rectangle you can use the trowel to lever out the whole lump in one go. The larger handle lends itself to the job perfectly, but to do so may damage the structure of the tunnel, so avoid doing so until you become proficient at it. Take two, even three pieces out, as none of us is faultless in what we do; but make the slightest error and the mole will punish you. Therefore cut a small piece out, and insert your hand. Feel for the direction of travel of the tunnel: is it as you first thought? If it is, then continue to remove the rest of the soil carefully with the trowel, and finally by hand – remember the mole has no natural fear of you, so you can ignore those who claim that your scent will repel the mole from the site.

With the trap site exposed, take a mole runner or other suitable tool, and smooth the base to obtain a clear overall look at the shaft and potential trap site.

Inserting the Trap into the Tunnel
Now take your trap and insert it into the tunnel; as you should have cut this hole slightly too small, you will have to push it in at an angle. Insert it down, align the trap with the tunnel at one end, and then push down the opposite end. It should fit tightly in the tunnel for the length of the hole you have cut. Now remove it again by tilting one end up, and lifting it out; this will not change the fit, so when you look down into

the trap site you will now see the shape that the trap has made in the tunnel. The two side edges on the trap body act as two blades and will leave two lines, which may require further soil to be scraped out. You can feel into the tunnel entrances at each end and pull out any loose soil that may have dropped in – but if you have used a sharp, straight-edged trowel there should be only a minimal amount of soil, or none at all, as you will have cut it in the same way as a sharp knife cuts a cake.

Do not go poking around in the tunnel with your hand: you have already determined the direction of travel with the probe, and have confirmed it with your fingers, and that should be it. Poking into the tunnel with a stick, bent wire or other gizmo will inevitably cause damage in the tunnel, however careful you think you have been. There will possibly be loose soil in the base of the tunnel, and many will immediately firm it down with the hand. This will be with the back of the hand, as it is the only way we can reach down, due to the limitations of our wrist. It will directly form a bowl shape, so firming the tunnel floor will mimic this shape. Some will firm the base with the handle of the T-bar probe, but this is too small in diameter and risks being used impulsively as a hammer to tap the base, having the same effect as the hand.

However, you do need to leave the base firm and smooth, and to do this I use what I have called the 'mole runner'. This is a nylon billet on a wooden handle, and I simply place it on the tunnel base and slightly into the entrance of the tunnel, and then roll or rock it from side to side. Do not press or tap down, just roll it gently from side to side, which is sufficient to achieve what is needed – and the runner from its weight and size is perfect for this task. The same needs to be done to the other end of the tunnel, so again the runner is slipped carefully into the tunnel entrance and rolled from side to side.

There will be those more adept at mole catching than myself who will consider there is no need for such meticulous preparation, and will declare they don't need such a tool. The truth is, they probably prefer long-handled spades, T-bar probes and a plastic bucket – but this is how I catch moles, and any guidance I can give to resolving those annoying occasions when the mole has compacted traps with soil, then this is one.

The Importance of a Tight Fit

So we have the trap site open only to the size of the trap, and the base is now smooth and firm. Replace the trap into the position, remembering to enter it an angle to ensure the correct fit. If you do cut the tunnel slightly too wide then you can pack a small piece of turf between the trap body and the tunnel walls, but only alongside the trap springs or in the middle of the trap body. Never pack anything near the trap loops as this could impede their operation upon release. I cannot stress enough the importance of setting the trap in the tunnel so that it fits tightly – it must not move when the springs are released, because if it does, some of the force will be lost, and it is essential that the full force of the springs impacts on the mole. It is just as important, if not more so, that the tunnel and the trap body line up without any gaps.

To reiterate, the only way that you will achieve a tight fit is to cut the hole slightly smaller, and to push the trap in at an angle, and then down into position, and to use a trowel that is sharp enough, and is used in close contact with the soil to cut its way in, and not rip. And this is important because of the mole's unique ability to detect the airflows and pressures in its tunnels. As already explained, the mole will create positive and negative airflows as it goes about its business: moving along the tunnel, it will create positive air pressure in front of it, and in the main tunnel, where it will be moving at a steady pace, this pressure will be greater than in tunnels where it is not moving with such intent. If you leave a gap in between the tunnel entrance and the trap body, any pressure will

straightaway be lost upwards into the gap above the trap, and the mole will be alerted immediately and will respond by closing off the tunnel.

To the mole, any loss of air pressure must mean there is a problem with the tunnel roof and one that needs fixing. And this is something that you as the mole catcher cannot fix, despite many trying – cut your trap site too long and you might as well forget it, and if you move to another location, take care. Plugging the ends with a piece of turf will not work: although it will seem to have done the job, inevitably the turf will dry out, and then it will drop down or shrink, and again, the positive pressure created by the mole's forward movement will be lost and it will be alerted to the change in the tunnel.

Always ensure that you line up the trap body and the tunnel roof accurately, and it doesn't matter if the trap loops have to be pushed down into the tunnel floor to achieve it: failing to take account of airflows and pressure is so often the mistake made by many people.

The importance of this can be experienced by anyone who has travelled on the London Underground or other subway transport. As a train approaches the platforms a rush of air will be felt: this is the pressure created by the train, in the same way as that created by the mole. The rush of cool air is often a welcome experience to those on the platform due to the temperatures below the city pavements. And these cool, positive airflows are exactly what the moles experience as they go about their business, and it is essential that we should consider their ability to assess these airflows in our efforts to catch one.

You must combine all this information to be successful. Moving around their tunnels, the moles will be controlling the airflows from these negative and positive pressures, and these will in turn affect the tunnel temperatures and the humidity – and we know the mole also has an acute ability to decipher any change in these. The mole environment will remain constant until any impact from the weather causes a natural change. The mole would expect this sort of change from the information it perceives from the circumstances around it, whereas any unexpected change would require action. A sudden increase in fresh air would be an unexpected change in air quality, from one with a low oxygen level (*see* next section), and will immediately alert the mole – so there is a lot to bear in mind when it comes to covering the trap site.

Covering the Trap Site

People have their own opinions as to the best method to cover the trap site. Some will insist that you should sprinkle loose soil on to the top of the trap, though I would immediately ask why you need to do this if you cover the trap over at the surface? The answers are mystifying, with some proposing that should someone open up your trap site they will see the trap. If they do, it has to be for a reason, so leave your trap site as both the mole and any third party expect to find it, and no one will be any the wiser. Therefore, we have no need to cover a trap with soil if we are going to hide it at ground level.

When covering the trap site you must shut out, as well as light and moisture, the main enemy of the mole catcher: air. Air is your worst adversary, as the mole lives in an environment that has an elevated level of carbon dioxide, on which it relies to feed its acute nervous system. Nervous systems are stimulated by carbon dioxide, but the mole can control the levels of carbon dioxide both in its body and in its environment, by producing bicarbonate in its body, which it expels in its urine as carbonic acid

In fact the mole can survive in levels of oxygen as low as 6 per cent, which is a unique phenomenon on earth. It has evolved for a life below ground in its complex network of tunnels at varying levels, where the flows of air are minimal or non-existent. (*See* November section below: 'The Mole's Hypercapnic Ability'.)

A mole trap must be covered only at ground level and not below it, and so that it will leave the trap's location exactly as the mole would expect to find it. Many people will look out items such as a piece of wood, a tile or some plastic to act as a roof, but even under a second covering of soil these materials can affect the catch rate because they will influence the temperature and therefore the humidity. They will naturally warm up in the heat of the sun, or cool down in the lower temperatures, which in turn will have a direct influence on that void below. The void will contain a static atmosphere that will still have an influence on the tunnels. There are also airflows resulting from movement in the tunnels in other parts of the complex, and this may not necessarily be caused by moles.

Even when fitted tightly the half-barrel trap will not be able to keep out all movement from airflows or pressures. This is an advantage, as its shape will allow the air movement and pressure to be maintained, and also because of the holes and slots some influences will still be able to permeate into the tunnel, and this I have found is essential. The mole will expect to experience some changes in all parts of its environment, however small these might be. Keeping this in mind, I will explain how I cover the trap site and maintain the tunnel as the mole will expect to find it, and the reasons why.

Having opened up the shaft where you will place the trap, I advised to keep the turf, as this will form the roof. Turf is perfect for this task as it is a natural covering, and the one that was possibly covering the tunnel before your intervention. The first clue to trap covering is to use what was covering the tunnel before you removed it, because it will be the influencing factor on the trap site when you replace it. You must consider those influences and how they can be replicated in your covering. Whenever possible turf should be the first choice, as it will always mimic the environmental conditions. However, it must be used as nature intended, and that is grass side up, not down, and for a very good reason.

To use the turf it simply needs to be put back over the top of the trap shaft to form a roof shape. It may be worked in the hands to spread it slightly, and then bent into a concave shape. You may need to slice it so as to thin it if you have cut a thick clod: it needs to be just over 1in thick (30mm), but no thicker. If you can't shape it, just cut another slice from the ground next to your trap site and use two pieces to form the roof shape.

The turf needs to be grass side up, as this will influence the access of rainwater or dew. Any water source will travel through the ground at a certain rate according to the prevailing conditions, and the presence of grass is significant in this – which is why the turf must be green side up. Its structure reacts differently if it upside down or soil side up. Try this for yourself: pour water on a turf grass side up and monitor the speed it penetrates through the turf, then take another turf and pour water on it soil side up, and you will see there is a considerable difference. The turf therefore needs to be set as it would be naturally, to mimic or retain this travel of moisture so not to change the natural rate of saturation.

Obviously, if you just place the turf over the top, the water would just pass through the turf covering and then drip down into the trap site, and this would not be as the surrounding areas, including the tunnel, as the water still needs to pass down through the depth of soil to the tunnel. To overcome this, cover the turf with soil taken from the molehills provided by the offending mole. The soil provided by the mole is perfect for the covering, which must be the same height as the depth of the tunnel beneath, so that the influences above the trap site will be the same as in the tunnel on each side of the trap.

Having made the roof of turf, place soil around the outer edges to apply some weight; this will prevent the turf roof from collapsing downwards or imploding. With the outer edge weighted, the rest of the roof can be completely covered, and to the depth of the tunnel. There-fore, a tunnel roof that is 6in (150mm) down will need the same height of soil piled on the top. If it is 12in down (300mm), then again the same applies.

If you cover your trap in this way it doesn't matter what the weather throws at it, as the impact will be the same: the water will soak down at the same rate all around, thus affecting the whole location in the same way. So whatever the weather – wet, cold or hot – the area below the covering will be the same as the surroundings. If you are in any doubt, cover it with more soil than you feel you should, as it is better to be on the safe side.

If you could see air flows you would see how they flow across the ground following every contour, and you can be sure that a mole will also detect the slightest change in conditions in its tunnels. (I will cover some extra points in relation to trap covering again when we look at traps set in different locations.)

Dealing with Stones

If you encounter a stone in your chosen trap position and it is preventing the trap from sitting tightly in the tunnel, my advice is to push it into the tunnel rather than try to pull it out. You won't know the size of this stone, and to remove it could damage the tunnel, so simply use the probe and push it into the tunnel wall or floor. The probe is ideal as you can place its tip against the offending stone, then apply pressure along it and directly on to the stone; hold the probe close to the tip to prevent it from slipping, and place the flat end of the bar against the surface of the stone. Then holding the handle in your other hand, push the stone steadily into the tunnel wall until the trap can be located without hindrance.

Trap Efficiency Depends on Trap Placement

Correct trap placement is vitally important to the operation of a half-barrel trap or any other trap employed to capture a mole. The force of any trap is provided by the spring or springs, and their full force must be utilized. If the trap is able to move when set in the tunnel then some of this force will be lost. The trap needs to impart as much velocity as it possibly can to the trap loop on its journey upwards when the spring is released: this draws the mole upwards quickly, and it also needs to terminate abruptly to apply the sudden shock and injury to the mole's thorax region to kill it. If the trap is not held firmly, a proportion of this velocity will be lost as the trap is jolted upwards.

Think of it as running into a wall: if you set your trap in a hole that is too big it will allow this movement, and cramming soil around it is not the answer. Any soil packed all around it will possibly still be subjected to natural movement and subsidence as it dries, releasing the pressure and again allowing the trap to move upon release.

A Month of Change

October can bring the first frost, to remind those of us who work outside that nature is preparing for a change. The change will be shorter days and a colder night, though until winter really decides to impress with her presence, this will have little influence upon the moles. October is also a time when the gardeners drift back into hibernation – lawnmowers rest and the barbecues are allowed to rust. Mole catchers are still prowling the fields, however, and like their forefathers, from this month forward will have to compete once again with those freed from the grip of the fiscal summer, as pest control companies once again start trawling for work during these harder times.

Whether it is the same today as it was in times past, when those agricultural workers once again picked up their traps and ventured forth to compete with the old molers, at this time in the year the modern pest controllers dust off their gas applicators and set out to compete for every opportunity to source a mole. So

it is this month, and more than ever before, that the traditional mole catchers need the support of their agricultural and regular customers if they are to continue working the land.

Moving with the Times

Traditional mole catching has changed very little for hundreds of years, but if it is to compete and continue it has to move forwards into modern times. Many bad practices and old wives' tales are now prohibited under the terms of acts of cruelty. For example, it is not permitted to attempt to gas the mole with vehicle exhaust fumes, drown it with the hosepipe, or pour foul-smelling or toxic substances into the soil. Many will view the mole trap as a cruel and barbaric form of dealing with a creature that features in childhood books, despite the damage caused to the land. But as you will understand from these pages, a mole trap is a humane, quick and effective way to remove a target mole, providing it is operated by those proficient in its use. However, some operators abuse the use of mole traps, and both amateur and, more disturbingly, professionals are guilty of this.

It is not acceptable to place a mole trap in the ground to target a mole, and not return within a reasonable time to address any possible suffering. If you employ a mole catcher or place traps yourself, you are required even under the heading of pest control to take reasonable measures for the welfare of that animal. This applies to all animals under the control of man, and the current animal welfare acts require that reasonable measures be taken to provide for the welfare of animals under the control of man, and traps must therefore be inspected to avoid unnecessary suffering.

There are those who see this in a different light, but it has been stated by government departments that 'it would be down to the courts to decide what measures could or should have been taken, to reduce any possible suffering caused to an animal whilst under the control of man'. Now I am in favour of a set or designated period of time between a trap being placed and its inspection, as any trap, even one that has been set correctly, can be influenced by forces out of the direct control of the trap user. Tampering from third parties, whether accidentally or maliciously, can hinder the operation of a trap and cause that trap to inflict suffering. A change in the weather can cause a mole to disturb the dirt, and it may be found cushioned by moist soil pushed into the trap site, alive in the trap, and subject to the stress of capture, starvation, dehydration or haemorrhaging until it expires.

Strange as it may sound, traps that are used for moles are currently exempt from any formal rules, however the very intricate wording contained in the animal welfare acts provides for prosecution should a mole be found to have suffered. So the mole catcher has an obligation to inspect traps daily to prevent any unnecessary suffering to the mole. Under current legislation, an animal becomes a protected animal when it is captured, or when the trap releases. Prior to this release it is not, as no potential harm has been directed at the target species.

There is a moral requirement to inspect traps for any target species and you have a responsibility to do so, especially in relation to the control of moles, as the traps are working in a hidden environment, and without physical inspection it is impossible to determine if they have sprung and made a catch. Those who place traps and leave them uninspected forfeit the right to be called a mole catcher.

There is also a professional obligation to meet the health and safety requirements of risk assessments and liability insurance constraints, and to constantly monitor any changes that could lead to any unforeseen mishap, such as harm to a non-target species or person. Daily inspection of any mole trap shows diligence in sorting out any situation that might incur prosecution, or that might be interpreted as neg-ligence leading to unnecessary suffering. You have been warned.

NOVEMBER

This month can be wet or warm, dry or cold, and more than likely a bit of them all. The weather station is invaluable under such circumstances as it records information allowing you to respond accordingly, especially when wet ground is subjected to a sudden frost. Temperatures can drop rapidly over one night, and you will need to inspect and possibly reassess where you have placed traps to see if the change in temperature has affected them, or will affect where you put any others. Heavy rainfall in the evening could result in soil coverings sagging or dropping, if you have not covered your trap sites correctly, and if this is followed by a sudden freeze it could prevent the springs operating properly, or at all.

The Changes Affecting Mole Behaviour

Soil can turn to mud, and moles then move to feed in higher grounds, causing exclamations from the public, or worst from mole catchers, that this is another mole population boom. Now whether this is a useful comment or not is open to debate: certainly it highlights the need to control moles, but it also results in many more inhumane attacks on moles from those in the 'let's have a go' brigade.

November brings warm, damp soil, with the annual leaf fall bolstering the organic layer, on which the worms in the epigeic layer will feed. This is important, because this increase in food supply provides enough for all the moles competing for food to maintain a healthy bodyweight and a good layer of fat. Worm casts are more evident during this month, and are one way for even the most inexperienced of mole catchers to understand the demands of the mole. This is because molehills without question will be prominent in areas where moles are feeding, and these mole workings will be accompanied by the deposits of worms in the form of casts spread on the surface. It is nature's way of providing for all.

The natural world's cycle of life can never be questioned, as evolution has provided a systematic procedure to ensure the survival of all those sharing that ecosystem. As the days become shorter the leaves of deciduous trees will start to fall, since less sunlight reduces their ability to photosynthesize – to convert the water absorbed through their root system and the carbon dioxide through their leaves into glucose and oxygen – and with diminishing light, the trees prepare for winter. The chlorophyll that colours the leaves green is lost as the trees begin to rest and feed on the store they have built up during the summer. The leaves dry and fall to the floor, and form part of the next stage, as decomposition will take place and the soil-rotting organisms will provide an enriched soil that the tree roots will exploit in the spring.

The earthworms assist the decomposition progression: every day they consume their own weight in fallen leaves and other organic materials, grinding large particles into smaller ones. Soil micro-organisms such as rotifers and nematodes consume the small particles, completing the conversion of once-living foliage into living soil. The worms deposit their waste just like a mole on the surface, as opposed to passing back into the tunnel they have created as they work through the soil.

Soil can be very different from one location to another, but essentially is made up of minerals, rock, organic and inorganic materials, water and air. The inorganic materials are rocks that have been broken down into smaller pieces, to as small as a grain of sand. The organic material is decaying living matter, such as leaves or even dead animals. The amount of water in the soil is closely linked with the climate and other characteristics of the area, and it is the water content in the soil that dictates how well it will be aerated. The wetter the autumn or winter, then the higher will be the moisture content of the soil, which brings the worms to the higher levels, resulting in worm casts appearing and the moles close behind.

As far as the mole is concerned, this reliance on the combination of soils, weather and available food goes on each and every day of every month, but it is often not until November that some people fully understand the intricate life of a mole.

Locating Mole Tunnels in November

Many mole catchers placing their traps at these testing times of the year will make a simple mistake when locating mole tunnels, and that is to inadvertently insert an apparently innocent fallen leaf into the shallow tunnel. This happens when probing over ground that has brown, fallen leaves lying scattered around, often not noticed by the mole catcher, so when the probe is pushed down in the normal manner it will often drag down a leaf into the mole's environment, and this acts like a warning to the mole. And when opening a deeper tunnel it is easy for a leaf to blow down into the trap site.

A leaf in a tunnel where the mole would not expect leaves to be present will obviously cause it concern. The mole is, of course, familiar with its surroundings, and will in fact drag down leaves and suchlike to use as bedding for its nest, but leaves out of place will, despite what many may say, alert the mole. It is easy to push a small, crisp leaf from an oak tree through the moist soil and into the tunnel with a 10mm diameter probe. It is not so easy with an 8mm diameter probe, which will become obvious if you use such a size, as the probe will pierce the leaf, which often results in it picking up every leaf it makes contact with, until it resembles the spike once used by litter pickers. Those who select a probe of a larger diameter must always consider the risk of this, and it may still happen even with a probe of thinner diameter.

The solution is always to brush the leaves away from your chosen location before you begin to probe for your tunnel. Simply scrape them to the side with the blade of the trowel, and at all times be alert to leaves falling into your trap site.

The end of November normally heralds the arrival of winter: the days turn colder, with more persistent frosts penetrating deeper into the ground with each morning as the daily temperatures fail to rise. The moles, as you will now understand, must turn to the available warmer areas, spots that feel the touch of the sun, locations where they find vital food supplies.

Health and Safety: Wearing Gloves

Those whose hands are constantly in dirt will always have reason to wear gloves against the risk of cuts and scratches, when hygiene must be of first importance. I will wash my hands more times in a day when out at work than most people will in a week. Garden taps provide a welcome source of clean water, and it is always advisable to keep an aerosol of instant soap and water, and a towel in your carrybag. For anyone working in the soil there is always the risk of possible contamination from bacteria, and for the mole catcher a clostridium bacterium is probably one to consider.

Some people may not have heard the term clostridium, but names that may be more familiar to you include tetanus, gangrene and botulism, which are types of bacteria in the clostridium range. However, as long as any cut that you incur is cleaned and covered, and your vaccination injection is up to date, then really it is up to you whether you wear gloves or not.

Some people claim that if you don't wear gloves then the mole will detect your scent on your traps and will avoid them, resulting in a failure to catch. They also maintain that you

should boil every trap in nut oil, bury it in the soil for six months, and store it in a vacuum. Now who would spread rumours such as these? In fact the belief that the mole will smell human scent on traps comes from days long ago when mole catchers used traps made of porous materials. Clay and wood are both absorbent, and any obnoxious smells from other substances would soak into them, possibly alerting the mole.

However, this advice came from a time when working men enjoyed chewing or smoking tobacco or taking snuff. These substances had an obnoxious and repellent odour and a smell unfamiliar to the mole. Therefore, advice to keep traps free of this sort of contamination would have been very relevant, as would rubbing the hands in soil to conceal these smells. However, the old mole catchers never wore gloves, and there is no reason for concern with the metal traps of today, as they will not be contaminated by our human scent.

When I am asked to produce moles for media production and when working with live moles, there is a requirement for a duty of care to fully provide for the needs and welfare of that mole. To achieve this, I hand feed the mole, which is quite happy to eat in this way, showing that it is not in the least stressed, and has no natural fear of human scent.

Look Professional!

The traps used today still need maintaining to be fully operational, and could be contaminated by liquids such as diesel and other spirit-based products. It pays to keep your traps, and the tools used for their placement, safely contained so they pose no risk to others, and to this end it is best to have a designated carrier to transport your gear, and a designated place of storage. For the professional mole catcher, the carrier will be an important part of the first impression that you make on your customer, so choose sensibly to reflect your level of professionalism.

First impressions will boost customer confidence in any trade, and providing you are competent in what you do, the combination of a professional appearance and an air of self-confidence will promote you and your services. A professional attitude and an appropriate carrier for your tools is the prelude to success, so I would always say consider what it is you offer, and at what level you as a mole catcher want to be recognized.

The Mole's Hypercapnic Ability

As the month ends and December looms upon us the temperatures are probably dropping, and moles will be under pressure to survive. By this time it should be obvious to the mole catcher that they are moving to warmer areas, or to lower soil levels, which are also warmer. It is here that the mole's ability to adapt to the conditions of its chosen environment makes it unique: working in tunnels at these lower levels presents the mole with a new predicament, but one that it has evolved to cope with.

We have established that the mole's environment is a sealed, complex network of tunnels of various depths. In such an environment, the levels of oxygen in the atmosphere will obviously fluctuate, dictated by the airflows or air movement in the tunnels, and the amount of exposure to the open air. The control of air is maintained by the mole itself: as I explained in the importance of correct trap placement, the mole acts like a piston so actually moves the air around the tunnels as it travels along, and monitors those levels from information absorbed with its Eimer's organ.

These levels of oxygen, temperature and humidity will vary in many ways; the shallower tunnels will allow fresh air to enter, which will raise the levels, where deeper tunnels will not. The lower levels will therefore have reduced oxygen content, as they may not be replenished from constant mole movement. The amount of air will be further reduced by the mole's respi-

ratory demands. The moles have the capability to survive at these depths in what is termed a hypercapnic environment, where the levels of carbon dioxide are much higher than in the atmosphere above ground. The carbon dioxide will be produced naturally, as exhaled breath contains carbon dioxide, which is produced in our bodies and discharged via the respiratory system. The process of breathing, passing air in and out of the body, and because the environment is confined, will naturally result in the moles' tunnels holding a higher level of carbon dioxide and lower levels of oxygen, the latter believed to be as low as just 6 per cent.

It is because of this exceptional ability to survive in such conditions that the mole can escape the attentions of any marauding weasel. As a comparison, the human body cannot survive in such a hostile atmosphere because it requires a minimum level of oxygen of 16 per cent to sustain life – in normal air there is 20 per cent. We breathe in air at 20 per cent oxygen and breathe out at 16 per cent. Like us, the weasel would be unable to follow the mole down to levels and depths with such low levels of oxygen, allowing the mole an easy escape.

Living creatures that are not adapted for such conditions would soon demonstrate symptoms of hypercapnia, such as elevated blood pressure, panic hyperventilation and convulsions, and which might lead to unconsciousness and even death. The mole can survive as it has the ability to produce bicarbonate. Bicarbonate is an alkaline chemical (buffer) that keeps the pH ('power of hydrogen') of the blood from becoming too acidic. This is especially important for protecting tissue in the central nervous system, where pH changes that too far outside the normal range in either direction could prove disastrous.

The mole has an acute nervous system, so controlling this carbon dioxide by producing bicarbonate is vital for its survival, not just to protect the nervous system but also to control the environmental levels. The mole passes the bicarbonate through the kidneys and out via the urinary tracts, thereby buffering the levels in the tunnels. Bicarbonate in water turns to carbonic acid, and that is the buffering agent for the atmosphere in the confines of the mole's tunnels, and for such low oxygen levels.

The mole also has a remarkable ability to detect drafts: should any fresh levels of air be allowed to enter the tunnel complex, either by the trap operator or from a natural occurrence, the mole will react immediately. Tunnels will be blocked, as any changes in air quality or flow indicate a source of possible danger. The mole controls the levels of oxygen and carbon dioxide in its chosen environment at all times, and this is why the mole catcher's main concern must be to ensure that traps are set correctly, and that coverings are appropriate to the location.

The control of air flows is not always confined to the colder months, and in a dry summer it is not uncommon to find a single molehill surrounded by evidence of shallow raised tunnels because the mole is running spooked. The mole is possibly not up in the shallow tunnels in search of food, but quite the opposite, because dry soils in a hot summer will lack vital food supplies. In fact the food sources will be in those lower levels where moisture is higher, which is clearly another reason why the mole is arduously working some hard soils – it is because it is having to sustain itself for prolonged periods at these lower levels.

It can, and will, return to the shallower tunnels for a breath of fresh air, but working at these lower levels will result in an increased respiratory requirement, so oxygen levels will diminish more quickly, and the labyrinth of deeper tunnels may become deficient in oxygen and therefore hypercapnic. Thus the mole will need to flush the tunnel system with new levels of oxygen at a controlled rate. The single molehill mentioned above will be the result of a central shaft down to the lower levels, and the running spooked, a collection of shallow tunnels that will allow air flows to enter, and

the air pressure and currents passing over the surface of the ground will filter new air into the mole's environment. The mole will then shift the air through the tunnels by creating positive and negative pressures of air using its own body movement. Moles will always control the levels of air in their environment, but at the amount required and only in circumstances when they can do so safely.

November Fog

Regular mornings of frost are not uncommon at this time of the year, but the climate seems to produce more challenges each year, with environmentalists shouting out different reasons for such events. Fog is another variance on the weather that is often experienced in November. It consists of droplets of water suspended in the air: in this winter month with clear skies, the land cools overnight, reducing the ability for the air to retain this moisture, and this will result in condensation or fog to appear.

This saturation occurs close to the surface of the ground, and it will disperse soon after sunrise as much as the sun warms the soil. This will increase the moisture level of the soil in some areas, and is why moles can be found in these, but not in others. Fog can accumulate in both large and small valleys, or in river valleys, and it can persist and remain quite dense as the warmer air often passes over the valley and therefore has no useful effect in dissipating the moisture in the air, and the fog can remain trapped.

For a mole catcher, it is important to consider what the local influences are upon the moles, and when working hills and fields, fog will have a direct effect on the land and therefore on those moles. It may have a freezing effect on the upper horizon (organic layer) when the cold air flows over warm land, so listen to the weather reports for cold fronts coming to your area, and if working the hills, be aware of the effect of the air being blown up and cooling to dampen your working areas. This moisture from changes in warm and cold air is different to every topographical area, but for the observant mole catcher the observation of the combined effects of fog, worm casts and molehills, provides many an answer to the client's questions.

DECEMBER

The work of a mole catcher is not determined by clocking in and out for the daily working shift, or the need to be sitting at a desk at a given time. And although I may not have the comfort of an air-conditioned, centrally heated working environment with fresh coffee on demand, I would not change my office in any way. There have been difficult times due to the rigours of Mother Nature herself, but whatever she decides to present us with, she will have her reasons.

As the days pass in the countdown to the end of the year, as with every year it is time to reflect on the influences that impacted on mole catching in the previous months. The glow and warmth of the home fire provides the perfect place to sit and recall the trials and tribulations of the battles that have gone before, and to contemplate what, if any, changes could or should be made to our mole-catching practice in the forthcoming year.

Whether you are a seasoned mole catcher or new to this fascinating practice, you should recall each small piece of experience gained, and then store it away in your memory. In this one-on-one battle with the mole, it is in fact Mother Nature who decides the level of the playing field when and wherever man and mole confront each other, and with the year not quite over in December, she often has one more trick up her sleeve. It is a month in which you could face every conceivable situation that you have already experienced during the preceding year. It can be mild, cold with rain or snow or stormy, and temperatures can vary from mi-

nus to double figures. It will also be the month when many choose the comfort of their home fire, rather than the call of the mole. However, to a mole catcher who depends on the income he derives from mole catching, December is a tribute to their skill and understanding.

There is a strange comfort in working in the countryside in the dark and cold winter month of December, possibly from the reassurance found in the security and contentment of returning home, and the cheer of the festive atmosphere. Although many people wish for snow for the celebration of the birth of Christ, unless you live in higher altitudes the month often fails to provide – but to the mole catcher working in such locations and under the snow, my thoughts are with you.

Myths and Superstitions

Now I would not consider myself a superstitious person, other than to worry about catching a white mole (*see* below), but I was taught to respect nature, and was told as a boy to observe certain rules, the memory of which remains with me today. For example, never curse the farmer with your mouth full, and never shoot on a Sunday, as everything deserves at least one day off a week. Also, always come home with a bullet or cartridge in your pocket, proof that the last shot you took didn't leave the quarry wounded, and you with no means of resolving the situation. Above all, never take life on Christmas Day. In respect of this therefore, in the days before the 25th, normally traps are removed and any requests for mole removal are delayed until after the big day.

Moles have featured in most of our lives, either in our imagination through childhood stories, or in the reality of devastation – but for many, the mole holds a unique charm fashioned from the mystery surrounding them. Many country folk will tell of myths of moles, and strange tales of a creature rarely seen and never heard, but such tales actually often origi-

Who needs a dentist?

nated from the mole catchers themselves. Who would spread such a rumour, that should a mole successfully tunnel all round a house, then someone from that household was doomed to die? Who was it that people called upon when they were afflicted with toothache? The mole catcher again, because it was claimed that if you were to hang a mole's front paw around your neck, it would relieve the pain, as it would also that of rheumatism.

Beware the White Mole

Witches would use moles and mole parts in spells or curses against others, so to get rid of moles would save people from the attentions of the local witches – so moles had to be removed. However, there is one curse that all those who place a trap to capture or kill a mole deeply respect, and that is, to beware of the white mole. The person who captures the white mole foretells their own death, a myth or legend that any mole catcher will relate in order to deter others from embarking on the task. In fact, I have personally known people who have made such a capture, and unfortunately some are no longer with us, and many have fallen into ill health.

And whether you are a believer on not, should you place a device in the ground to take up battle with a mole, take time to think of this curse and maybe say a little prayer.

As a boy I was told of the white mole, and its portent has been with me ever since; so I wrote this prayer to remind me of the need to be respectful when taking the life of a mole.

The Mole Catchers' Prayer

When I am called from life's hard toil
To lie and rest in the cold damp soil
I will lie in peace when it's my time to go
And lie with friends that were once my foe
What I do, it can be cruel, but I abide by one simple rule
Every trap, set in the run, the check next day is always done
I understand the landowner's plight, the farmer's fear, the gardener's fright
Also of the needs and strain to ensure the task – it is humane
A wanter's trap the tool of death – may leave a captured mole with breath.
So have respect, avoid the curse and check your trap and not your purse
If financial gain is your main aim you might just find you're in the frame
The curse they send for your delight, a single mole that is pure white
So keep in mind your daily check, and not the draw of the payment cheque
So when your call is finally made, before the digger lifts his spade
Before your chosen day has dawn, before those standing by do mourn
Before your ashes have gone cold, even before you have grown old,
Respect the mole and what you do – the next hole dug could be for you

Jeff Nicholls

Mole Colour Variations

White moles do exist, and many claim to have caught the white mole, and boast that they are very much alive and have broken the so-called curse. However, most will not have caught a white mole, but an apricot. Moles come in many shades of colour, normally grey through to black, but the apricot is quite common, and it comes from a pigment deficiency. Cells fail, and this is referred to as leucism, so if you see a leucistic mole it will be apricot in colour. Also the apricot colour may not always cover the whole mole, but may be in patches. There is also a darker colour of apricot, which could be from a mutation in the mole's pigmentation known as erythrochromism: this produces an apricot to reddish colour.

Such coloured moles may not remain that colour, because after a moult they can in fact change to the colours normally associated with the mole. The true white moles of the curse are extremely rare and are albino moles, though just being white does not necessarily make the mole albino – it must pass the eye test to be classified as a true albino, in that the eye must be red. It is quite possible to catch a white mole, but it will have dark eyes, normally a dark blue, and these are another form of leucistic mole. Albinism, although very rare, can be hereditary, with offspring possibly having a combination of genes, thus placing further pressure on the unsuspecting mole catcher.

Referring to moults, the European mole has two moults in the year, in spring and autumn, and it was thought that they possibly had a third – a summer, or intermediate moult. I have not experienced this personally, but talking with other mole catchers around the United Kingdom they have affirmed that they are catching moles in moult at these times of the year, and it perhaps confirms that, like the breeding seasons, the mole's habits are dictated by the climate that prevails in the locations where they are found. So collectively, it would certainly be feasible to assume that some have three moults.

The spring moult depends on the prevailing temperature, and no mole would shed its warm winter coat when the cold remained in the ground; from collating all the information, it seems that the spring moult can be from as early as February to as late as May. Visually, a mole in moult is a strange-looking mole, with areas of thick fur sculpting shapes over the body. The autumn moult normally begins in September, but moles in moult can still be found in as late as this month of December. The shapes made as the fur is exchanged can be clearly seen when the skin is removed from a mole, because on the flesh side the patterns of change are visible, with a black coloration where the new fur is growing.

Moleskins and Pelts

Moleskins were once a sought-after commodity, and have been put to use for thousands of years. The Romans used the fur as clothing, as its thermal capability, comfort and strength is ideal for such a purpose, and of course moleskins have featured as linings and as garments for centuries – and what mole catcher would not have a real moleskin waistcoat? My own was made for me from 260 moleskins, though despite it being a full waistcoat, in that the fur is all round front and back, it did not take the full amount to complete it. The skins had to be graded first to ensure they were of a

Once a sought-after commodity. The pinholes in the moleskins show how they were stretched and dried to fit the size required.

Augustus C. Edwards & Sons,
MANUFACTURING FURRIERS,
16, 17, & 18, HIGH TOWN, HEREFORD.

Are now Buying MOLESKINS, and pay

2/- per doz.
For Best Large Blue-Black Skins, Air Dried in full Winter Fur, properly squared, and free from Black Markings on Skin, and for small Skins equally good in Fur, 1/6 per dozen.

Note.—Skins off-colour (rusty brown at edges) marked with black on the skin side, patchy in fur, changing from winter to summer coat, or badly dried, are of little commercial value. For such skins we pay **6d.** to **1/-** per dozen.

PUT NO SALT, ALUM, OR CHEMICAL PRESERVATIVE ON THE SKINS.

When thoroughly dried, Skins can be kept several weeks. It is cheaper to send several dozens in one parcel by post.

Do not send less than two or three dozen at a time.

This is the Shape to Square and Dry Moleskins.

DIRECTIONS.

Skin the Moles the same day as trapped.

Cut open straight down the centre of the belly.

Draw off the skin.

Stretch out square by hand.

Tack the skin to a board, fur down, by a tack in each corner.

DRY SKINS IN THE OPEN AIR.

DO NOT LET THEM GET WET OR DAMP.

FULL SIZED SKINS SHOULD MEASURE **5** inches long by **4** inches wide.

THE SIZE OF THIS SQUARE.

DO NOT TAKE THE SKINS OFF THE BOARDS UNTIL THEY ARE QUITE DRY AND STIFF.

A. C. E. & Sons remit Postal Orders FOR PARCELS OF SKINS ON THE SAME DAY AS RECEIVED.

A. C. Edwards & Sons are also buyers of other British Skins.

AIR DRIED AS MOLES.

OTTER SKINS at **5/-** to **7/6** each.
WILD CAT SKINS, **6d.** to **9d.** each.
FOX SKINS, **2/6** each, with Brush and Pads.

PINE MARTENS, POLE CATS and SQUIRRELS, but NOT Rabbit or Rat Skins.

Advertisement for the purchase of moleskins, complete with guidance on how to prepare them.

quality suitable for the finished garment. The preferred pelts have always been what are known as 'clears'. The best pelts were the moles' winter coats as these were thicker, being 11–12mm thick in comparison to summer pelts, which were 9–10mm.

The coat on a mole is a collection of three hairs of different length: the fur hair, the intermediate hair and the over hair – the intermediate hair acts as a support, as it is shorter than the fur hair, and the longest hair of the three is the over hair. The intermediate hairs are not so prominent, but the fur and over hairs appear in equal numbers. The long over hairs retain their thickness throughout the length, whereas the fur hairs are whip-like, terminating in a thin point. This is what creates the lack of lay or set in the fur, which enables it to move in any direction and allows the mole complete freedom of movement.

Although the winter clears were the first choice for the fur dealers, all moleskins were considered, and the grades varied. The best clears were the 'super' clear pelted winters, which were the best full-bodied thick pelts with no faults and of a good size; then there were the 'firsts', the clear pelted winter skins, not quite the quality of the 'supers'. 'Seconds' came next, which were clear pelted summer skins, and then came the 'thirds'. These were marked winter and summer skins, or pelts from moles that were in moult; the skins in moult may have been thick, and good skins, but they were not clear in that they were not of a consistent colour or thickness throughout. The last grade were the 'smalls and tainted', and these were sold for plumbers' wipes.

The grading of skins was important as only the best moleskin made it into a garment to merit the work of the furrier. Those of inferior grade were made into tobacco pouches, purses and trimmings. The moleskins were air dried and stretched out to the required size of 5 ×

Full moleskin waistcoat.

many pelts allows for a constant and natural colour throughout the whole garment. Today we would simply dye the fur, and authenticity and accuracy is difficult to find, but I learned that another reason for needing so many skins to make a garment was that the skins were not sewn as a rectangle or squares, but in small hexagonal shapes so that the skins created a fur fabric that moved with the wearer.

Today our moleskin clothes are an imitation man-made fabric, and not as soft to the touch or as tough or warm as real moleskin; but it is no longer fashionable to wear real fur, and I wear my waistcoat with caution.

THE TRUE WANTERS

Traditional mole catchers, the true wanters, whose quarry is exclusively the mole, will continue to be an elusive character, and not just of the fields and lanes but now of the gardens and parks, as the changing face of the country continues. These new characters will be the small important piece of future history that will enable this old traditional skill to continue. These individuals display no greed or swank in what they do, nor do they boast about their achievements, out of respect for the moles they take. The custodians of this knowledge are gifted with this ability, which can only be gained from the discipline taught from the teaching provided by every mole they come across.

You may not wish to become a full member of this élite membership, but I sincerely hope this explanation of a mole catcher's year has educated, enlightened and entertained, and has brought you an appreciation that very few comprehend. From this, I hope now that you will truly understand the term — and that now you know what it is to want, whatever the weather.

4in; the poster for the purchase of moleskins explains the requirements in detail.

The best price is for the winter skins with no black markings on the flesh side. This denotes the best clears, as black markings would show that the mole was in moult at the time of its capture. The smaller best clears fetch the second best price. The Note in the poster states that off-colour skins marked with black on the flesh side, patchy in fur (meaning in moult) and badly dried are of little commercial value, but would be purchased at a reduced rate.

Of those moleskins that went into the making of my waistcoat many were discarded as unsuitable as the large number of skins required were graded for colour as no one wants a patchwork quilt for a coat, and the grading from so

Chapter 4

So You Want to be a Mole Catcher?

So you have been bitten by the mole, and been infected by the strangest feelings of both conflict and compassion that in combination create a respect for the mole that only those who have experienced it will ever fully understand. Whether you are professional or amateur, you will never admit to knowing all there is to know, but I truly believe once bitten, its influence will be with you until your last breath. Needless to say, this has not been a physical bite, but a psychological one, an introduction to the extraordinary existence of one of nature's most timid and secretive soil dwellers.

When I teach people how to catch moles I cannot emphasize enough the importance of attending every lesson, and the lecture will be given by every target mole that you will be fortunate enough to have some level of conflict with. Throughout your mole-catching career it is the mole that will be your tutor, and you will always remain the scholar.

Catching a mole is not actually difficult if you follow some simple rules, and these have been explained in the previous section, the mole catcher's year, but let us now look at them in more detail so we are competing on a level playing field.

EARTH IMPLEMENTS

We have referred to the tools the mole catcher might use in the course of the mole-catching year, and many will have their own favourites – and if it works for them, then there is no need for change. Let us now look more closely at

these items, and why and how they are used in the removal of unwanted moles.

The Mole Probe

The first tool that anyone wishing to become a mole catcher will need, is something to locate and determine the mole's underground tunnels. The mole catcher will have calculated where the mole is likely to be from his local knowledge, and from the evidence of its working in the locality. From the position and pattern of the molehills, and the possible line

The diameter of your probe is more important than you may think.

of travel because of features providing natural drip, and the impact of flora, use and the weather, the mole catcher will have immediately decided where to place his chosen device. Now he needs to pinpoint the exact position of the tunnel, with minimal damage and as little disturbance as possible so as not to alert the target mole to this intrusion – the more damage you do to the mole's environment, the more it will do to yours, or worse, the client's.

Minimizing the damage can be achieved by the size or diameter of the tool you use to puncture the mole's world. Rods that are too thick will cause unnecessary damage to the mole's tunnel, and there is no reason to use a rod that is any more than 10mm in diameter. With use and practice the mole probe, as it is termed, becomes an extension of the mole catcher's arm, enabling him to feel a path through the soil. The probe need not be too long, but also not so short that the user is bent over it – constant use of a short probe will certainly result in backache. With the handle fitted and the probe held in an upright position, its ideal length would be from 6in (150mm) above your knee to the ground.

Having a probe in proportion to your height means it will be comfortable to use, as you will be slightly bent over; the initial penetration of the probe into the soil will be made by straightening the arm, which is then assisted by the upper body leaning over and adding weight to the movement downwards. With this extra bodyweight the probe's entry into any tunnel is felt immediately with the sudden rapid drop or 'give' as the probe breaks through its roof. With a probe of the correct size, shallow tunnels that are less than 6in (150mm) below the surface are felt immediately just when the arm is straightened, with little if any structural damage to the runs.

I prefer the wooden file-type handles for ease and comfort in use, and would advise avoiding a T-shaped handle as this style encourages force rather than precision.

The mole probe is a key part of the mole catcher's armoury, and once conversant with its use and feel, he will be able to interpret the information it discloses almost instinctively. With practice, stones, roots, voids and changes in the soil are all revealed as the mole probe tells the story of what lies below.

Hand Trowels

Physically entering into the mole's environment must be done as precisely and cautiously as when using the mole probe. Therefore the choice of implement again must be fit for purpose so the task can be carried out effectively, but with as little damage to the tunnel as possible. This cannot be achieved with long-handled tools, so a hand utensil is the preferred choice, and a garden trowel is ideal. This should be a trowel with a flat straight blade and of quality steel, which will allow it to be sharpened and honed on abrasive stones.

The flat blade allows for precise use and so better trap placement.

The blade should be sharp, as it must cut into the ground, and not rip its way in. Moles are found in a variety of soils and locations, in soil that may be light or heavy, and under grass that may be short and tended or long and thick. The preferred trowel must cope with all possible soil types, and one with a sharp, flat, straight edge will do the job asked of it except in the heaviest of soils; in these, a Japanese garden trowel would be best as its construction allows for more leverage. The blade forms the tang, which enters firmly into the wooden handle, and the thick steel blade takes all the force required to prise out heavy clay soils, where thinner-bladed trowels might bend.

From its blade width the Japanese garden trowel resembles a large knife in appearance, but it is a garden tool, so if you are looking to purchase one, source it as a trowel. Despite the lack of width in the blade, it must be an addition to any mole catchers' equipment, as when times get sticky it will come into its own.

Modern trowels may look the part with their rubber soft-touch handles, but many are just not suitable – this one comes complete with a curved blade.

The mole catcher will have to work in a range of soils, and for clay soils, many will prefer longer-handled tools, but the problem with these is that you can't work up close when installing the chosen trap. I advocate getting up close and personal with what you are doing when cutting, entering and placing any device for the capture of a mole, and this will mean kneeling on the ground and looking closely at what you are doing, if you are to carry out the procedure correctly. Long-handled tools distance the operator from the task, and this can result in simple mistakes being made – even though at this point they may seem an easier option, you still have to kneel down to complete the task.

Never cut corners when considering your personal choice for the hand trowel: refrain from running to the garden centre, builders' merchants, and browsing the internet, because your ideal trowel is waiting for you in the antique shop.

The Mole Runner

I have described this tool already, and it is not always necessary to use one, however if you do, it can often make the difference between catching the mole and maybe not. Any countryman

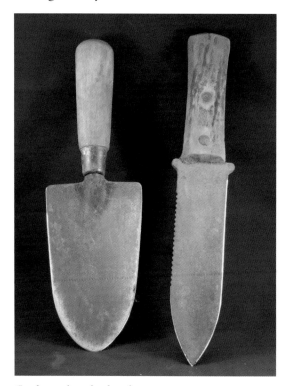

Good trowels make the job easier.

will tell you that mole runs are always smooth, so you must also leave the run smooth, as the mole expects to find it. It is amazing how frequently this is overlooked.

The mole will certainly smooth the tunnel by its movement through them, and it is almost impossible not to cause some damage to the tunnel when we enter to place our trap – the sharpest of trowels will cut a fine edge, but soil will undoubtedly be left as spoil somewhere in the process. The hands will be plunged into the shaft, and soil pulled from the darkness into the light, followed by tapping and prodding with a reversed T-bar gas dibber, the round head of the handle at the end of a long bar etching patterns and shaping the base to a basin. Those without such a tool will compress the tunnel floor with the hand, and in the only way possible, which is with the back of the hand, resulting also in the natural shape of the hand and another basin. The mole runner completes the smooth

The mole runner.

base without any force or tapping; it removes the guesswork, and leaves the tunnel as close to how the mole would have left it.

The secret is in the weight, as the body of the runner is made from industrial nylon and the length and thickness are such that it requires little pressure. The small wooden handle prevents excessive force from the way it is held in the fingers, to avoid creating a basin shape to the tunnel floor. It is inserted into the shaft cut for the device, and merely rocked gently from side to side, moving it along the tunnel slightly to ensure an even coverage of the base. It should only be allowed to enter into the tunnel a little way at each end to join the smoothing with the existing tunnel. Remember, if the entry has been made with a sharp blade then the result will be a clean, smooth cut so there should be little spoil actually inside the mole's tunnel at either end.

I stress again, never poke anything up into or along the mole's tunnels: the damage you cause might only be minimal, but it will be enough to alert the mole to change. The mole runner just smoothes the tunnel in the same way that the mole would in its everyday movement – you are only smoothing the tunnel to allow the air pressures and flows to remain as the mole expects them to be. This is the reason for not creating a basin shape or changing any direction of travel, as the air flows and pressure will travel ahead of the moving mole, and it will detect such changes and undoubtedly its response will be to pack the area with soil.

CUTTING TOOLS

Cutting tools are included here because at some time you will need to cut something in your work, and in relation to mole catching, this is most likely to be roots. Obstructions from roots, either from plants, shrubs or trees, is something that mole catchers have to deal with on numerous occasions. The mole likes nothing more than the sanctuary of tree roots as a roof for a tunnel, because not only do they provide a path to follow to moist areas, but a solid roof often prevents any predator gaining access to that tunnel.

The roots when thin can be cut, and garden secateurs are a good choice when they can access the shaft and there is enough room to make the thickness of the cut. When the shaft is deeper, access is limited and hand-held secateurs take up the whole of the shaft, which makes cutting the offending roots difficult, even if the cutters are held between fingers on both hands. In the deeper runs, a good large knife is best, the sort that was once permitted to be proudly worn by boy scouts and countrymen everywhere. A stout handle with a good grip is needed, as the hands are often wet and slippery, and the all-important blade should be a minimum of 6in (150mm).

The sheath knife is best for this purpose, as it can be slid down the side of the shaft, and as it makes contact with the offending root it slices it off neatly and flush with the side of the shaft. The knife should be kept sharp, and the large blade will be capable of removing the thicker roots with a few cuts and not damage the shaft; a blunt knife will rock the root and cause damage.

TRAP MARKERS

The importance of marking where you have placed your traps must never be overlooked, as you are responsible for any incidents that may arise from your actions, and the placement of a device that will capture or harm must not be undertaken lightly. Often the location of a trap is best kept secret, as to publicise its position could encourage tampering or theft. It is possible to disguise the location if the site has been covered correctly, so that the only chance of the trap being revealed would be if the site were examined closely or exposed by accident. Recollecting the trap position is often quite easy for the mole catcher, as from their scrutiny

of the area they will be reminded of where they placed it from their initial assessment. However, in areas where more than a few traps have been placed it may be necessary to visibly mark the positions.

A few pebbles or stones, or a simple slice of turf removed in the construction of the covering can suffice, but in operational areas such as agricultural land where machinery is working it will be necessary to mark the locations prominently. Hazel is the preferred choice for this; I call it the forgiving tree, as it never fails to provide, and has always been a prominent part of the British working countryside. If left alone, hazel can grow for eighty years; however, if it is cut and coppiced it can survive for hundreds of years. The thatcher, hurdle maker, furniture maker and gardeners all used the produce from the hazel tree, as did the traditional mole catchers. The old mole catchers never had reason to mark their trap positions as they rarely left them, but if they needed a suitable timber they would choose hazel or willow.

I like to think that they would have used the humble hazel in the same way that we do today. I cut hazel whips to manageable lengths of approximately 2ft (90cm), and paint one end white for easy identification. Pushed into the soil they provide a perfect marker for others to avoid, such as other land workers, tractor drivers, and anyone you wish to inform not to trample over the area. It is easy to source these simple but effective markers, and time spent in the hazel copse is time never wasted.

However, hazel has its other friends, and rabbits, deer and sheep all are attracted to hazel, and like chewing it either for enjoyment or for food. This can sometimes result in the markers being pulled from the ground, and therefore indication of the trap positions being lost, so where it is known that such companions are to be found it is best that hazel is exchanged for nylon. The modern substitute may cost a little extra, but it is not liked by livestock so they will ignore it. The white nylon markers with their bright red painted tops do stand out from the crowd, and certainly come into their own in times of snowfall, and where and whenever they are used they do present that impression of professionalism that is expected in this modern world.

SHARPENING STONES

I carry two grades of stone for hand sharpening the items I carry with me when out mole catching: a rough cigar stone for maintaining the blades of hand trowels, and a smooth flat stone for the knife. Any cutting tool needs to be as sharp as possible at all times – it is the blunt blade that cuts the user, not the sharp one.

MISCELLANEOUS

Every mole catcher will have a few miscellaneous items they feel are necessary for their work in their mole-catching kit. Personally I would include a pair of small wire cutters, pliers, a ball of string, and the most important two items, a towel and a nailbrush. The wire cutters are carried because I am slightly superstitious, in that if I discover a trap has not operated correctly or for any reason, and a target mole is found to be still alive after its capture, then I will cut through the trap loops so that it can never be used again, as I feel the device is unlucky. And if you ever have reason to discard a tunnel trap, then always remove the retaining bars, as these can be lost so it is useful to have a few spare.

The pliers are for those times when a trap may be slightly damaged, and they can be used as a hand-held vice to make repairs. The string has many applications, but its main use is to leave proof of mole removal, for those who require confirmation that the task has been completed before they make payment. The target mole is hung somewhere out of reach of predators, and also out of the sight of those who are more sensitive to the work of a mole catcher. Yes, this practice has been accepted

for hundreds of years, but sadly today it can be frowned upon as disrespectful – and in truth, I do agree with this side of the argument; but it has become almost compulsory as a result of some deceitful practitioners dishonestly claiming they have removed moles when in fact they haven't.

The nailbrush helps scrub the mud from your nails under the garden tap, and the towel mops up the mess it makes in your vehicle.

THE MOLE CATCHER'S BAG

Having constructed or obtained all the items or equipment required for work it is important to not just to keep them safe, but ready to hand when required. I designed my mole catchers' bag for my personal needs, and although you may not have the service for what I use, a bag is ideal. It should be strong, large enough to carry all that you have need of conveniently, and be fit for purpose. The old postman's bag, paperboy satchel or canvas game bag would once have served as the perfect solution, but these no longer seem to be available. The large bag will not only cart round the tools of your trade, but will have room for the devices of capture, too.

My bag will hold everything as well as fifty tunnel traps, and if someone tells you that they will need more traps than this in their exploits, they are either working a large area or they lack the skill and knowledge to encounter the mole. If you are working large areas then another bag will help, but you will soon find that loading yourself like a packhorse will in time cause wear and tear on the joints and back, and the will to trudge over heavy ground. The bag over the shoulder is comfortable, and portrays your professional appearance and attitude towards your work.

If possible, separate your hand items from the traps, as even a trap that is not under tension can become a hazard to hands as you rummage to remove one on a cold and frosty morning. Always ensure that traps are never returned to the bag under tension. I have a compartment in the main body of my bag to keep tools and traps apart, though you could simply insert a box into a bag for the purpose. The probes hang through rings sewn on the end, and front pockets hold the smaller items – and when the bag is laid down next to the trap positions, the large flap that covers all can be knelt on to save your knees from the damp and cold. Trap markers wait in a quiver for use and everything is protected from tampering and contamination.

There are canvas and nylon manufacturers who can provide a bag, and you can ask them to add some personal touches to make your working day even easier – or you could always find a plastic bucket!

Everything you need and close to hand.

Chapter 5

Modern Mole Traps

Ask most people who use traps to control moles how they work, and many will say that they break the mole's back or crush it, or maybe squeeze it, while to some it will be of little interest. The doubt often comes from not really understanding the fate they intend to administer to the target mole, or the information provided by the internet, that all-perceptive source of knowledge.

No mole trap currently available has the strength or the ability to break a mole's spine, nor does it have the power to crush or squeeze it to death. These claims have come about as a result of misguided, insincere sales and marketing, or misinterpretation of what is termed 'approved'. The truth is that from the very character of the surroundings, there will always be a level of uncertainty on the part of the person responsible for setting the trap as to how effective and humane the mole's capture will be.

It is vital that we understand how these implements of affliction operate in the way they eliminate life so that not just those who use them today, but also those who will use them in the future, may ensure that any modifications and changes in practice progress for the better, so that this traditional craft will always remain a part of the British countryside. Every trap that claims to kill a target mole uses a spring, of which there are only two types: a flat spring or a wire shape. The flat spring consists of two flat plates of steel that oppose each other to provide the power, and a wire shape is a coil of wire that will store the energy until it is released.

These types of spring can be found in an array of traps, both old and new, that are used against moles.

It is therefore essential that any trap operates correctly, cleanly and as humanely as possible in order for the chosen spring to be fit for purpose. It must provide enough energy to administer the necessary force immediately upon release to deliver an instant and irreversible level of unconsciousness. Many traps for mole control that are currently available do not, but to many people this fact is of little importance because the trap is in the ground and out of sight, and therefore out of mind.

The very fact that the traps are placed below ground immediately places extreme demands upon them. Metal will be subject to attack from moisture, and despite protective processes such as galvanized surfaces, within a short period of time the trap will yield to the effects of the environment. The springs will become weaker and less effective over time as a result of being under constant strain and tension in the mole's demanding habitat.

Also some styles of mole trap require that in operation, parts of the trap must thrust through soil that has been back filled, which again will place extra effort on the spring when it is released. Often in manufacture springs are simply not fit for purpose, and lack the ability to provide sufficient force; and another main factor is the mole catcher's skill in placing the trap for use.

Let us look at some of the mole traps available and how they operate, so that you can make your own comparisons as to choice and capability.

THE SCISSOR OR PINCHER TRAP

Still available, the scissor trap remains the mole trap that most people can identify with, and can still be found rusting in garden sheds until it is needed. These traps have not changed much since their conception in Victorian times, except for some twentieth-century modifications such as a choice between flat springs and wire shape springs – and occasionally serrated jaws, which must be a topic for concern. Other than that it remains very much the same, and I affectionately refer to it as the lazy man's trap.

The trap is placed in the ground with its arms held up in full view of all, and to check it, all that is required is to glance at it occasionally to see if these arms have spread. So time passes by, and the traps remain with arms aloft

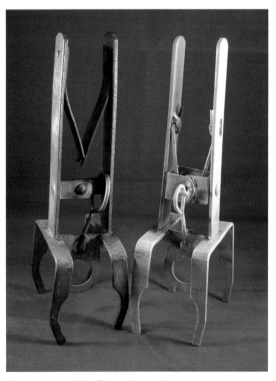

Scissor traps with a flat and wire shape spring.

until the day comes when they are pulled from the soil to reveal that the mole has backfilled them – which would have been apparent if a proper inspection had been made, and the trap repositioned. It is not possible to be lazy when mole catching, as traps must be inspected to determine exactly what the target mole is up to. Scissor traps can certainly imply from their soldier-like appearance across the lawn that the mole catcher is working and on the case, when the truth is that the only cohort working are the moles.

The advantage of using this style of mole trap for many was the ease of inspecting them, because the prominent part of the trap remains above the ground surface. However, the action of the trap is such that the arms must be able to spread if the trap is operated. This maximum span is 4in (100mm), which prevents the trap being set in the correct location in the main tunnels of the depth normally used by moles when travelling to and fro, or in any tunnel greater than 6in (150mm) deep.

The mole is actually captured when the jaws close once the centrally positioned mumble pin – often referred to as a plate, but let's keep tradition alive – is knocked out as it enters. On average the distance between the jaws of all scissor traps when set for use is approximately 2in (50mm), and never any wider. This would seem sufficient for a mole to pass through – but that is all, it is sufficient, and a large buck will undoubtedly contact the open jaws with its body as it enters. This means that when the jaws are released they will only have minimal, if any, travel prior to contacting the mole's body: there is no actual strike, only a closure, and it is around the strongest part of its body, the shoulders.

Its immediate reaction is to tense these muscles, and sadly the mole can endure the power of the scissor trap for a considerable time. Because there is no actual strike on the mole, there is no level of sudden shock, and the wrestle between the target mole and the trap springs can be prolonged. The springs will eventually win when the mole succumbs to fatigue, dehydration and starvation, the more fortunate moles being those that are monitored and despatched by a watchful mole catcher.

These scissor traps lack the force to impart any level of unconsciousness, and certainly will not cause any form of injury other than to restrain the captured mole; claims that the mole is despatched or that these traps will kill the target mole are only made by those who spend very little time and effort inspecting their traps. They are certainly not a trap to consider if trapping in areas where discretion is required, and personally are not a choice of mine – but everyone has their favourite, and to many the ease of use and inspection appeals to the more indolent mole catcher.

THE GRIPPER TRAP

The gripper trap has appeared in the United Kingdom again after a short break, having travelled across the English Channel from Europe,

predominantly the Netherlands. It has some trade names that are used to refer to it, but in essence it is another form of the scissor trap but with a longer span between the jaws and a shorter length in the arms. More recently, some gripper traps have had extensions added to the arms, ostensibly to improve their operation by providing a better mechanical advantage to opening the jaws – however, this is no more than a marketing guise, where a more powerful spring is said to help those with a weaker wrist or grip. Claims that the power in the spring will break the spine of a target mole are without proof, and personal tests have not substantiated such claims.

The 7kg wire shape spring in the form of a coil of wire set along the length of the trap does have some noticeable force, but this force is required so the trap can operate successfully when it is in use. This trap is designed primarily for placement in light soils, and is set in the tunnel at an angle of forty-five degrees so that the mumble pin is held in the vertical position – although the gripper trap can still be positioned

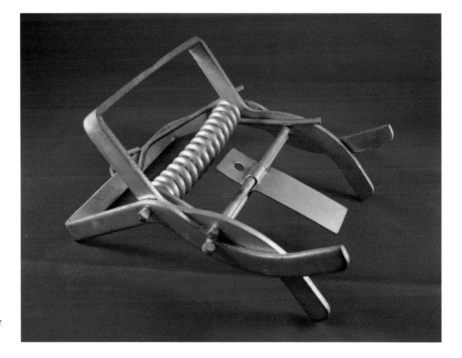

The modern gripper-style trap showing the full wire shape coil spring.

so that the mumble pin is horizontal. With the mumble pin in the vertical position and the trap at an angle, when the target mole enters the trap site, the trap jaws upon release will close with one jaw travelling down and one jaw upwards from below so as to strike the mole as claimed and break its spine. If set with the mumble pin in the horizontal position, the jaws will close around the mole from the side as it enters, as with the scissor trap – so claims that it will break the target mole's spine are quite unfounded, as it will close around the mole at the point of the shoulders.

The power of the spring at 7kg is required not to impart a force upon the mole directly, because correctly used, these traps are placed in a tunnel and then backfilled with soil by the operator. Reinstating the damaged tunnel the target mole will dig through, dislodge the mumble pin, and release the trap jaws. The spring strength is required so it can travel through this backfilled soil; lighter soils will offer less resistance than a heavier soil, but any velocity lost in the trap's operation as a result of friction must reduce the efficiency of any strike.

It must also be considered that when set in light soils and backfilled, once this soil is wet from any rainfall it will become heavier, and this must impede the force in the trap's operation. In addition, the single mumble pin is fully dependent upon where it is positioned by the operator between the jaws as to where it will strike any mole and does not compensate for the size or direction of any mole entry.

There is only a small area in a mole's spine where a strike could be made, which is directly behind the muscle group in the shoulders. To make a strike at this point on a mole could not be definite, nor can the force of the trap be guaranteed to break the spine, which will result in the trap only restraining the target mole. Front paw capture will occur with any further movement in the soil as the mole attempts to reinstate the tunnel.

TRAPLINE TRAP

Imported from the United States of America, this trap resembles those metal puzzles that you could get in a Christmas cracker. The market-

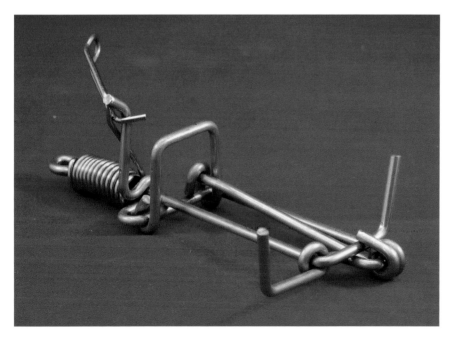

The trapline trap.

ing may claim it provides an 'instant' kill, but the truth may be different when compared with the manufacturer's own instructions, as this trap must be fixed with a cord to the eye behind the spring and secured to a small stake to prevent the mole from dragging the trap back and down the tunnel. Clearly this is not a kill trap, but a restraining trap, which upon release will result in the mole being caught like a fish on a hook. Struggling to free itself from the grip of the two tines that will close around its body, the mole is subjected to unnecessary suffering until it dies from exhaustion, dehydration and starvation.

The manufacturer's description of the trap states that it is equipped with tines that will close around the mole, and this assertion places further reservations on the use of this trap against a British mammal, as tines are described in the English dictionary as being found on forks to 'stab, impale or pierce' – and under the current regulations in the United Kingdom it is an offence to stab, impale or pierce any animal.

You will need to use two traps, as this trap can only operate from one direction. Its small size certainly refutes any claims of any level of strike on a target mole's body, as the travel distance between the tines in the open and closed positions will not be sufficient to inflict any level of irreversible unconsciousness. The position of the wire square as a mumble pin is fixed so that the mole releases the spring with its face. This only permits the tines to enclose around the mole depending on the size of the mole that has operated the release, in the lower or rear areas of its body and held from the side.

PUTANG TRAP

The Putang trap is very similar in use and operation to the trapline trap. It is imported from France, and consists of a single bent wire shaped to form a spring that is opened and held by a square wire shape until its release by the target mole. These are not new, and another French mole trap of similar design, the Arouze trap, can also still be found.

As with the trapline trap, these also require staking down, and two are needed per tunnel. The disturbing point of these traps is that they

The Putang and Arouze trap with the setting tool used to hold the jaws apart prior to positioning the wire square.

are permitted for sale in the United Kingdom, and whether they are humane or not seems to be of little concern either to those who sell them or to those who use them. People seem quite happy to accept that these two trap types, for some unknown reason, may be placed and then left almost indefinitely, possibly because they think that if they are staked down, then they must be safe and secure. The wire shape employed as a mumble pin for the release must be tied to the trap so it is not lost in operation, and the advice is that the string used should be long enough to maintain the same point of release every time it is used.

At first this may seem a good recommendation, but the length of the string cannot compensate for any difference in size of the target mole, so the point of contact in striking a larger mole will be different to that in striking a smaller mole. The best point to strike the mole is said to be just behind the head, so as the jaws close around the neck, the force is sufficient to cause asphyxiation after a short time – but it is questionable if the jaws connect with the mole in the correct area every time.

Any new trap should be left to weather to allow the metal to tarnish and rust, because then the wire square will not slip but will remain firm until the mole dislodges it; obviously prior to any weathering there is a risk of premature release.

The advice to peg the trap down immediately casts doubt on its capability, and it is essential that both the trapline and Putang traps are inspected several times over short periods when they are used for mole control.

LIVE CATCH TRAP

Unfortunately these traps may still be found lurking around in garden sheds after their rise in popularity in the late twentieth century amongst people who would see no harm come to the mole, but whose preference was to capture and release it into another person's land.

However, there is no reason to imprison a mole alive unless it is for study or research, when the welfare and duty of care for that captured animal is completely catered for.

To many, these live traps were considered as an alternative and humane method for mole control – but in fact this could not be further from the truth. The trap is a plastic tube with a simple metal flap as a door at each end, allowing for entry but no escape. Any unfortunate mole that enters is immediately confined, and its future entirely depends on the clemency of the person responsible for its placement.

Designed for amateur use, the mole would be incarcerated alive until the trap was inspected, which in respect of any live capture or restraining trap, is required to be at least twice a day; however, there is no such direction or advice on any of the packaging or instructions supplied with these traps. Thus the stressed, starving, dehydrated mole would be left until such an inspection was made, entirely at the discretion of the trap user, fitted into the everyday hustle and bustle of his own life. The mole found to be still alive in its plastic tube of terror was then subjected to the next part of its traumatic journey to possible survival.

It would be taken to fields afar, and with or without permission would be tipped into an environment that might, or might not, have the capability to support it. To many, releasing it into an apparently suitable environment might seem the answer to its survival – *except* that it always has been, and still remains, an offence to release an animal into a location whose carrying capacity you know nothing about, and equally its chance of survival. A mole must source two-thirds of its bodyweight in food per day, and it must work and dig to find if any suitable food is available – so in short, the starving, stressed, dehydrated mole will probably die before it finds its first meal.

Many will release their mole into an area that may have evidence of moles present, in the pretext that it can share the rest of its days with its friends – but we know the outcome of such an action. These live catch traps have been removed from sale, and the government has advised that any mole captured alive must be humanely despatched – so why would anyone wish to put a mole through such unnecessary suffering, especially in the mistaken belief that what they are doing is humane.

THE HALF–BARREL OR TUNNEL TRAP

The half-barrel trap is, without reservation, the ideal trap for the British mole catcher. The in-stinctive thoughts of a mole catcher led to its invention, and it has served us well for a hundred years, and with changes to improve it, could continue to do so for the next hundred. I have already described the half-barrel trap in detail, and how I place it under normal working conditions. Because of its compact design it can be located in any depth of tunnel, and its independent operation enables a double catch of two moles, one at each end. It is versatile in that it may also be used sideways, so can be slipped under obstructions, but its main feature is that it is the most humane trap currently available used for moles.

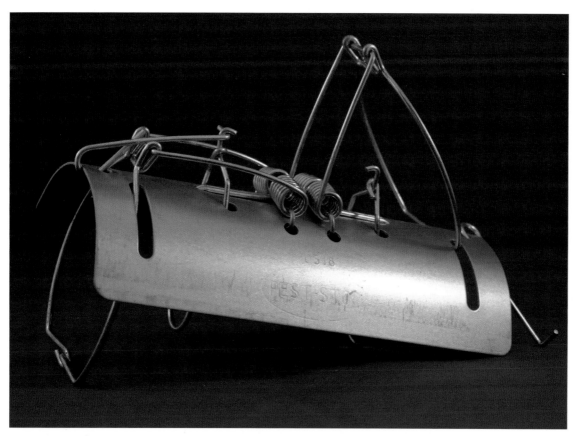

The modern half-barrel mole trap with a batch number to ensure the quality is not compromised.

Chapter 6

The Power Behind Mole Catching

You should have very little trouble with the traps you use providing they are fit for purpose, and in good working order. Many will advise various tricks and tips to make the device more efficient or less detectable by the target mole – for instance, they say that on the half-barrel trap the length on the hook needs to be cut smaller, as it can snag on the trap loop as it is released. But no, it doesn't, unless the quality of your chosen trap is poor, and operated by a spring that is weak and therefore slower in its action.

If the spring is less than 6kg in strength, sometimes on release it doesn't throw the retaining bar up and out of the path of the rising trap loop fast enough. This results in the hook on the retaining bar catching the top of the loop, thus stopping it from achieving its full travel. This can happen with any half-barrel trap that has been set incorrectly, such as when the roof covering is allowed to contact these trap parts upon release, or if a heavy covering of soil rather than a light sprinkling has been placed over the top of it. This can result in the mole being unintentionally captured alive in a kill trap, which is an offence under the current animal welfare acts.

Soil can be a problem to the gripper traps when they are set and require backfilling with soil, as heavy soil will also impede the travel speed of the closing jaws. A quality gripper trap may have a 7kg power spring fitted, but when surrounded by soil it poses the question whether this is enough. It has become accepted that if the spring requires some force to depress

it, then it must be suitable, but what is resistance to compression to one person may not be to another. It has even been suggested that to test if a half-barrel trap is of acceptable quality you should depress the loop down slowly and insert two fingers into the loop and then allow the trap to grasp these fingers. If by holding the trap, you can slip the fingers out then it is of inferior quality, but if the fingers are held firm then it is acceptable.

This very unacceptable means of classifying the ability of a trap to carry out its task effectively highlights the lack of appreciation as to how it operates to capture a target mole. Apart from the half-barrel trap, all other spring traps used against moles operate on a system of closure from the side, with complete disregard to any direct point of contact on the target mole. The opinion is that providing it closes around the mole then the job is complete, and it will asphyxiate the mole eventually. We know this to be incorrect, but the truth of how the springs in mole traps operate has eluded many people for a long time.

SPRINGS IN TRAPS

Let us therefore look more closely at the springs, the power behind the force that is the core of trap operation, and understand what goes into a spring. Commercially available mole traps employ two types of spring, as explained earlier: a flat spring or a wire shape. Flat springs are primarily found on scissor traps, with wire shapes foremost on all others. To many, a spring is just a piece of wire that when depressed, bent or stretched, will return to its original position when it is released. In fact, a spring is a store of mechanical energy, which is used to apply or absorb force. In relation to mole traps, springs are used directly to apply force towards the target mole. This is their duty and is all they carry out, so it is important to understand what the springs may be in your trap choice.

Torsion Springs

The favourite spring is the torsion spring, either singly or in doubles. Examples of this are the single torsion spring found in the gripper trap, and the double torsion springs used in the half-barrel trap. The torsion spring exerts a radial force or a rotational movement, as opposed to a vertical or horizontal movement. The spring applies torque from its physical dimensions and the deflection. The torsion spring is a coil with two legs, and the spring rate is determined by the number of coils and the tightness.

The spring rate is the amount of force it takes for the arms on a torsion spring, or the compression on a coil spring, to travel 1 inch, or in metric 1 millimetre. The measurements are now calculated in kilograms, but previously were once pounds per force per inch (lbf/in), or Newton's per millimetre (N/mm). Spring torque is calculated for the specific purpose with the degrees of deflection multiplied by the spring rate, and requires accurate measurements to be efficient.

Those old mole catchers who at one time powered their devices with a simple bender stick, certainly considered that the number of sticks used, and the lengths of them, were an important factor in the capture of moles. Those who boast on media channels about producing home-made traps for moles should reflect on what they create, and judge with honesty as to how humane they are. The spring force must be fit for purpose, and in the modern spring, even the diameter of the wire affects the spring's

rate of travel. Examine any mole trap today employing a torsion spring, and you will see the legs and a central coil. The legs as found on the gripper style of trap and some scissor traps will be of equal length. Others as found on the half-barrel trap will have a longer leg, which operates the trap loop in relation to the other, slightly shorter leg that is fixed to the trap body.

Should you compare these two torsion springs it is easy to believe that the larger coiled spring found on the larger gripper trap should provide more force or power than those smaller torsion springs that supply the power to the compact half-barrel trap. This is the science of springs, as the smaller torsion springs actually provide only slightly less energy, but from the design of the trap, can direct that force to the target mole at the point where it will cause the most efficient damage.

Big is not necessarily better when it comes to torsion springs, because it is all down to that spring science again. By increasing or decreasing the wire diameter, you can change the strength. Increasing the wire diameter will increase the strength, as decreasing the wire diameter weakens the strength. This happens because the larger diameter wire makes the springs coils tighter, which will reduce the spring index. Spring index is the correlation between the mean diameter of a spring and the wire diameter of a spring. The diameter of the coils influences the force, so if the coils are tighter they are said to have a smaller index that gives you more force, and if the coils are larger, the spring will be weaker.

It does not stop here, because you can also adjust the number of coils. In a torsion spring, if you reduce the number of coils working together to provide that torque, so the spring will be stronger, but will be under more stress. If you add coils, it will increase elasticity: it is all about the correct mixture for the task. The torsion springs on the half-barrel trap are set in pairs, a pair to power each trap loop, and these are a left- and a right-handed torsion spring that work jointly with a combined number of twelve coils. The quality half-barrel trap has springs of a tighter coil made from a wire diameter producing an almost equal force to that of the larger single torsion spring on the gripper trap.

The Spring Travel

The next consideration is the spring travel, and a torsion spring's travel is determined by the length and position of the legs. The torsion spring has two legs and a central coil, and travels in a rotational path: if you consider the position of the hands on a clock, then the torsion spring also has its legs set in what is termed the free position, like a position of time on a clock. As an example, imagine that one leg is pointing to twelve and the other to the seven. If you were to move the leg pointing to the seven in a rotational direction clockwise to the leg pointing to the twelve, it will travel, and wind and twist the coils to produce a torque as the coils will want to force this leg back to the original position at seven. This is the spring travel, known as the degree of deflection.

Depending on how a spring is constructed these legs can be set at different positions and have different lengths. On the half-barrel trap the length of the torsion spring legs are one longer than the other, with the longer leg attached to the trap loop. The shorter leg attached to the trap body again affects the calculations of spring rate to provide for the full efficiency of the spring.

The Scissor Trap

The most common of mole traps remains the scissor trap, as the mechanical advantage over the spring from the legs allows the trap to be set with confidence that it will not grasp the hand in any effort to disable a finger. The trend for mole control may have changed, but still the scissor trap sells as well as any other device. It may be that the elderly still recall their presence when in their youth, when the gardener had one, and the gamekeeper and the father. The truth is that these scissor traps have changed little since their conception, and the springs today remain much as they were then. More common were the flat springs, but more recently the wire shape springs have been used as the provider of force.

Force is a term I use loosely, because it must be said that these traps were originally being made when trap manufacturing was at its height and vermin control was at a premium. But at that time there was no heed to the mole's welfare or concern to its suffering, and the only thing of interest was the prize to be had. Maybe for the modern day user, the same remains today, as these scissor traps produced for retail have the same spring strengths as they did then, and only questionable modifications have appeared, such as serrations cut into jaws or an additional spike.

Single Torsion Springs

The trapline trap employs a single torsion spring, and the suppliers stated, 'They were designed through trial and error, and not with the benefit of any real understanding of spring design equations.' This would explain the lack of strike in the trap, and combined with its inappropriate fixed point for the body strike, is clearly a device that is not fit for purpose.

The Putang and Arouze mole traps use just a single torsion spring, a continuous piece of wire coiled to form a spring, and no specification has been obtained on the mechanical energy this spring provides. The concern when a Putang trap is employed is the point of contact with the target mole, as there are no allowances to determine the point of body strike from any movement of the target mole at the point of trap release. The position of the mumble pin is at the discretion of the operator, and although it can be repeated with a determined length of cord used to retain the mumble pin upon release, it cannot allow for a mole that raises its head at the point of release of the spring, or the release is made with a paw, resulting in an unpleasant capture. The strength in the Putang trap spring may seem forceful, but it lacks sufficient spring travel to strike a fatal blow, and clearly relies on a prolonged retention of the target mole to kill it.

When asked how to judge the power of a spring, a United Kingdom importer and supplier replied: 'If you trap a finger it hurts, and you can't remove it without a setting tool or pliers.' Clearly, concern for the welfare of any target mole is lacking in both the Putang and trapline mole traps, and the question is – should these devices be a choice for either the professional or the amateur working to control moles? Those who either sell or use any form of device that indiscriminately inflicts unnecessary suffering must question their attitude towards animal management.

A DEVICE FIT FOR PURPOSE

Whether a device is fit for purpose is down to the operator, as with no current approval for mole traps, any contraption can be offered as a mole trap, promoted in the media, and sold for use, and sadly alleged adversaries of animal management often support both the experts and the products. The issue of any type of trap being unfit for purpose may, to many, be a contentious point, as to what is perfectly acceptable to one person will be unacceptable to another. Some people will ignore best practice or spurn regulations, sadly more so in relation to involvement with and management of animals than in any other topics.

Mole control is no different, and many who employ the use of traps will look for the easy way, favouring those that are easy and uncomplicated to operate or position. Often methods or devices that are simple to use are so for the very reason that they are not fit for purpose. The original mole catchers had simple traps that required knowledge and expertise to position, skill that they gathered from experience, which simplified the task. It returns us to that old adage 'It is easy when you know how', though today the answers are found on the internet, and for many it provides all that is required, whether it is accurate advice or not.

Chapter 7

Mole-Catching Problems and Solving Them

There are always problems when mole catching, and the majority of them are created by the mole catchers themselves, for not taking heed of what they can learn. Some will fall into this category, and will look for excuses as to why they have not caught that particular mole, and others will want to know why they did. Therefore I will assist you here with further advice and information to augment the guidance that you will have learnt in the mole catcher's year.

SOILS

Often the reason for catching or not catching a mole is because you have not taken into consideration the soil condition or type in the location that the mole has chosen to make its tunnels. The soil type and what it reveals must always be accepted as a form of assistance to a mole catcher, providing you can understand the clues presented to you. Soils can be broken down into five basic types: chalk, clay, loam, peat, silt and sand. Moles will not be present in some soil types because they do not support any of their preferred food sources, or because they are difficult to work.

Chalky Soils

Chalky soils are often shallow and free draining, and are low in fertility; moles will appear in a chalky soil if it has a content of clay, because then it will retain a level of moisture and nutrients. Normal alkaline chalky soil often has

lumps of chalk present, and for the mole catcher these can present a problem when it comes to trap placement should they appear in the structure of the mole's tunnel that has been exposed. Like a hard stone, you should not remove such a lump, but push it into the tunnel walls or floor with the probe. If you can't do this because the soil is too hard or the lump too big, then because chalk is soft you can break it up. The Japanese garden trowel is strong enough to double up as a cold chisel so you can tap it on the end of the handle, and it will quite easily chip away at the soft chalk.

The lack of fertility in chalky soils often means that moles are not the slightest bit interested in the area: combined with their free-draining properties these soils offer little in the way of sufficient food sources. However, the calcium carbonate – lime – in the structure does sometimes attract worms as they require calcium for good health, and it helps to neutralize the pH in the soil, so never rule out moles in chalky soils. It is normally due to the changes or use that humans have made of the area that will result in the presence of moles. So look carefully and ascertain the full picture before making a hasty decision.

Clay Soils

Clay soils are really hard work to dig over and cultivate, and moles will avoid the task too. They drain slowly after rain because they will hold the water, which is a consideration for mole catchers as this could influence the water table of that area. If there is a horizon of clay below the upper horizons that are being worked by the target mole, this should be taken into account because it will naturally retain the water, dry slowly in the summer warmth, and remain colder for longer in the low temperatures in winter.

Loams

Loams are a mixture of clay, sand and silt and can be quite easily worked; this is the gardener's favourite soil as it is the best growing medium – it is the soil that gardeners fuss over.

Peat Soils

Peat soils are very high in organic matter and hold moisture, but this type of soil is rarely found in the domestic garden at any depth for moles to frequent so as to cause a problem. However, if they are, because the consistency of the peat is so light, it will fail to hold a constructed tunnel – but this does not mean that a mole cannot work through it. There are occasions when gardeners do mix large quantities of peat and compost as a soil conditioner, and if there is a problem mole then this is the only point of access for trap placement.

Proceed as you would catch in a shallow tunnel, using a set half-barrel/tunnel trap. You will probably find the mole's tunnel is clearly visible, so under this exceptionally light soil composition you should use the hand to feel the tunnel through its roof. Slowly pick out the roof and only expose the tunnel for a few inches, maybe 4 (100mm) at most; then push the trap at an angle into one end of the tunnel, and push the other end directly down into the tunnel. Then leave it – don't try to pull it out again for any reason.

Cover the trap lightly with more of the peaty soil – the mole will expect some debris in the tunnel, and being light will just push through. Because of its construction the half-barrel trap

will effectively replace the tunnel, so it is an ideal choice for such conditions.

Silty Soils

Silty soils are fine soils that are easily worked; they can be washed away or eroded by the wind, and it is the planted flora that stabilizes this type of soil and keeps it in its location. They are actually quite fertile, so it may not be a surprise to find mole activity; however, the mole catcher should consider the light content, and land that is being worked will often have an organic mixture added.

Sandy soil

This soil is light, usually low in nutrients, and fails to retain moisture; it can, however, be bolstered with fertilizers and organic material.

Catching moles and not catching moles often depends on your understanding the soil of that particular area, and what influences it has. Of course, the moles are not alone and you must consider what other living creatures are present – and of course the main diet of the mole is just as dependent upon what the soil has to offer.

SOILS AND WORMS

Most people will call out 'worms' whenever the question is asked, what do moles eat? Certainly worms and worm cocoons will form the main part of the diet of most moles – they create the very environment in which the moles live, and in fact it could be said that worms feed the whole world, because without them we would not be able to grow anything. They plough their way through the soil consuming almost their own weight in organic matter every day, and through its ingestion produce the nutrients that make the soil fertile. Evidence of their work is often visible, and the mole catcher depends on such tell-tale signs to understand the reasons for the presence of a mole.

Castings are the waste from the workings of a worm; they are often visible on the soil surface, and they contain the vital ingredients of nitrates, phosphates and potash, which provide for plant growth. Different species of worm will provide this service at different horizons in the soil. Thus surface castings are from a species of worm that prefers the variable temperatures and moisture conditions found just under the surface. They are known as epigeic worms, and because they depend on high organic matter they will not be found in the deep layers or horizons where such matter is lacking. They are not a large worm, which is evident in the size of their castings when visible on the grass, but these castings are the clue for any mole catcher as to why moles are feeding there.

When worms work in the deeper horizons they also improve soil quality because their movement, and their consumption of matter and small particles, also aerates the soil, providing arteries for air and water to penetrate into the lower levels, neutralizing acidity and alkalinity and promoting healthy roots in plant life.

The worms that frequent the upper levels are called the endogeic species. They patrol the soil, just moving through, eating and consuming matter as they go. Their waste is extruded into the burrows they have created behind them, spreading and conditioning the dirt. They do not have permanent burrows, like the worms lurking in the darker depths of the horizons: down here, these are the anecic dwellers. On a dark night, how many of us have crept carefully across the dew-wet grass in search of the night crawler, the lobworm, the largest of the worms in the United Kingdom?

Lobworms have always been a favourite of fishermen. When lobworms feed they come up from the depths of their sanctuary, but remain in contact with their vertical shafts; to catch them needs a precise and positive finger to prevent them dropping back into the deep again. Once a worm is in hand, it needs to be gently eased from the shaft, but are a prize to anglers and moles alike. These anecic dwellers live in a semi-permanent burrow that can plunge down into the soil for over 6 feet (2 metres): look for the evidence, as explained in Chapter 3.

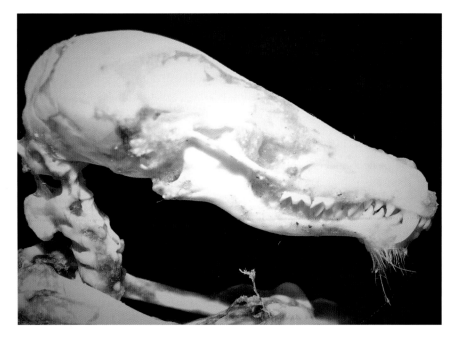

Moles do not eat the roots of plants, and the evidence is visible here.

Moles do not feed on all worms: they avoid the flatworm and redworms, but like the occasional wireworm – but for an animal that needs to fill itself with food, you would think anything would do. However, they do consume other bugs and grubs, so always deliberate the reason why the mole is present.

WORMS AND MOLES

Evidence of what the mole has chosen to eat can always be identified in its stomach contents if it is dissected, as long as the food has not been excessively masticated. Also the mole's food waste is often discovered in molehills, as they deposit tunnel waste. I have witnessed pieces of earthworm and worm cocoon in the fresh soil, before the ever-attentive robin or blackbird has devoured them. The mole is driven by its need to feed, and therefore the mole catcher should always take account of the information presented to him. The mole does not hibernate and must feed all year round; obviously locating that food if it is available will determine the amount of food in the stomach. So the mole will have to take what food it can find, and source it from wherever it is available.

The food that is readily available all year round is without doubt the earthworm, and the amount available will again be a huge contributing factor. In the spring, these worms will be in abundance, but in different locations – for example, the worms will breed in their own preferred environments, and this will have a bearing on the moles. I am no expert on worms but it seems that, like all living creatures, they prefer the easy means, and they seem to be happy to have their offspring under grass rather than in open soils. Worms are always present in the soils, under topsoil or below grass, but you can always find evidence of worms breeding under grass, as their worm cocoons are more prevalent there than in the open soils.

I know that worms mate on the surface, and damp grass may provide more comfort; they move faster over wet grass, so again, like the moles, maybe it is simpler to locate another worm in the breeding season. Whether grass provides the right temperature, or moisture, or a safe haven for the worm cocoon, as a mole catcher I have yet to discover the motive, but it will always explain why it is a preferred location for a mole.

DO MOLES MOVE IN BLOCKS OF TIME?

We have looked at claims that moles move in blocks of time in the mole-catcher's year, but now, armed with that information, we must also consider the variable nature of the mole's food – what it will be – and when and where it is available. Also consider the amount of food that a mole needs for its size, and it is easy to disprove the claims that moles move in blocks of four hours or any other designated time slot.

The mole is a wild animal, it will sleep when it is tired and eat when it is hungry, and the daylight doesn't influence it, as it lives in an almost permanently dark underground world. However, in our research into whether moles move in blocks of time we might easily be prejudiced by the findings of captive moles, even those marked in some way and used in field tests, because when I have filmed them for myself or with other media production companies, I have found they are quick to take advantage of us as humans and any of our efforts, and quickly exploit us in any way they can.

Remove any mole from the soil and you have an immediate duty of care for that animal. Your principal requirement is obviously to provide sufficient food for the mole's insatiable appetite. As soon as the mole consumes food it will either look for more to meet its full requirement, or if you have supplied an adequate amount, curl up and sleep. The metabolism of the mole seems to revolve around the simple need to feed and sleep. If moles have no reason to toil to locate their own food, then they will not – which explains why, when they acquire an excessive number of worms, they will immediately stockpile them in a larder.

If they have stocked up on worms they may often be thought to have left an area, when in truth they are feeding on stocks acquired from previous excursions in the soil. Under test conditions in a laboratory environment, the mole is dependent upon the test or research establishment staff to provide it with food, and this will often be after it has been weighed, examined for changes, poked, prodded and probably subjected to changes in light patterns. The only pattern the mole will very quickly understand is when that false environment determines when it will be fed. Maybe when the person begins work at the start of the day, again in the middle of the day when most take lunch, and then again in the afternoon when another tea break is taken. The mole will become accustomed to the regime it is permitted, the rules of the establishment in accordance with the research.

Captured moles tagged and released back into a natural environment are also influenced by the pattern of disturbances from study. The mole may not be so dependent upon its source of sustenance, but it will certainly feel it is constantly under the pretence of threat from movement in and around its location, and as with the inside environment, will respond accordingly.

Whether the method of research is inside or out, there is little evidence of mole activity in the night hours. Most recorded information is documented between 8am and 4pm; information available during the night is limited, and the methods used inevitably disturb the area, which must again influence the accuracy of the information.

Any mole in its natural environment when at rest or at work will be constantly wary to the threats and dangers around it. A wild animal cannot afford to be a creature of habit or routine, as this would threaten its very survival; a mole may have few predators, but it still shares a unique world with other living creatures. I have witnessed moles moving soil at various times in the day, evening and night, but these movements rarely fall into any fixed timetable of activity as so many references claim, and which is bizarrely accepted as how moles live. I will take a lot of convincing that moles in the United Kingdom live according to a regimented daily timetable in the same way that we do.

Chapter 8

Mole-Catching Tips and Tell Again

The reason why many mistakes are made when mole catching is normally from a lack of attention to detail: it is those small differences that can actually make all the difference to being successful or not. Small errors such as unnecessarily damaging the tunnel when probing, opening the trap site so it is too large for the chosen trap, or failing to cover it and leave it as the mole expects to find it – these are but a few. In this chapter I will try to explain some of the more obscure tips that can be used to get the edge over the target mole.

WORKING IN HARD GROUND

Working in hard, dry ground may seem a little daunting, but actually, once you have located the position for your trap placement, the hard ground can be the mole catcher's friend. You will have located that main tunnel, the one the mole is constantly using and which it considers to be a safe route. Entering into a tunnel when the ground is exceptionally hard, if you can do so without breaking the tunnel structure, will almost certainly bring rewards. Even a slightly badly positioned trap can entrap the mole, as it will abandon the extra effort needed to tunnel around or under it, and will keep going providing the trap is not loose, and is free of any obnoxious odours.

In really hard ground the mole will still need to travel to the desired feeding area, though many mole catchers will fall into the trap of conflicting interests and will seek to place their trap in this feeding area. It is vital to remem-ber that in any softer areas, the mole's hand of mattocks and spade will be ready to exploit the slightest change in an area it can work more easily. Do not be tempted to scatter fresh soil over hard ground for the sake of dissembling and sculpting your trap site, which many would consider a place to avoid. The tunnel passing through the hard soil is the original tunnel, the trusted and dependable run, and the mole will have faith in the security it provides.

WORKING IN HARD, FROZEN GROUND

Hard, frozen ground is actually slightly different to dry hard ground because despite being cold, it normally holds a higher level of moisture. The probe requires more precise use in hard ground because of the sudden 'give' in travel when it breaks through into the run. Under these hard conditions, the smaller 8mm diameter probe comes into its own, because the thinner probe has enough strength if used vertically to penetrate, rather than bend, under the required force. The difference when probing in frozen ground is easily experienced, as the moisture allows for a smoother travel as opposed to a forced one. A forced probe needs a lot of effort and almost crashes the tunnel when it enters. The smooth journey in frozen ground is completely different.

The possibility of probing in frozen ground is often questioned because of the initial feeling of breaking the frozen crust: to some it is almost a sign to give up, in the belief that the ground must be as hard and solid throughout. However, use a thin probe – 8mm is ideal – because it punctures the crust, and then allows for an easier passage downwards. The problem most people have is interpreting the information from the feel of the probe in their hand, especially when it enters the tunnel. It requires practice, and that can only come from experience when winter mole catching.

WORKING IN MULCHED AND LIGHT LOOSE SOILS

When you scrape aside the top cover in a shallow tunnel the sides will begin to collapse into the tunnel; however, you can often get away with this if you set a half-barrel trap into the tunnel. The mole will often accept the presence of a small amount of subsidence in light loose soils, as it will be a natural occurrence. Should this happen, then the half-barrel trap set in the tunnel may be packed in with moist soil. It may seem strange to employ moist soil in a location that has dry, loose, light soil, but packing moist soil along the sides of the trap will fill any gaps and recreate the tunnel shape. Importantly when the moist soil dries, it will mimic the tunnel structure, or as close as can be, and in drying, a small amount of this soil will drop into the tunnel, but in the same way that the tunnel would naturally suffer a little subsidence.

Always ensure the length of the trap site is not compromised, and that the half-barrel trap body is tight at the points of entry. Hold the trap in place with one hand, and press and pack the moist soil along the trap body with the other. Hold the trap firmly so it doesn't move and remains aligned within the tunnel. Cover the trap site as the mole expects to find it, so a sprinkling of the light soil or mulch over the top will suffice, but ensure that the amount used will not impede the trap operation or reduce the body strike. If you estimate that the amount of soil required to cover and mimic the

tunnel roof could impede the operation of the trap, then build a pitched roof structure over the trap site with turf, and then cover it using the sprinkling of light soil.

It is always important to calculate the amount of covering you will require, and how it may influence the tunnel. Using a good 6kg spring-operated trap will allow you to sprinkle a little extra covering, as the power of the spring will compensate for this; if you are using a weaker spring then the only option available will be to cover the trap with a pitched roof of turf and covering. It must be remembered that the pitched roof of turf will reduce the penetrating light, and could create a tunnel that is different to what the target mole expects, causing it to tunnel under the trap.

DEPTH METHOD

A trap may be discovered to have been sprung on one side only, and a small amount of soil located in the trap but no mole. This may happen when the mole is working very shallow runs in loose soil; however, I have discovered a method to prevent the mole from escaping. Tunnels in loose soil will slightly collapse or reduce in diameter through natural subsidence, as the tunnel has little support in its structure. As the mole travels along it will need to recreate the tunnel to return it to the required size for it to travel through it easily. The mole will have created these tunnels to the diameter of its body, so it will be reinstating the tunnels to that original size.

The mole will move along the tunnel on its side, and it was from catching moles in traps sideways that I realized this was the reason for failing to catch previously. The mole works along the tunnel, and in a motion similar to that of a swimmer carrying out a front crawl stroke, it places one front foot down and then reaches forwards and pushes the collapsed soil up and over its head, raising the roof. In making this movement the mole naturally dips, and if it has entered a positioned half-barrel trap, it will in fact move into the trap loop – but in moving its front foot upwards and backwards, it will push against the mumble pin in the wrong direction, so the trap spring is not operated and released.

It then repeats the process, and this time will release the trap spring at the opposite end by operating the mumble pin – but it will not have entered the trap loop, as it has travelled from the opposite direction. This will result in a trap being lifted up out of the tunnel and a trap site full of soil, a trap loop operated, and a disgruntled mole catcher.

The solution is simple: set the traps in these tunnels of loose soil so that, contrary to normal half-barrel trap positioning, the roof of the trap is approximately 1 inch (25mm) below the tunnel roof. So do not align the top of the trap and the tunnel roof, because now the mole, when dipping forwards, because the trap is lower, will strike the mumble pin with its head or forward-positioning front foot. The mole will be caught, but will be found to be sideways in the trap.

This can only be achieved with the use of a half-barrel trap as the technique relies upon the mole opening the diameter of the tunnel and not reinstating the existing tunnel. The method of completely filling in the tunnel, as when using other types of trap such as the gripper trap, can work, but in shallow runs, the less disturbance the mole is confronted with, the better the chance of a quick catch.

WET WEATHER

I have spoken earlier in the book about catching in flooded tunnels, and I cannot stress enough that these often ignored tunnels will produce moles to the trap. You must find the main tunnels, and these will be under areas of natural drip. You will recall that it is from this drip that a percentage of water content will always be present in the ground beneath; following prolonged or heavy rainfall, water could filter down quickly and result in the tunnels being flooded much more quickly. Always look in these tunnels, and on opening your trap site never be put off if you are confronted with a fully flooded tunnel.

Set the trap as normal, and ensure it is tight in the tunnel. Cover it as you would expect for that location, and return as normal the next day. The moles will be using these tunnels, and the level of water in them will drop just as quickly as it rose, should the rainfall cease or diminish. You will be surprised to find that the moles continue to traverse these very wet tunnels, which may be flooded for considerable lengths or in sections, though we may never discover by how much without opening the entire length.

My experiences of catching moles in completely water-filled tunnels have led me to believe that they could possibly swim underwater for some significant distances, and can possibly hold their breath for some substantial length of time. Never underestimate the ingenuity of the humble mole.

COVERING THE TRAP SITE

Shallow Runs

If the tunnels or mole runs are shallow and you have scraped the roof to expose the position for your trap placement, then it may be possible to simply sprinkle light soil over the trap as a covering. As the mole will expect a certain amount of light to penetrate into the run, to block this light from the tunnel with a heavier covering would be a change that could alarm the mole. However, if the shallow tunnel is under the grass then you will be working with a raised tunnel, in which case you must cover any placed trap with a pitched roof made from turf and then covered with loose soil. Light will not penetrate this organic horizon and will not reach these tunnels beneath the grass. Many will consider a sprinkling of soil to be sufficient and the quick option, but it will

Evidence should be considered carefully.

not be equivalent to what is taking place along the rest of the tunnel.

When constructing a pitched roof, or any covering over a trap, be sure that the full operation of that trap is not compromised so as to impede its action. Never cover any trap with soil that could for any reason reduce the efficiency of its operation, or even for no apparent reason, such as when traps are set in tunnels of any depth, as the moisture in the soil could freeze and again hinder the trap function.

Normal Runs

Where trap sites are at a depth that the trap will obviously operate unimpeded, it is important not to cover it over with a slate, or plastic or a piece of wood, even if you intend to then cover over with turf. If you require your turf to be supported, then a couple of sticks placed across the shaft to hold the turf is fine. This is because pieces of slate, plastic or wood will naturally act as a solar panel and warm the air beneath in the shaft, and the mole will detect such a change. The turf placed over the trap site must be covered with mole dirt to the same height as the depth of the tunnel. There is always enough soil to complete this; use the molehills from the excavations of the target mole, and for that little extra just scrape away any flattened molehills with the blade of the trowel.

Deep Runs

Traps in deeper runs still need to be covered so that the tunnel and the trap environment remain the same; furthermore in the lower tunnels, the mole will be more sensitive to any loss of air pressure, and will detect it more quickly. As well as ensuring the trap is set tight so as not to allow air pressure to escape from the movement of the target mole, it is important to shelter the trap site from change – so if it is over a foot (30cm) down, then place over a foot of mole's dirt on the top.

ESTIMATING THE NUMBER OF MOLES IN AN AREA

Calculating how many moles may be at a location is not easy, because the population of moles can move at any time in relation to the influences of location and seasons. It is quite common to attend a location of some considerable size, and to be confronted with a mass of molehills, yet be confident that it is just the one mole, much to the disbelief of the landowner – until the production of that single mole results in no further activity. For many, coming to terms with just how much damage a mole can do is daunting. Likewise, the same amount of damage could reveal several moles, so it is important to consider all the facts and what is occurring in the world of the moles in that locality.

Estimating the Food Supply

What is the size of the area and where are the points of mole damage? How many moles do you believe could be supported, and how long do you feel this area could sustain a mole or moles for? The quantity of earthworms in an area of land is difficult to ascertain, but the formula that many people use is to mark a square foot of pasture and trim the grass off: they then count the number of wormholes in the square, and if you carry this out across the area at random points, it will give you an average number. Twenty-five worms per square foot will average one million per acre – although this has its flaws, as the land will obviously vary according to the condition and depth of the horizons and their carrying capacity for worms.

From the mole catcher's view, if there is a mole at work in a particular spot, then something is attracting it, and it could be that there is a supply of worms in the pockets where mole damage has occurred. Therefore we look at these pockets of mole damage and consider why the mole is feeding at these points – which then takes us to our next stage.

Natural Features: Water Table, Natural Slope and Flora

The natural features of the area are the next consideration, as these will possibly explain why the food that the mole is working to obtain is present – the possible species of food, especially earthworms, will point towards these features. Consider how deep the moles could be working, also how big the molehills are in the area, and how many – or are the moles running spooked and working shallow tunnels?

What is the water table like in the area – does this area remain damp all year round, or only in times of prolonged rainfall? Is there any incline or slope that will cause the water to pocket in certain areas, or run to a certain part? Are there any large trees that will provide areas of damp from their foliage dripping water from rainfall, or is the soil dry because the trees need to absorb water from the ground, drying out the earth in times of drought? The presence of the mole or moles is the next point, and just how they arrived here.

Perimeter Features

What borders the land – hedgerows, walls, post and rail fences? Moles don't fly, so they have tunnelled to the location and out into the areas, and it is all about natural drip. Remember that under every post and rail fence is a mole motorway, you will not see any molehills, but the runs are there. The soil is perfectly moist to maintain a tunnel, and as the ground is not

The mole will work the perimeter of a field from the hedgerow.

disturbed the moles can scurry around undetected. Under hedgerows and walls the run-off and drip provides a network of travel for all the moles to share, and share they will, as they all need to make their way from point to point.

From a mole catcher's point of view you must consider every opportunity for an area of moisture, and these hidden infrastructures are prime points for trap placement. Moles will exploit all, and never fail to probe under watering systems, and the dribble pipes laid along borders or snaked through flowerbeds even when these are not in use. Rainfall will run off these and drip constantly below and you will often discover hidden tunnels there.

Additional Influences

Additional influences might include livestock, and permanent or temporary structures. It is amazing how quickly a pasture that has had little previous evidence of moles will suddenly become overrun with them when livestock is put out to grass. There may have been some oc-

casional evidence of moles in the paddock, but as soon as livestock moves in, then molehills seem to erupt everywhere. Sheep will soon encourage the moles to move in, as their grazing of the ground will rouse the worms and other soil-dwelling bugs and grubs. Depending on the time of the year, their manner of nibbling the organic layers, treading over the ground and depositing natural fluids and waste turns the soil into a playground for worms, larvae and insects.

There will also be occasions when moles will appear after the livestock has left, keen to exploit the opportunities provided by the attentions of their agricultural companions – the livestock moving around will have stimulated the worms, and equally this movement is a call for moles, and if the location will support them, they will come. It is also quite usual that the moles will move away when livestock competes directly with them – that favoured feeding corner of a field when conditions are perfect is suddenly trampled under heavy hooves and their possibly shallow tunnels are squashed and crushed.

Very soon a pasture can become a battlefield.

The reason for moles to be present is not confined to livestock, and you need to consider every possible influence, so always look for other reasons – a leaking water trough, wrapped bales stacked in a field corner, even field shelters can all provide points of natural drip, and the same applies to domestic circumstances, too.

Seasonal Influences such as Breeding

The moles may, of course, have arrived driven by their natural need to exist as a species, and the location could be the nursery for the next generation of moles. The activity might be the workings of pregnant females, or it could be the movement of travelling males seeking the attentions of any available females yet to conceive. You will soon become used to the shouts of alarm and claims of a mole population boom, fuelled by the increase in damage caused by mole activity, declared by those who are ignorant of the ways of moles, and who can't imagine just what it is like to live like a mole.

The Weather

The weather is a vital consideration in determining why and how many moles are present in a location: if you have considered all the previous points, the influencing factor could be the climate – the period in the year, and the impact that the meteorological conditions are having on the area. Rainfall, air and ground temperatures, and direct sunlight will all play a part in explaining the presence of moles in a location.

LOOKING AT THE AREAS MORE CLOSELY

If you are requested to remove moles from a large area, possibly a field, take time to position yourself in one place and contemplate these points in your mind, and build up a picture of the contributing factors that could possibly explain why the moles are there. This is the same for any area where there may be more than one mole present: you will be able to determine the overall picture, which will help you identify whether the location has more than one individual mole, or if it is a single mole working different areas. So before you consider making any disturbance, take some time to stop and look at the overall picture.

How many separate areas of mole damage are there, and how far apart are they? From your vantage point you should be able to see the overall layout of the affected areas and the distances they are apart. The mole can create a vast network of tunnels, and the soil evident in the molehills will reveal how deep it is working. If this activity is close to the outside of the area, then these could be feeding grounds that are being accessed from the field boundary. Look at this closely, because this could be moles entering from other areas, or a single mole following the outer line of the area – but whichever it might be, the choice for trap placement is without doubt the tunnels under that natural drip, or the tunnel linking the perimeter and the first or nearest molehill.

You may find there are molehills in the middle of the field, or some considerable distance out into an area, especially in large fields. As mentioned before, mole activity might suddenly appear in obscure positions in fields, because there are tunnels that once followed a fence line or a hedgerow now taken down or grubbed out. This could be the reason, but if you can actually see the lines of molehills extending out either between areas of damage or as a single artery, this will be another point of interest.

The tunnels linking the areas of damage will be an obvious position for trap placement, to intercept the mole as it travels from one to another. Be sure to find the tunnel between two of the molehills that are furthest apart, as it will allow for a run where the mole will have some distance to travel and should be moving more quickly, so when it enters the trap it will encounter the full force of the strike.

If the tunnel is not linking two areas, but is maybe just being pushed out from a feeding ground, on most occasions this is because a mole has detected food in another area, and is responding to it. In doing so it will create an obvious line of molehills.

In creating this tunnel, the mole will be cautiously making spurs off this main run in its search for the source of this newly available food. This tunnel can be used for trap placement, but it is important to locate a position where the mole has not already spurred off, and to do this you will need to use your probe and follow the line of the tunnel. The molehills are your friend, as they will show you the direction the mole is travelling in, but will also indicate possible spurs or branch tunnels. You must examine the content of these molehills, and feel the moisture content of the soil that is contained in them. Good moist loam will allow the mole to compact much of the soil workings, so these molehills could depict the branch tunnels, as more soil has had to be worked to create junctions. Probing to the side will reveal any such runs, and you need to stay away from these areas.

Similarly molehills that are close to each other, especially in a straight line, indicate that the mole has created a double tunnel. Similar to the central heating system in our homes, they will have a flow and a return tunnel. These tunnels will be running adjacent to each other and may be installed to allow the mole an escape from another mole or potential predators, as it will have links between the two. Rather than placing a trap in such a tunnel, probe around to locate a single tunnel, with no other adjacent one.

Also, take the time to look a little further out from the tunnel, as there may be branch tunnels and often a series of runs that the mole has created because it has discovered food – which is the reason it dug there in the first place. Again, if you locate other tunnels, then

Look closely, as sometimes you can miss evidence to a mole's presence: here the mole is running spooked, to the point where it decided to create some more obvious clues to its being there.

consider another point along this route. It is a good opportunity to intercept a mole moving across a span of land, but it has its hazards for the mole catcher who fails to consider fully the information before him.

This opportunity can present itself at any time of the year, so close examination is required, but is time well spent.

PROBING FOR TUNNELS: GET IT RIGHT

Use of the probe should be second nature, and with practice, it can be. Practice makes any task easier, and this certainly applies with the mole catcher's probe. The probe is the only contact that you have with the mole's environment from above ground, so you must learn to interpret all the information it can provide. If you can find a location where there are plenty of moles, and where you can use the probe to improve your skills in this essential ingress into the mole's world, it will certainly be an advantage. It would be a mistake to go stabbing around in someone's pride and joy turning it to a pincushion and giving the obvious impression that this may be an early stage in your mole-catching career. Practise where any damage that you cause can be tolerated, as any damage you do to the mole's environment will be returned twice over.

I cannot stress enough that this first contact with the mole's underground world is vitally important. You must not trample over the area, or allow anyone else in his or her enthusiasm to divulge their extensive knowledge of what the moles have been doing, which they have gleaned over the past three weeks prior to calling you. Molehills provide so much information about the location, and how the moles are working, but never forget that you should be looking to ascertain the route the mole has taken to arrive at the location.

Try not to walk in front of the probe – in other words, if you believe from your initial considerations that the tunnel could be at a particular point or place, then probe in front of your steps. From the distance from any natural drip and the size of the first molehill or molehills, you should have an inkling as to the possible depth, and should immediately concentrate on the movement of the probe at that approximate depth. Trampling over and amongst the molehills will possibly damage any shallow tunnels or runs, and this can alert the mole into a cautious approach.

The moles will always find an annoying route for any mole catcher to follow – tunnelling under tree roots is so irritating – but there is one problem that is no fault of the mole, and is becoming more common in today's modern mole-catching world. You may be confronted with molehills that hold a rich dark loam content, leading out from the perimeter in a methodical fashion, indicating that it should be a straightforward tunnel to find. That is, until you start to probe, only to find aggregates, when every push of the probe stops abruptly with the tap, tap and tap of stones. Waste materials have been spread over the land, and a blanket of soil strewn over the top. The mole is happy in the depths, in the soil below, which it is depositing up through the intricate pattern of pebbles and crushed brick.

The solution I have found is to use the thinner 8mm probe, and patiently search and survey for what you believe to be the tunnel. Mark the depth and then use the Japanese garden trowel to repeat the process; it will penetrate down more easily because of its wide, thin blade. The sturdy construction can often reveal the tunnel, but it will take practice. Any probing with the Japanese garden trowel should only be used under such described circumstances, because in softer ground, although it will locate the tunnels, it will cause unnecessary damage. At your training ground, do use the Japanese garden trowel to experience this way of locating tunnels, and feel for yourself the damage it can cause under normal conditions.

Probe use is the foundation of mole trapping: get it right, and you should have no trouble with trap placements, get it wrong and you could be struggling to catch that particular target mole for some time. Take your time, and always be sure of what lies beneath before hastily opening up runs and tunnels. Ensure the chosen tunnel is straight for the trap alignments, that there are no annoying tunnels entering in from the side, and that you are not damaging the tunnel with any of your actions. The layers below will always be a challenge to your ability to use the probe, so your full concentration will be required whenever you put it to use.

Chapter 9

Some Frequently Asked Questions

I hope that I have covered most circumstances to help those both inexperienced and experienced in the craft of mole catching; however, there will always be occasions when the mole presents us with a new problem, and you have to compare what confronts you with previous experiences and solutions, and come up with an answer. Some questions that I am often asked are worthy of inclusion, as they may assist others with similar problems.

I have located the tunnels under a fenceline and have had the trap in position for a couple of days, but have caught nothing – no trap disturbance or anything – but out in the molehills there is evidence of the mole working, as fresh soil is being worked. What should I do?

If the mole is not using the tunnel that you located to access the area, then stand back, and observe the area again. It often helps to move to another part of the area and look at it from a different approach. It is easy to become complacent with habit – so the fence has a tunnel beneath it, but the mole in this circumstance is not using it. We can become drawn into perceiving every obvious possible location for a tunnel as the place to position our trap, but the mole could be using another travel direction to the area of damage.

I would always stay with what I know should be the normal point of possible entry to an area, in this case the fenceline, and I would position a trap there, but if you can obtain some further information from the client it may assist. The

first molehill always helps, and if you can ascertain which one it was from advice, then it may help you consider another route. Remember the fenceline tunnels could have been there for a while, and this target mole has another path from which it arrived. You may not be fortunate to have information provided at times when you are having this same predicament.

So no matter how accomplished a mole catcher you believe you are, never refrain from looking outside the box. What is on the other side of that perimeter fence on all sides, and if you were that mole, why would you not have travelled along the fenceline tunnel? But as the mole catcher, you can still position a trap there, but look elsewhere, too.

I understand that I should try to locate the tunnel that leads out towards the molehills that are the obvious feeding ground, but I just can't seem to find them – any tips?

This problem quite often occurs because you are not probing at a deep enough level. If the molehills contain the same soil content, and there is no other soil type – aggregates or sand – to help you determine any depth, then the mole could still be coming up from a deeper level than you are considering.

Go to the nearest molehill from the direction you have considered the mole has entered the area. Probe down approximately 12 inches (30 centimetres) out from that molehill on the side or towards the direction you believe the mole came from. The tunnel should be found, and it will reveal the depth it is located at: mark this with a pinch of the fingers, remove the probe, and note this distance downwards. Then probe down where originally you considered the main tunnel linking the molehills to be, and ensure you are working the probe at the same approximate depth as you discovered the other tunnel to be at. It only takes a very short distance to miss the tunnel depth, and is a mistake we all can, and will, make at some time.

I have caught several moles in one location where I have placed a trap; do I keep that trap active even though it has stopped catching?

Definitely not – it is not acceptable to leave any trap for any species in a position set for use if there is no reason for it to be positioned there. The pretext that another mole may come along at some time and may be caught is no excuse. Any trap left down may fail to be inspected, and suffering could be caused, to a non-target as much as to a target species.

Furthermore the current position is that it is not permitted for anyone other than the person responsible for placing the trap to carry out the inspection. Therefore if someone, maybe a client, had agreed to make such an inspection for you, this in fact contravenes current regulations.

It is important to remember that as soon as any animal enters into a trap it becomes a protected species under the Animal Welfare Acts, and if it is found to be caught alive, even unintentionally, it must be immediately humanely despatched. It is not permitted for the person making the inspection to seek assistance from another party, as this unnecessary suffering is considered to be current, and any further delay in despatching the captured bird or animal is an offence.

There are also technological devices being developed that will be alerted when a target species is captured and remains alive, which will in turn immediately alert the person responsible for the placement via the use of an 'app' or a call to a mobile phone. Thus when the device is triggered that person is required to inspect the trap immediately. Inevitably, however, there will be some who will claim they had no signal, or their mobile device was out of charge, or it was switched off, and they will ignore this summons.

People in the modern world seem devoted to the alternative approach to any task, but to combine technology and mole catching will without doubt make the mole catcher's task harder, especially those willing to respond to an alert in the early hours of the morning. Of course, those providing such a technological state-of-the-art service will promote the humaneness of their system, when in reality it is only another cloak for the new breed of mole catcher to hide behind.

In a small garden is OK to trap amongst the molehills?

Whenever possible you should avoid setting your trap amongst molehills; here the mole has a network of tunnels and you may have difficulty finding a suitable placement, and it will not be moving at speed so as to enter any device positively. It could be moving soil as it sources its food, and could release the trap prematurely, resulting in a foul, improper strike. However, if you are struggling to find any link from another location, then your only choice could be this area of molehills.

You can look on the farthest side of the molehills to see if a new molehill is present on the far side of that hill. Alternatively, you could place a trap in the longest tunnel – you can possibly estimate this from what is revealed to you on the surface. Though remember the molehills bear little evidence to what the tunnels are below ground.

If you can see two molehills that are together in line but have the greatest distance between them compared to any of the others, then you may find a slightly better tunnel to work with. You will need to probe to identify the tunnel in some detail, and it will probably have some adjoining tunnels, but if you can identify a tunnel that is reasonably straight, then set your tunnel trap in there. Try to set it where there are no connecting tunnels that will interfere with the entry of your target mole: you can be sure that if there is any tunnel entering into your trap site in addition to the one you want the mole to travel through, the mole will use it.

What advice would you give if I saw a molehill moving when I entered an area?

The mole will probably have been alerted to your presence, but this may not inconvenience it, and it may continue to work the area – so providing you move slowly and cautiously, you can set your trap to try to catch it. Look to ascertain the entry direction to that area: this may be from the perimeter of the lawn or field, and even at the other end of a row of molehills, especially if it is working along an area of natural drip.

Have your trap set and ready for placement – look for the farthest point back from where the mole is working, and before probing, examine the overall picture to determine the possible location and direction of the tunnel. Probing down to find the tunnel, you need to work positively, and concentrate so you take the least amount of time possible. Immediately you begin to probe into the ground the mole will possibly respond, as it will detect that something is happening below ground level. This may be slightly delayed if you are a distance from the molehill that you witnessed moving, but when you begin to disturb the tunnel to insert your trap, the mole will certainly be aware of your presence.

Having found the tunnel, open it quickly and cut to the trap size, clean out any soil – smooth the base, place the trap, and cover: this should be easy to achieve in less then two minutes at the most. Ensure the covering is correct, as the amount of air you allow into the tunnel will be detected very quickly as the mole returns to the safety of the tunnel that takes it back to the perimeter.

The speed the mole may choose to travel back to the original tunnel from your disturbance may create a higher positive pressure than it would normally, and this greater pressure acts as an advanced warning that the mole will be relying on to tell it of any changes or disturbances to the tunnel. It is vital that you cover correctly so the mole continues along the tunnel for a clean entry to the trap site. As a proficient trap user you should be able to place a mole trap in a tunnel well within a two-minute time frame – to take longer will also allow the atmosphere to change dramatically, and the mole will detect the change and react accordingly.

If you are catching on a regular basis you may find that having opened a tunnel and placed your trap, a mole straightaway runs in and it immediately operates. As you become more proficient in mole trapping you will be able to carry out your work with little or no disturbance to the environment, so avoiding alerting any mole that may be present. Juvenile moles may fall prey to this occurrence in their bid for the sanctuary of the main or deeper tunnels. Be warned, however, that when you place the trap under these circumstances and a mole enters and it operates, it will not be a pleasant experience, because you will witness at first hand the trauma of the mole's capture.

If you are using a good quality trap, one that upon release will strike the mole correctly, then this will be less stressful for both parties. Should this happen, then immediately remove the trap and despatch the mole if it shows any signs of movement – and even if it does not and is quite still, it may be in a state of unconsciousness but be still alive, but will be mortally wounded from the injury inflicted: so the humane decision is to despatch it and so prevent any further unnecessary suffering.

It cannot be stressed enough that, depending on the point of strike on the mole's body from the chosen device, inevitably the target mole will be experiencing a degree of suffering. Never take anything for granted when inspecting any device placed for a mole. Just because the mole is not moving does not necessarily mean that it has expired: it could be in a state of unconsciousness, or worst still, paralysed from the point of strike. If the mole has been struck in the lower abdomen, it may well have a paralysed body but still be alive, so please always check the state of the mole at every occasion and be ready to react to the possibility that it is still alive.

If you experience a moving molehill and have to set your trap in a position that is a considerable distance from that molehill, it is possible to encourage the mole to your trap placement. Having placed the trap, walk wide and back to the area where the mole was, or still is working. Wait and see if your disturbance has moved the mole – this could be a few minutes depending on the area and what you can see happening with the molehill. If it is still working, insert your probe into the ground and tap it with the trowel. You don't need to insert it into any tunnel, just into the ground is sufficient, and the tapping will alert the mole to possible danger and send it scurrying back to the safer tunnels towards the perimeter and the trap's position.

Do moles sometimes leave on their own accord?

Yes, and many an old wives' tale has been born from the fact that moles will sometimes be seen to create an area of damage, and then that activity will suddenly cease. The mole may have left, or it could have harvested the worms and stored them in a worm larder for later. Whichever the reason may be, the activity of soil being moved will no longer be seen.

This can happen during the spring breeding season, as the male moles, looking to perpetuate their species, leave the home territory in search of female moles and travel into other areas where they will feed opportunistically. They will create tunnels to extract the available food, and will then continue on their journey; they still have to consume enough food for survival during the breeding season, but driven by the need to multiply will not stay at that location. This can result in new areas experiencing mole damage, where moles may not have been observed previously. They might not always be suitable for supporting moles, but can provide a snack, but the sudden and frequent occurrences of these moles often gives rise to claims of a mole population boom.

But these moles will leave, and the mole catcher must always consider the time of year and what influences may be the reason for the activity. Moles can enter into an area at any time in the year and for many reasons, and it is down to the mole catcher's experience to deduce the true circumstances, if or why that mole may leave.

What is the most common mistake that people make?

I have referred to many of the simple mistakes people make, but without doubt the biggest is due to laziness. This is down to two main failings: the first is using too many traps for the location, and the second is not inspecting trap placements correctly.

To define these points I would say that many people are led to believe that the more traps they have down, the better their chance of a catch. You now know this to be wrong, because the more traps that are placed, the more disturbance is caused to the mole's environment. It is important to remember that less is more when it comes to mole catching. The fewer traps you have down, but crucially, placed in the correct location, will produce more catches. If it takes only one trap to catch a mole, why employ, say, five at the location? People boast of having hundreds of traps down, which to me only indicates a lack of knowledge and skill for the task – and which leads me to the second point, that of the importance of inspecting the traps correctly.

Clearly, traps must be inspected at least once a day, and those with vast numbers of traps down cannot do this, and will not provide an assessment that meets risk or welfare issues. Moreover, many who do examine their placements in a larger location such as a field or paddock will take the easy way to get round them, whizzing round in a four-by-four vehicle or on a bike. In fact it is far more useful to get out of your vehicle and walk – agreed, you need to get to the location in such a vehicle, and I am as guilty as the next mole catcher of driving a four-by-four to the fields, but then, as with placing the traps, the inspection should be made on foot. That new area of mole activity can slip by unseen as those eager to get to the next job swiftly pass by in their enthusiasm to test the all-terrain tyres to the limit as they plough through freshly deposited soil.

This idleness can be very costly, as further complaints of mole damage will almost certainly be received from the landowner, together with the insistence that the mole catcher returns or continues until the task is done. If the inspection, as the placement, is conducted with care and consideration, then the results will be achieved more quickly and be more cost effective.

What records should I keep?

You should always keep a record of the number of traps used, and their location; it doesn't need to be a detailed map, just a note of how many traps you have put down, and where. It is important that you retrieve all the traps down, or ensure that you have inspected every one. It is easy to forget a trap site if for any reason the location has changed since that placement – markers may have been removed, or some third party may have tampered with, or disturbed the location.

Furthermore if, when you inspect your traps, you move one, or more importantly, add to the number of traps used, then you must record this: it is easy to forget to do this, and then you find that the next day you are scrabbling about looking for that lost location.

There is no requirement to keep a record of how many times a trap has been used. In 2004, the United Kingdom Department for Environment Food and Rural Affairs (DEFRA) stated that a mole trap has a default value of twenty, which means that it may be used twenty times and then it must be replaced. I questioned this new ruling, as the tunnel trap and other professionally manufactured mole traps employ their springs in such a way that they do not pass the yield point. The yield point is the 'break' point, and if a spring is stretched beyond that point its correct operation will be seriously compromised. As an example, if you remove the small coiled spring in a ballpoint pen and stretch it, it will not work properly when you replace it because you will have stretched the coils past the yield point.

This cannot happen in, for example, the half-barrel trap, as the spring is attached to the trap loop, and in the raised position cannot be pulled or stretched past the yield point as the loop will not pass through the trap body. Likewise, if you push the spring down and place it under pressure it cannot pass down through the trap body, so again, it does not pass that yield point.

DEFRA agreed, and said that it was information used in a report for a comparison of methods for controlling moles in the European Union, and that other methods such as poison and gas applications required additional products to be purchased, and they considered it a fair inclusion that traps should have this default value. However, this ruling has now been repealed, and there is no requirement to keep a record of how many times a trap has been used. Nevertheless, as a best practice, do consider replacing them on a regular basis, or when you feel a weakness in their operation.

Which is the hardest mole to catch?

There are no easy moles to catch; only difficult locations. You will find the answer to this question in your own ability to decipher what is presented to you.

What do I do if the mole is alive?

Whenever you inspect a trap, there is every chance that if it has captured a mole, that mole may still be alive, whatever claims are made concerning skill levels and trap efficiency. Always have a suitable tool that you can use to despatch a mole if you happen across one that is still breathing. The hand trowel is perfect, and will be with you in your mole kit. With the half-barrel trap, one or both trap springs may have operated, which means you can lift the trap out of the shaft with a finger looped in the spring. It also means the trap can be used as a secure method to hold the mole.

Never remove a live mole from a kill trap as it will have sustained injuries from which it may not recover. You must now be positive: hold the trap up and out from your body, and in a vertical position, and the mole will lean forward because of the larger upper bodyweight and present its head, to which you deliver a quick sharp strike with the hand trowel. Be careful not to strike the trap if the trap has not operated on the other side, as it could release with the jolt and the spring will clout your finger. If the mole bleeds through the ears, this indicates that its blood pressure is high, and it has not been suffering for long; a lack of blood loss indicates a low blood pressure, which means it has been in the trap for some time.

Chapter 10

Cruelty to Moles

Talk to anyone about moles and how to rid yourself of one, and you will be inundated with old wives' tales and advice. What people fail to understand is that much of this advice is no more than cruelty. Professional advice can now be found on the internet from sources that are considered by many as respected providers of information, but when examined closely are equally as guilty of subjecting moles to harmful attacks as the aficionado propping up the bar in the village pub. Much of the advice intends well and for no harm to befall any mole, but often it is quite the opposite.

Animal welfare organizations as well as horticultural experts will endorse the 'live and let live' approach, giving good reasons why it is better to allow the mole the freedom of the lawn. Those more determined to be mole free will be advised of the relocation process, or as popularly known to most, 'not in my back yard' – although in fact the advice of animal welfare groups is that a live captured mole should be just that – released back from where it was captured from. Although this policy of capturing and relocating is slowly being recognized as an act of cruelty by respected groups, it will certainly be difficult to persuade everyone that this is an unkind future for any mole to endure. It is human instinct not to inflict suffering on another living creature, which is why people prefer the thought of the live capture of an animal, as opposed to killing it.

As a mole catcher I fully understand and respect everyone's opinions on this subject, and openly refer to myself as 'the bad man in the village', but what I do and how I undertake that task must reflect the opinions of others. An acceptance of other people's perspective of what is involved in mole catching should be of value to anyone catching moles. With more people now understanding the implications of the pressures inflicted on a mole, which conflicts with what has previously been considered as a humane release, the honest values of a mole catcher are the future for this old tradition. Government advice now is that a live captured mole should be humanely despatched, and animal welfare groups' guidance is that there is no scientific data to confirm that this policy of live capture and release is humane; these conclusions therefore support the mole catcher in his role of continuing to provide the current best practice and most humane form of mole control.

Currently mole catchers provide the optimum service for the control of moles: this change in attitude towards live capture, the withdrawal of the use of poison, and the industry restrictions on gas applications, has placed trap use at the top of the tree for mole control – nevertheless the judgment remains that what we do is without doubt cruel. This necessitates explaining, and for people to understand, that if moles are to be controlled – as with any animal requiring control – they will be caused a certain degree of suffering. But the reduction of suffering must therefore be paramount now trap use is once more at the heart of mole control, and it is up to those who employ mole catchers, as well as the mole catchers themselves, to regulate best practice.

Moles have a basic protection from cruelty under the Wild Mammals Protection Act 1996, which makes it an offence to stab, pierce or impale any mammal. This is of importance when choosing which mole trap to use. It is also essential to know that any animal, even under the terms of pest control, is protected under the Animal Welfare Act 2006. Thus when a mole enters any trap, even under the terms of pest control, and is captured unintentionally alive in a 'kill trap', it is an offence to cause it unnecessary suffering, especially if it is held in a device that needs pegging down and it is held like a fish on a hook.

The capture of a mole alive can happen, and although a high percentage of bad captures are down to inappropriate trap placement by the operator, choice of device or failure to inspect traps, often a mole will be captured alive due to the circumstances – for example, a mole moving soil can be caught by a front paw, especially in heavy soil, while in lighter soils it may be caught by its back legs, as it pushes soil along its tunnels with the rear legs. It should always be of prime importance to consider that even an ostensibly humane action might cause suffering to a mole, and those who are paid for mole control services are responsible for the wellbeing of any mole they are being paid to remove.

As a mole catcher, we can ensure that our device for capture is fit for purpose, and that our trap placement is to the best of our knowledge correct and presents no harm to non-target species – and it is also our personal demeanour to the provision of welfare that is significant. The need to supply the highest level of welfare towards the target mole at all times is the difference between those who merit the title of mole catcher, and those who do not. Those who worked the fields with spuds and traps and horsehair string, never failed to monitor the sprigs of willow, nor did they neglect to respect their foe, and the same should be true today.

The world today has changed, however, and despite mole catching having not changed for hundreds of years, for it to continue it is essential that it is conducted in a civilized and considerate way. The trend today is to set and leave traps, with no thought to the target mole. Because of the methods those old catchers used, they may have had little choice but to set their sprigs and wait, removing them at the end of the working day. The modern trap we use today is much the same as those used a hundred years before, but the mind-set is to place them and abandon them until circumstances allow a return – circumstances such as when other workloads permit, the welfare of an animal superseded in the interests of greater fiscal gain.

Nevertheless anyone working in mole control, if proficient in the skill, would have no reason not to inspect any trap they had placed to capture a target mole. Integrity is relative to the person responsible for placing and inspecting the trap, which also speaks volumes about the person employing the mole catcher or any operator.

We as humans never cease to inflict suffering upon animals either intentionally or unintentionally – sometimes ignorance fuels such actions, but the professional has no excuse. People will never fail to explore the advice given by others, which might involve hosepipes, broken glass, and an array of unapproved substances, all with the promise to rid the mole from the location. The mole can avoid these attacks, as it can and will avoid any improperly positioned device, but what actually occurs below the ground and out of sight when a capture occurs can only be determined with a physical and visual inspection, and the mole deserves at least this much respect.

When such an inspection should be made is subject to the circumstances prevailing at each location, but it should be a minimum of once a day. It should be a priority that is not gainsaid by the pressures of a professional working day, or the time schedules of those governed by windows of time, or by competition from the day's leisure. Having previously placed a device it is the catcher's responsibility to inspect it at least once a day, which is not a major interruption to any 'to do' list in a working day.

SO YOU STILL WANT TO 'WANT'

If you still desire to become a 'wanter' then I hope you have enjoyed this look into the strange world of the mole, and I welcome you to join those who have, and who still strive to remove them. To become successful you must attend every lesson that every mole provides for you, when and wherever that may be. Choose your tools wisely, and be even more astute in your choice of traps as it is 'these that work for you and not you who works for them'.

Remember in mole catching that there are no easy outs, no simple ways to do things. There are bad practices, and there is always some level of suffering, but avoid the bad practices and the suffering will be reduced.

Respect your new friend the mole and be honest in what you provide, and together you will have a long relationship and one that will bring enjoyment, enhancement and enrichment. You will never forget the privilege of being a part of this world both above and below the ground.

Index